KELLEY T. JANSSON

"Hatched"
— in —
Newtown

The Family Story that Led to a Wild Generation X Childhood with World War II Parents

CENTER CHIMNEY
PUBLISHING

Sandy Hook, Connecticut

HATCHED IN NEWTOWN

CENTER CHIMNEY
PUBLISHING

Sandy Hook, CT
www.centerchimneypublishing.com

Book design by TLC Graphics, *TLCGraphics.com*
Cover: Monica Thomas, Interior: Erin Stark

Red background: ©iStockphoto.com/Nic_Taylor and ckphoto.com/billnoll
Retro pattern: dreamstime ©Helena Öhman | Dreamstime.com

ISBN 978-0-9910530-0-1

Library of Congress Control Number: 2013952738

For my mother and father

Author's Note

This book is a memoir and, as such, written from my own memory or from stories related to me by my mother, father, or other individuals. I have done my best to confirm the accuracy of the details contained therein, and others have vetted the manuscript to confirm my depiction of events. Still, errors unknown to me may exist. Some names have been changed upon request to protect the privacy and/or anonymity of individuals named in the book.

Table of Contents

Table of Contents

Figures

Figures

Figures

꧁꧂

Prologue

In 2011, I convinced my elderly parents to forego Christmas gifts for the first time. They were already well into their eighties. I had no interest in waiting for Christmas as a pre-determined date to express my love with gifts. I bought them whatever they needed, whenever they needed it.

Still, Christmas had been so special to the family over the years that I wanted to give Mom and Dad something special to unwrap for the holiday. I remembered the homemade gifts that had given them such pleasure when I was young–a drawing for the refrigerator or a craft project for their bedroom. After a bit of thought, I decided to write a book of stories about my earliest childhood memories. I wanted to say "thank you" to the parents who had filled my childhood with love, fun, and laughs.

My parents were elated by the gift. Mom sat in her recliner and read the vignettes aloud to my father one at a time. They chuckled over the tales and added colorful commentary. As they remembered more funny events, I wrote more tales to add to the original volume. At the end of Christmas week, the story book documented some of our family's most cherished memories.

Less than eight weeks later, my mother passed away. She talked about the book up until the time of her death. I was incredibly thankful that she had received so much joy from the project. I loved her so much. Several months later, I decided to rewrite the stories and self-publish them as a tribute to my parents. I also added more about my parents' lives. Every family should write its story before it is too late. I wrote mine, just in time.

Introduction
to the
Family

My father said that I "looked like a monkey." He had seen me for the first time through the glass of the newborn nursery at the hospital, but was embarrassed that my grandfather had declared that I was "the prettiest one there" so loudly that all the other new fathers had heard it. Dad thought that all the babies looked alike and were differentiated only by their names on their cribs.

The insult was aimed at my grandfather. Grandpa knew it was a joke, but Dad could not resist the temptation for a bit of humor. Both men liked to jest, although Grandpa clearly considered the subject of his granddaughter off limits. He could find no fault in me and was furious at my father. The two men argued over the brazen monkey comment and created such a ruckus that they were asked to leave the hospital. That was my beginning.

I had a Texan for a mother and a Connecticut Yankee as a father. Both were teachers. Mom adored horses and consumed books at a furious pace. She served as an elected local official in several positions and was so well known in town that I was often identified as "Ruby's daughter" rather than by my own name. Dad was crazy about Early American antiques, antique cars, and cooking. Mom

1

said that all her female friends were jealous because she had married a cook! A gourmet dinner of New England fare was served daily at 5 p.m. SHARP. The family ate together every night.

Mom and Dad met as fellow educators at a Connecticut high school. Mom taught English, while Dad taught science. Married shortly thereafter, they settled down in Newtown, Connecticut, where Dad had purchased a 1700s center chimney colonial farmhouse with two acres of land a few years earlier.

The old house had been condemned when Dad bought it, in such a state of disrepair that cows were walking through it at the time of sale! With my grandfather, a professional builder, nearby to help, my parents began the long restoration process, which never ended, but produced a home ripe with indoor and outdoor stimulation for two active children. Doris and I were born in the first few years of our parents' marriage.

When my sister and I were both very young, the family owned two ponies, two donkeys, one dog, two cats, chickens, pheasants, and a Box turtle. We grew our own vegetables in the garden and had a multitude of fruit trees (apples, peaches, pears, and plums), as well as a strawberry patch, blueberry bushes, and several rows of raspberry plants. For a short time, Dad grew grapes, but the grape vines blew down in a hurricane, and he never replanted them. Sorry, Dad!

The scent of the seasons filled the air with fresh snow, cut grass, tilled garden soil, or autumn leaves, and inspired us to live outdoors as much as possible. In fall, we raked the leaves of century-old maple trees and jumped in the leaf piles. In winter, we skated on the ponds and sledded on the hills. In spring, we dug through snow to uncover crocuses. In summer, we tended a large garden.

We all worked in the garden, maintained the yard, shoveled snow, and helped to maintain our old farmhouse that always required repairs. Dad owned a small fleet of tractors, riding lawn-mowers, and push mowers, of which only one or two ever worked at any given time; the need for lawn equipment was acute with two acres of land. More importantly, the whole family was together during the eight-week summer school break. We took many summer excursions around New England to explore the area's rich history and beautiful nature that surrounded us.

When I was three years old in 1970, Mom and Dad bought more than a hundred acres of property in the woods of Acton, Maine, and contracted with a builder to construct a cabin. At first, the cabin had only a roof and sides without electricity, plumbing, or interior walls. Slowly, the family worked to develop the 24' x 32' structure into a rustic retreat, performing most of the labor ourselves.

Doris showed signs of her artistic talent at a very young age. Mom and Dad encouraged her talent with lots of art supplies. By high school, she regularly attended art classes and participated in a special summer art program at a nearby university. Besides art, Doris was also famous for being singularly responsible to a certain plump gray cat, called Lollipop. "Lol" was Doris' cat from the start and pretty much lived in my sister's room where the cat received an endless supply of affection from Doris, along with a few bites of cheese on special occasions.

I was a rambunctious child with outdoor interests and played sports year round, including soccer, basketball, and softball. Mom took me to practices and never missed a game. By the time I was in high school, Title IX had been around for almost a decade, and there was no girls' soccer program at Newtown High School. Mom spearheaded the community effort to institute a high school girls' soccer team, and I took part in the fund-raising and political lobbying. I even addressed the Board of Education on the night of their deciding vote. Winning a girls' team by a narrow margin, I became a captain of the team in its inaugural varsity season. We won the conference title, and I graduated in the spring of the same school year. The championship was thrilling, but the greater victory was having won the political battle to establish a team.

Doris and I were never particularly close. A family friend used to comment that my sister and I were born of the same parents, but otherwise nothing alike. Doris collected Barbie dolls. I hoarded stuffed animals. Doris had a quiet personality, while I was an energetic prankster. Doris insisted on her favorite color of blue for all her toys, loved chocolate, and studied for endless hours each night to achieve good grades, whereas I was somewhat partial to green, preferred homemade goods, and skipped homework altogether. Doris dressed fashionably, while I lived in jeans. Doris pursued a college degree in art, while I went to engineering school. She remained a cat lover. I stayed an athlete. We both loved books.

I had a terrific childhood with two loving parents, a roof over my head, and the environment to make my own fun. I hit the family lottery, and a lot of funny things happened along the way to fuel the dinner table stories that we laughed about so often.

This is my family's story.

Paternal Roots

——— The Swedes ———

At nineteen years of age, Johannes Emmanuel Jansson of Uppsala, Sweden, desired a fresh start in life. In 1887, he boarded a ship in Göteburg for passage to America and said goodbye to his mother and father, two brothers and a sister, as well as two half brothers and a sister from his father's first marriage.

When Johannes left for America, he became part of a massive Scandinavian emigration wave in the 1880s. The flood of Swedish immigrants generally steered toward Swedish communities throughout the U.S. Johannes made his way to the Black Rock section of Bridgeport, Connecticut, and settled among other Swedes.

The Jansson family had lived a comfortable, middle-class lifestyle in Sweden, and Johannes was educated. The young man received hundreds of letters from his Swedish family and wrote back with the same tenacity. Addressed affectionately as "Manne," a nickname for his middle name of Emmanuel, Johannes was kept up-to-date on the family affairs in Sweden with great regularity. His father's accomplishments as a builder and brother's musicianship were central to the family's interest. Brother Joel sang in an Uppsala singing group. Johannes played the piano.

When Johannes announced his engagement to Emily Larsson, a Swedish immigrant from Gotland, his brother wrote to him, "… know for certain that all of us, from Mother and Father to the youngest brother, will participate with all our hearts, and we wish you…your continuous happiness…." They never wavered in their written expression of affection.

However, the family clearly expected Johannes to return to Sweden. Several times, his mother sent him the money for his return Atlantic passage, but each time Johannes simply spent the money. She sent a sterling silver tea set, and he sold that, too. It is possible that the money went toward clothes, as Johannes donned a suit with white shirt, tie, pocket watch, and hat, whenever he left the house. The style suited Johannes, as he owned a decorator (paint and wallpaper) store in Bridgeport and greeted customers. More importantly, a high hat made him look taller than his wife, who bested Johannes by all of one inch.

FIGURE 1:
*Johannes and Emily
(Larsson) Jansson in
Bridgeport, Connecticut.*

Johannes and Emily raised a family of two boys and two girls: Lawrence (my grandfather), Harold, Judith, and Mabel. Unfortunately for Lawrence, the hospital representative who registered his birth with the city of Bridgeport did not understand the pronunciation or spelling of Swedish names. When she repeated the name that she heard, the boy's birth certificate was formally issued with the phonetic spelling of his name, "L-o-r-e-n-z," instead of "L-a-w-r-e-n-c-e." The mistake so embarrassed the boy as a teenager that he legally changed his name to "Lawrence" to obtain a new document.

Lawrence learned Swedish at the Baptist Church. Johannes was not religious, and Emily was a Lutheran, but the Baptist Church was in their neighborhood, whereas the Lutheran church was on the other side of town. The Baptist church commanded that Lawrence should not smoke, swear, or drink. Behind the church, he could partake in any of it with the rest of the sinners, as long as they were out of view.

As a teenager, Lawrence worked at the decorator store, but disliked his father's Swedish mannerisms. When a customer entered the shop, Johannes greeted the person with greatly exaggerated enthusiasm.

"Oh, *hello*, Mrs. So and So, it's so nice to *see* you again," welcomed Johannes. He followed the magnificent greeting with prompt direction for his son to assist the customer.

"*Lawwwrrencce*, please help Mrs. So and So," said Johannes, as he settled back into his round wooden chair by the entryway. Lawrence summed up his father as "too heavy for light work, and too light for heavy work."

Lawrence endured the fact that he provided the bulk of the decorator store labor, but resented his father's frugal nature with the business. Johannes purchased retired horses from the local fire station to save money. The horses were used to haul a cart for paint delivery, but went berserk at the sound of a siren. Clothes may have been an indulgence for Johannes; business investments were not as essential.

When he was old enough, Lawrence built cars to race at the Danbury Fairgrounds in Danbury, Connecticut. Using parts from a cousin's junkyard, he once had four flat tires on the way to the racetrack. Despite the meager investment in his hobby, his success came in the thrill of the affair. Asked if he ever won a race, Lawrence usually shrugged uneasily and responded that he "wasn't last."

FIGURE 2:
Lawrence Jansson at the Danbury Fairgrounds, 1919.

A Man with a Baby

Around twenty years old, Lawrence married Florence Smith, who gave birth to Lawrence Jr. (my father's older brother) in 1917. Tragically, Florence never recovered from complications that arose during childbirth. At twenty years old, she died six months after her son's birth.

Lawrence was a young widower with an infant. Called into federal service for World War I, he did not serve long, as he was released to care for his son. Emily, Lawrence's mother, took care of Lawrence Jr. during the daytime for about two years, while Lawrence worked as a foreman in a motor plant in Bridgeport that charged batteries for electric milk trucks and peddler wagons. The job was interesting, but provided little to challenge Lawrence's mechanical talent. Soon, he formed "Jansson Brothers" with his brother Harold to build houses, paint, and perform general carpentry, while his father served as the wallpaper expert when needed. If a customer needed a car fixed, then Lawrence did that, too.

In 1920, Lawrence was hospitalized with influenza, a very serious illness at the time. When the hospital called on the phone to say that he passed away, his mother collapsed upon hearing the news. The undertaker, who knew the whole family, was sent to pick up Lawrence's body at the hospital. However, when the undertaker arrived at the hospital, he knew that there had been a mistake. The body he had been directed to collect was not that of his family friend.

"That's not Lawrence," he corrected the hospital officials.

"Yes, it is," they insisted. After a bit of wrangling, the mistake was straightened out. Johannes received a letter that apologized for the mistake.

February 16, 1920

My Dear Mr. Jansson:

My attention has been called to an error which was made in our office on Saturday, by way of informing you of the death of a patient, Mr. John Johnson died in this institution and for some reason or other you were notified that your son Lawrence has died. How such a stupid error could have been made, we cannot account for it, but when we informed you that three of our clerks have been ill, suffering from influenza, you can readily see under what a handicap we are working and more or less mistakes are made. However, this it the first one of the kind and we regret that this one was made.

We trust that nothing serious will come of this error, and that this letter of apology will help to straighten the matter out.

Believe me sincerely.

Yours very truly,

H.B. Lambert M.D.
(Signed)
SUPERINTENDENT
BRIDGEPORT HOSPITAL

A young father, Lawrence recovered from influenza and rejoined the family. However, his mother's health began to fail, which meant that she was no longer able to provide care for Lawrence Jr. Various neighbors helped with the child, but arrangements did not provide a great deal of stability. Requiring a more permanent child-care solution, he pursued a different option. He had heard that a convent in Bridgeport took care of children in need and went to discuss his situation with the Mother Superior. The nun agreed to have the convent provide the daycare needed. The arrangements were finalized, and a young Catholic novitiate, Albertina Bissonnette, was assigned to care for Lawrence Jr. The plan required Lawrence to drop off his son at the convent each morning and pick up the boy each night.

Albertina's roots were French Canadian, from Montreal. Her mother, Graziella (Desmarais) Bissonnette, had completed finishing school and achieved fluency in Greek, Latin, French, and English. Her maternal grandfather, Oliver Desmarais, was a relatively well-known professional Montreal photographer and had created 3D stereoscopic images of landscapes along the U.S. and Canadian border nearest Montreal.

Albertina's father, Napoleon Bissonnette, was an accomplished engineer. After Albertina, the first child of Napoleon and Graziella

Bissonnette, was born in Montreal in 1887, the family moved permanently to the U.S., where Napoleon worked for the Singer Sewing Machine, Inc. factory in Bridgeport, Connecticut, and generated a comfortable living wage due to the royalty income from his many patents. Graziella gave birth to fourteen more children over the next twenty plus years, of which nine survived to adulthood (Albertina, Camille, Wilfrid, Ulric, Elva, Flora, Stella, Hector, and Grace). Grace was born in 1909.

FIGURE 3:
Tina Bissonnette before marriage.

Albertina, called "Tina" by her family, attended a normal school (a school for training teachers) in Bridgeport and studied French to become a French teacher. Upon completion, she worked as a seamstress for several years before she entered the novitiate in the Bridgeport convent. It is possible that she was unable to find a job as a French teacher in an era when most students concluded their studies in the eighth grade. As a nun, she would have had the opportunity to teach French in a parochial school.

Tina embraced her novitiate duties and forged an immediate relationship with Lawrence Jr., so much so, that the child wanted to stay with her full-time, rather than return home with his father each night. The Mother Superior recognized the problem and issued stern instructions for Tina to take the boy to his home and "straighten him out."

As instructed, Tina changed into street clothes and accompanied Lawrence home with his son to tend to the boy's adjustment issues. A picnic or two later, the novitiate was no longer on-track to be a nun. In 1921, Lawrence and Tina were married at St. Patrick's

Church in Bridgeport, Connecticut, and began a life devoted to one another that pre-dated the *Sound of Music* by twenty years.

From Drunkeness to Resourcefulness

Tina called her husband "Larry," while Lawrence Jr. assumed the name Lawrence. They settled into a 1,300 sq. ft., three-bedroom house with one bathroom that Larry built in Stratford, Connecticut, an adjacent town that had roughly 10,000 inhabitants at the end of World War I.[1] The lot size for the small house was 50' x 100'. Larry also owned two adjacent lots that were the same size. The couple had two children together, a girl (Bernice) in 1922, and my father Kenneth (Ken) in 1926.

Ken's early years corresponded with the Prohibition era in the U.S. Characteristic of the times, Larry homebrewed beer; but when a bottle exploded in the cellar due to a fouled batch, he switched to drinking at local bootleg establishments. With his brother Harold and other men, Larry drank too much on paydays and returned home in a drunken stupor.

Tina refused to have anything to do with her husband when he was drunk. Lawrence Jr. put his father to bed on the sofa, and assumed the responsibility of protecting his adopted mother. He had been utterly devoted to Tina since he entered her care at the convent. He also shielded his young brother from the family problem. He did not allow Ken to see their father drunk, communicating only that "Dad was not in good shape."

Lawrence Jr. looked out for Ken and endeavored to build his little brother a racecar to drive in the annual boxcar race held on Boston Avenue in Bridgeport. Ken's car consisted of a metal frame with rounded hood and pointed back. The car had wagon wheels with a

FIGURE 4:
Ken Jansson as a toddler.

rope to steer. In heats of four racers, Ken finished last in his heat and did not advance further in the competition. His brother's efforts had emphasized style over function. In addition, the faster cars had wheels with bearings and a real steering wheel.

For some unknown reason, at the age of thirty-eight, Larry had a change of heart about alcohol and gave up drinking cold turkey. He maintained his sobriety for the rest of his life and reapplied his home-brewing skills to the production of non-alcoholic root beer. He kept the family in flush supply of the beverage that had become popular during prohibition for years to come. Likely, it was Ken to have suffered the only misfortune due to the "safer" beverage. Larry's 1926 Dodge truck tipped over on a rutted dirt road in Newtown, Connecticut, on the way to a cabin on Lake Zoar that was owned by Tina's brother. Ken fell on broken glass from root beer bottles that spilled out of the car. He opened a gash on his knee that bled profusely.

FIGURE 5:
From left to right:
Graziella (Desmarais) Bissonnette,
Tina (Bissonnette) Jansson, Ken Jansson.

Nearby farmers helped to right the vehicle. Larry left the uninjured passengers at the lakeshore cabin in Newtown and returned to Stratford with his youngest son where Ken received several stiches from the family doctor. Ken screamed bloody murder throughout the short medical procedure. He would never have a high tolerance for pain and somewhat blamed the top-heavy Dodge for his injury, describing it as "a phone booth on wheels."

Ken's parents pulled together to re-establish normalcy in the household. Ken was only eight years old at the time of his father's drinking metamorphosis, but he confronted further challenges as a child of the Great Depression. The Jansson children witnessed their parents' perseverance through the period of national hardship, as Larry and Tina worked tirelessly to provide Lawrence Jr., Bernice, and Ken with the basic necessities.

Larry resumed his hard-working lifestyle. He framed houses, built garages, or painted. If he did not have enough work as a tradesman, he chopped wood. Sometimes Larry received a portion of the wood as payment, which provided fuel for the Jansson home, or sold the wood for extra cash. On other occasions, he dug clams at Cockenoe Island (pronounced "kah-KEE-nee"), and exchanged some for a rack of pork ribs. No matter the job, Larry gained something that the household needed. The little cash that he collected was enough to cover the utility expenses. Tina wore white gloves for the trolley to Bridgeport to pay the bills in person. No woman showed her hands in public.

FIGURE 6:
*Bernice (left),
Lawrence Jr. (center),
and Ken Jansson (right).*

At home, both Tina and Larry tended a large garden. They grew roughly fifty tomato plants, as well as cucumbers, beets, carrots, squash, and potatoes. The family ate some of the fresh vegetables in season and preserved what they needed for winter. Carrots and potatoes were stashed in the cellar, while the cucumbers and beets were pickled. Tomatoes were boiled and jarred, or made into tomato soup or spaghetti sauce. The excess tomatoes were used in trade. One bushel of tomatoes traded equivalently for one bushel of apples or other fruit. Like the vegetables, some of the fruit was eaten fresh, while the rest was jarred for winter preserves. The Janssons also grew a patch of logan-berries. The sweet berries were used to make jelly or sauce for shortcake and cream as a summer dessert.

A chicken coop housed approximately a hundred chickens. Larry bought fifty baby chicks each year. The family ate fresh eggs all year long. When a chicken stopped laying eggs, she ended up in the soup pot. Larry killed and plucked two chickens every week to feed the family, but he could never get over the fact that he had killed an animal. Larry managed to swallow chicken soup, but avoided chicken meat during the Great Depression and for the rest of his life.

The family drank fresh milk from the Guernsey cow that lived next door. Every few days, Tina sent Ken with a dime to purchase a fresh pail of milk. Tina skimmed off the first few cups of milk to beat into butter with an eggbeater. The next couple of cups were put aside for Larry's coffee. Most importantly, the children had milk to drink in an era when milk was considered critical to their health.

The same neighbors raised one pig to slaughter each year for food. The day of the slaughter was known in advance throughout the neighborhood. The owners hung the beast in their barn and bled it slowly to death, as they collected its blood in buckets. The dying animal squealed throughout the process. Tina closed all the doors and windows in the Jansson house to dampen the noise, but the children still heard the pig's screams. In subsequent years, she

15

pre-emptively planned a shopping trip to avoid the situation altogether and avoided pork when she could.

The fish wagon visited the neighborhood on Friday afternoons. The owner announced his arrival with a loud foghorn. As Tina and her neighbors streamed into the street to buy fish, Ken's cat Topsy ran ahead of them. Topsy was a regular at the fish wagon and received a fish head for her efforts before she disappeared into the backyard to consume her prize. The selection of seafood from Long Island Sound featured flat fish and clams. The merchant cleaned the fish on the wagon's tailgate as they were purchased. For the Janssons, only sugar, flour, and coffee were purchased from the local First National grocery store. The store was located in the first floor of the owner's house in Stratford.

Groceries that required refrigeration were stored in an oak icebox, an insulated cabinet that pre-dated mechanical refrigeration. The unit had one compartment for ice and two separate compartments for food storage. Melted ice drained to a pullout tray at the bottom of the unit. Larry emptied the tray at the end of every day, but got tired of the chore and drilled a hole in the floor to drain the water continually outside the house via a long tube that he connected to the unit.

An "ice man" delivered ice to the Janssons several times a week. Carrying a big slab of ice in a truck, the man chipped away the amount needed for each household and collected a penny per pound of ice.

The family was occasionally treated to a fresh, commercially baked pie from Maurice Zowidowski, who lived across the street. Maurice drove a pie truck for the Frisbie Pie Company in Bridgeport. He delivered pies to the retailers who resold them, but a damaged pie often made it home with him. Lawrence Jr. and Ken devoured a strawberry pie that had been dropped upside down. The pie was a mess, but the boys never noticed a difference in taste.

Tina's exceptional cooking talent enabled the family to enjoy the garden's harvest all year. In addition to hearty dinners with meat and vegetables, the family enjoyed her bread, pies, and cookies. Lawrence Jr., in particular, hovered in the kitchen to consume his mother's freshly baked cookies. If Tina said that he could eat only the broken ones, he mischievously shook the cookies to break them before he helped himself. Lawrence Jr. never defied Tina.

When she was not cooking, Tina sewed clothes for Bernice. A gifted seamstress, she remade dresses for adults and re-used the old material for a new child's outfit. Ken was mostly attired in hand-me-down clothes from his cousin Donald Bissonnette (Ulric's son). Donald was just enough older than Ken to have worn knickers (short pants that gathered just below the knee and were worn with knee-length socks). The garment had gone out of style by the time Ken inherited the old clothes. He was mortified to wear the outdated items to school. Although he did not complain, he changed his clothes as soon as he got home.

FIGURE 7:
Ken Jansson wearing the knickers that he disliked.

Like his father and mother, Ken loved animals. Ken also liked trains and had a Marx train set with an engine, caboose, and several cars. The electric train used the center rail of the track for power. Ken decorated the train setup with small items that he purchased separately. Father and son liked to watch Topsy, the cat, chase the moving engine and cars until she knocked one

17

of them off the track. Father and son laughed hysterically and continually reset the train to repeat the fun.

Ken also had a pet squirrel, named Nipper. The animal befriended the family much more than the family sought the animal as a pet. At first, Nipper jumped into the laps of visiting relatives as they sat outside and encouraged the squirrel with peanuts. Before long, the animal was riding around on Ken's shoulder and lived in a box on the screened-in porch where Tina opened the door for the animal to get in and out as needed. The animal even knew its name and came running when it was called. Only once did Nipper behave like a wild animal. With Nipper on his shoulder, Ken walked across the street to see a neighbor. The neighbor's dog, although chained, ran toward them and frightened the squirrel. Ken received a nasty squirrel bite on the neck as his pet fled in terror.

While Nipper frequently jumped off and on Ken's shoulder, the squirrel injured itself in one of its landings. Unsure as to what was wrong, Ken took his pet to Dr. Leon F. Whitney in Orange, Connecticut, because the Stratford veterinarian treated only cats and dogs. Dr. Whitney was distinguished in the community as he was a prolific writer, developed animal foods, bred bloodhounds, and studied genetics.[2] His office was in a garage, attached to his home. Dr. Whitney gently examined Nipper. Although the exact nature of the injury remained elusive, the doctor advised Ken as to how to care for the animal.

At the conclusion of the office visit, Dr. Whitney invited Ken into his home. Ken walked into the living room and observed a plush couch with a skunk curled up in it asleep. Ken pet the animal, which responded to his affection and asked for more by pushing on Ken's hand as he scratched the animal's neck.

"I thought it was bad to de-skunk a skunk," questioned Ken.

"The animal that you're petting isn't de-skunked," responded Dr. Whitney. Ken was a bit shaken, but did not stop petting the animal. "Are you afraid of your dog biting you?" asked the doctor.

"No," said Ken.

"Well, I'm not afraid of my skunk spraying me," offered the doctor. Although Nipper had lived on the Janssons' porch, Dr. Whitney's skunk had the freedom to move in and around the whole house.

Ken returned home with Nipper, but woke up to find the squirrel dead the next morning. Ken was broken-hearted.

Ken also had a German shepherd mix with floppy ears, Brownie, as a constant companion and loyal friend. Brownie lived off the generosity of others and received the leftover meat bones and table scraps from the whole neighborhood. Dogs were expensive to feed, and friends contributed what they could to keep the dog around.

Ken attended the Stonybrook School in Stratford until the fourth grade. He and Brownie walked through the woods together to reach the school about a mile away. Ken crossed the street, while Brownie stayed near the woods to watch him enter the school through the boys' entrance. The dog returned home by herself.

In the afternoon, Tina let the dog out with the encouragement to "go get Ken." The dog followed the same path through the woods and waited across the street from the school for Ken to emerge. Ken united with Brownie, and the two returned home together via the same route. The dog never tired of the task, but Tina did not allow Brownie to make the trip in bad weather.

Ken attended the Nichols School for fifth and sixth grades. On his way home, he passed by Corda's Meat Market. Tina called the proprietor during the day and placed her orders for Ken to pick up on his way home from school. He stopped by as a matter of routine, to check whether his mother had ordered anything that day.

With two pets, their own home and food to eat, the Janssons fared well by Depression standards.

Idleness Unacceptable

As the children grew, Tina became actively involved in the PTA (Parent Teacher Association) and held several offices, first as secretary, and then Vice President and President. Although very involved in school activities, Tina also made sure her children were productively engaged outside of the classroom. Ken foraged in the nearby streams for frogs, turtles, and fish, although he disliked snakes. Otherwise, Tina kept him occupied with scheduled activities. Idleness was unacceptable for her children.

Tina paid a nickel each week for Ken to take piano lessons after elementary school. A few years later, Ken joined the Boy Scouts of America. He wore his uniform (shirt, pants, and kerchief) and spent one week during the summer at Camp Pomperaug on Lake Zoar in Southbury, Connecticut. The camp's accommodations offered single cots in a tent with four kids per tent. The boys enjoyed swimming and scouting lessons during the day and ghost stories around the campfire at night. To mark the occasion, Ken received the gift of an official Remington Boy Scout knife in a sheath with a small pocketknife. He cherished what he later called "the best gift that he had ever received." He barely used the knife, however, always afraid that he would lose it.

Ten cents purchased elocution lessons at the Sterling House Community Center for an hour each week. Ken learned how to walk, sit down, and shake hands like a gentleman. He also attended ballroom dancing lessons. His mother had learned that boys could attend the classes free, since the instructor needed them to couple with the paying female customers. Tina believed that the lessons had worldly value.

Once a month, Ken was allowed to attend the Saturday matinee at the Barnum Theatre in Bridgeport. The Stratford Theatre would have been closer, but the Barnum Theatre charged a nickel for the Saturday matinee, whereas the evening shows cost a dime. The Stratford Theatre maintained one price all the time, $0.15 for kids, and $0.25 for adults. Ken did not mind walking the extra distance to Bridgeport. He liked the movies a lot, and the cartoons were his favorite. A cartoon and Pathé newsreel were shown before every feature film.

On Sundays he attended the 9 a.m. St. James Church service with his mother and sister. Larry did not attend, but provided transportation for the family. Lawrence Jr. attended the Methodist Church; his grandmother Jansson had started him in the church closest to where they lived when he was a boy in her care, and Tina did not think it was right for him to change. Tina always arrived early at St. James to ensure that she could sit in the same place each week. Ken sat at one of the four entrances to collect the $0.10 or $0.15 charged by the church to sit in a pew. While a few people walked by without paying, others asked Ken to make change from a small cash box before they dropped their coins in the collection box. He also helped with the collection during the service.

Ken visited an amusement park on Pleasure Beach a couple of times each summer, usually with his mother or grandmother. The popular destination was situated on a 2½-mile barrier island that was partially in Bridgeport and partially in Stratford. The Bridgeport section included the amusement park, which was also called Pleasure Beach. Long Beach, which was part of Stratford, contained more than forty seasonal cottages. The island was accessible by a wooden swing bridge. Ken was entertained at Pleasure Beach by the rides and attractions, which included a carousel, roller-coaster, fun house, penny arcade, roller skating rink, and dodge-'em cars. The games of chance were easily identified as barkers lured customers to spend their money. If Ken and his family tired of the amusement park, they wandered along the water's edge to pick up seashells. The famous amusement park also contained a ballroom and movie theatre for nighttime visitors.

While the Janssons had money to expand Ken's horizons, he also had to work. His first assignment outside the home occurred around the third grade. A family friend with a farm had a crop of baby carrots that were about 1½-inches high. The plants needed the weeds pulled out from in between them, tedious and boring work that required child-size hands. The long, fifty-foot rows seemed endless to Ken. The experience was so monotonous that, when he walked home at the end of the first day, he vowed never to become a farmer. Teamed with three other children, the kids finished after about a week. Ken received six cents an hour for his work.

Ken escaped from work and school for special occasions. In 1937, the Hindenburg was to pass directly overhead of the Nichols School. The German airship's flight path was continually tracked and broadcast by local radio stations. The school's office staff monitored the exciting radio updates. When the reports indicated that the airship was approaching the school, the principal allowed all the kids to go outside to see it. Over 800 feet in length and 135 feet in diameter, the airship moved so slowly that Ken thought it might fall out of the sky.[3] With plenty of time for viewing, Ken's teachers explained that the long-range, passenger-carrying airship was called a dirigible and used hydrogen for lift. It was intended to provide transatlantic passage in half the time as an ocean liner. The Hindenburg had completed eighteen round-trips between Germany and the U.S. in the 1936 season.[3] Ken witnessed the first North

American flight in the 1937 season. Indeed, his premonitions about flight worthiness proved correct, as the Hindenburg crashed in a fiery inferno at Lakehurst, New Jersey. The disaster ended the airship era.

The Janssons actively participated in local events and participated in a ceremonious drive by the Republican Town Committee, that included Larry as a committee member, on the scenic Merritt Parkway prior to its official opening in 1938 (from Greenwich to Norwalk), and 1940 (from Greenwich to Stratford).[4] The group called themselves Minutemen and wore tricorne hats to distinguish themselves in public. Likely, some of them had been involved with the politics of the road's construction.

The road had been proposed to alleviate congestion on the Boston Post Road along the coast in Fairfield County. However, the project sparked a political outcry as Fairfield County residents worried about lower property values as well as an influx of New Yorkers into their community. The concerned citizens organized as the FCPA (Fairfield County Planning Association) to influence the design of the road away from a standard superhighway to that of a scenic parkway that preserved the natural beauty of the land and served local residents. Amidst a torrent of political wrangling, the voice of the organized residents, who were also politically connected, was heard at the statehouse, and the road was developed to aesthetic design guidelines such that it became known as the "Queen of the Parkways."[5,6]

While many of the Stratford residents thought that the road was worthless due to the fact that it did not connect anywhere, Larry had a clearer vision of the road's future. "Don't worry, they'll tie it up," assured Larry. Indeed, while the parkway was initially completed from Greenwich and stopped at the Housatonic River in Stratford, it eventually connected to the Hutchinson River Parkway in New York and the Wilbur Cross Parkway east of the Housatonic River in Connecticut.

The small procession of vehicles with the Janssons drove from Stratford to Greenwich on the unfinished road. At least one of the bridges had not yet been completed. The small stream of cars bypassed the bridge construction by driving up and down a nearby embankment. The Jansson family enjoyed a celebratory picnic at a large estate in Greenwich where town leaders presented speeches to mark the occasion. As they listened, the Stratford residents were well aware of the controversy regarding the lack of an exit in the Greenfield Hill neighborhood of the Town of Fairfield. The residents of the exclusive area did not want any added traffic in their section of town and blocked the creation of an off-ramp. As a result, the parkway included a long stretch of more than five miles, dubbed "no man's land," without an exit.[6]

While Larry used his vehicle for work and ceremony, it also served in Stratford emergencies. On a bad-weather day in September of 1938, Larry and his brother Harold hurriedly collected Ken and all the kids in the neighborhood from Nichols School to take them home. With no advanced warning, a Category 3 storm had hit Connecticut. The hurricane now known as the "Long Island Express," created 40-foot waves on Long Island and winds that exceeded 100 mph in Connecticut.[7] Ken watched as his family's apple tree blew over in the yard. The eye of the storm passed through Stratford to create an eerie calm. When the wind changed direction as the storm passed, the tree blew back to its upright position.

Ultimately, more than 700 people were killed by the hurricane, with nearly 9,000 homes and buildings destroyed, and 15,000 damaged.[7] Ken was aware of the severe damage to the town of Stratford and surrounding area. Ocean-side cottages had been devastated, and Ken knew that the home of a local politician, Helen Lewis, had been swept out to sea, killing the stateswoman and her husband. Helen had been a member of the Connecticut state House of Representatives and been nominated Secretary of State only a week before the storm.[8] While the effects of the storm had been traumatic for the community, the wind-blown apple tree survived the ordeal. Larry placed stones around its roots to keep it upright, and the tree produced fruit for several more years.

More festive, the popular Memorial Day parade provided annual entertainment for the whole family. Larry usually marched with the Minutemen, while Ken marched with the Boy Scouts or his school. The most notable participant was Truman Parsons, Stratford's last surviving Civil War hero.[9] Dressed in his Union soldier's uniform, the veteran marched ably for many years before riding in an antique car later in his life. His bastion of respectability left a long-lasting impression on young Ken.

In the summer of 1939, the Janssons joined in the revelry of the Stratford tercentennial. Puritans founded Stratford in 1639. A number of special events were organized to celebrate the occasion, including a special train to the 1939 World's Fair in New York. The train left from Stratford and went directly to the fair with the Janssons among the revelers. At the fairgrounds of Flushing Meadows-Corona Park, the family witnessed the introduction of television to the American public, with Ken especially amazed by the new technology that looked like a movie theatre screen in a small box. The thirteen year old plunged

FIGURE 8:
Ken Jansson after carrying the flag for the Boy Scouts in the Stratford Memorial Day Parade.

from the 262-foot Life Savers parachute jump and collected a souvenir Lucky Strike book. The family had so much fun that they went back to the fair the next year by themselves.

In September of 1939, they received an invitation from Larry's friend and Stratford entrepreneur, Igor Sikorsky of Sikorsky Aircraft Corporation, to witness the first helicopter flight. No one at the time even knew the word "helicopter" or understood the concept of direct lift. The skeletal structure with a four-cylinder, 75-horsepower engine, a single main three-blade rotor of 28-foot diameter, and a tail rotor, lifted off the ground for a few seconds piloted by Igor Sikorsky himself.[10,11] The onlookers stood in amazement as Sikorsky made headlines and history. The Janssons relied on the subsequent newspaper reports and photos to remember the occasion. Tina had stayed at home and her expensive Kodak Brownie camera that cost about $1.00 never left her possession. Sikorsky Aircraft Corporation went on to become a leading helicopter manufacturer in the U.S.

Lawrence Jr. expanded his little brother's horizons as well. He took Ken to the midget auto races at Union Field in Bridgeport or Savin Rock in West Haven. The small cars were low to the ground as the drivers raced with their feet outstretched in front of them while their torso and helmeted heads were exposed to the open air. The track was likely no longer than a quarter mile oval of packed dirt with surrounding bleachers for spectators. Concessions vendors sold Coca-Cola, orange soda, and fresh roasted peanuts to the spectators. As soon as Ken heard the first call for "fresh roasted peanuts" from the stands, Lawrence Jr. obliged to buy the snack for his brother.

Larry continued to work in painting and construction and in 1939 built the family a bigger 1,600 sq. ft. three-bedroom home with one and a half bathrooms on one of the lots that he owned on the same street. He allocated the second vacant lot for the garden. The master bedroom was downstairs, and two bedrooms were upstairs for the children. The new house contained a major kitchen upgrade, as electric appliances were installed, replacing the old icebox and large kerosene-burning kitchen stove/oven that the family relied on in the old house. A shower was also included in the bathroom, whereas the old house had only a bathtub. The children had taken baths on Saturday nights and shared the few inches of bathwater that was expensive to heat. Bernice went first, followed by Ken, and then Lawrence. Tina added a kettle of hot water to the bath before Ken and Lawrence each used the tub.

FIGURE 9:
The second house Larry built on Klondike Street in Stratford, Connecticut, 1939.

Larry worked non-stop, whether at his own business or at home. He tinkered on cars, worked in the yard, or helped Tina in the garden. He relaxed only by listening to the radio and tuned in to CBS news or the popular radio programs *The Shadow* and *The Green Hornet*. Tina sewed constantly, made dresses, or constructed intricate doll clothes for a personal doll collection. Between the two of them, they never sat still, until Tina got sick.

Sickness and Wartime

As Ken entered his teenage years, Tina was diagnosed with rheumatic fever. Before too long, Tina was in a wheelchair and barely mobile. Larry and Ken managed the household together while they cared for Tina. Ken assumed the role of cook, while his father washed the dishes. Bernice, a bit of a prima donna due to her incredible natural beauty, did little to help. Lawrence Jr., nine years older than Ken, was already living on his own away from home, but the family had grown with the addition of a new dog, called Snooky, that belonged to Tina.

FIGURE 10:
*Tina (Bissonnette) Jansson
at Veteran's Park, St. Cloud, Florida,
October 29, 1942.*

Tina's condition had worsened when her doctor suggested a change of climate was needed to improve her health. Taking the doctor's suggestion seriously, Larry arranged for Tina and her sister Elva, who was trained as a nurse, to live in St. Cloud, Florida, for the winter. Elva, an incredibly generous person, did not blink at the interruption to her nursing career. The two sisters traveled to Florida by train and stayed in the room of a small house that had one bedroom set aside as a rental. After several months Tina's health had greatly improved, and the pair returned to Connecticut.

As the nation headed toward World War II, Tina resumed her management of the Jansson household. Having lived through World War I, she also anticipated a sugar shortage. By the time sugar sales were officially rationed in 1942, Tina had stockpiled more than fifty pounds of the substance, which she stored in Ken's closet. If a friend needed sugar during wartime, Tina always had some to spare.

The Jansson Brothers enterprise also had its privileges during wartime. While every American had food rations, business owners received additional rations for gasoline and rubber tires. Although gasoline was readily available, the government rationed its consumption due to the scarcity of tires, which were made from natural rubber, a scarce foreign resource. Building supplies for the business, such as wood, nails, and lumber, were easily purchased from Connecticut lumberyards.

At its peak, Jansson Brothers employed more than sixty men who were organized into small groups with varying expertise. The team had the manpower to paint the largest buildings in town, as well as churches with tall steeples, including both the Christ Episcopal Church and the Congregational Church. Harold proved himself fearless on a ladder and painted the tall steeples himself.

FIGURE 11:
Jansson Brothers painting the Christ Episcopal Church in Stratford, Connecticut. Lawrence Jansson is second from left. Harold Jansson is on the far right.

Lawrence Jr. painted with his father, but liked to pull pranks on the workers. He sneaked up underneath other men on their ladders and painted the bottoms of their feet or tied their shoelaces together. Larry was known as a jokester himself. He often imitated his father's speech and used a thick Swedish accent. When Ken was asked how long Larry had been in America, he ratted his father out and confided that Larry had been born in Bridgeport and spoke English perfectly. The customers gained great amusement from the charade and gave Larry a hard time the next time they saw him.

Larry charmed the customers with his own humor. He stained houses from a big bottle labeled "VO." When someone asked him about the mixture, he happily revealed the high quality contents as "violin oil." His customers admired that Larry did not use "cheap stuff," but in reality, Larry had mixed his own stain with tar and kerosene. The commercially manufactured substance contained the same ingredients, but cost more and was not labeled "VO" to impress customers.

The success of the business was little consolation during the war, however, as Connecticut men became fallen heroes. Tina sat with the mothers who had lost their sons, including her own family members. Ken's cousin Donald was reported missing in action. Donald had served in Europe as a B-17 pilot, and his plane had reportedly been lost.

Tina's friend from Bridgeport, Helen Martin, also suffered unimaginable loss. Helen's husband and two sons all served in the military. When Helen's husband and younger son had been killed in Europe, the War Department recognized the sacrifice and recalled the oldest son to serve stateside as a test pilot. Sadly, the test pilot assignment provided no relief from danger, and the oldest son was

FIGURE 12:
Donald Bissonnette,
B-17 pilot in the
U.S. Army Air Corps.

killed in a plane crash. With her entire family lost, Helen was nearly inconsolable.

To change Helen's environment, Tina provided her friend with constant companionship. The two women called each other every day at 10 a.m., ate lunch together, and traveled together for errands. Tina did not drive, but Helen had a car. Accompanied by their two dogs–Tina's Snooky, a Maltese mix, and Helen's Rusty, an Airedale Terrier mix–the women spent the afternoons together. The dogs were never on a leash and got along with one another fabulously.

Two women who traveled around town with their dogs was an unusual sight during wartime; people stared. Nevertheless, the routine helped Helen to cope.

Ken attended seventh through twelfth grade at Stratford High School during the war. His favorite subject was science, an interest influenced heavily by a terrific teacher, Ruby Wheeler. He was president of the Photography Club and also a member of the Music Club. He sang as a bass in the chorus and in the a cappella choir. The a cappella group performed every year at Christmas time on the local radio station, WICC (AM 600) in Bridgeport. A radio announcer named Bob Crane, who later became famous in the starring role of the popular television series *Hogan's Heroes*, introduced the group.

At one point, the choir staged a minstrel show that featured Ken as one of the black-faced entertainers.

"Do y'all know where the bugs go in winter time?" acted Ken.

"Search me," responded a female choir member.

"No, thanks, just wanted to know," replied Ken flippantly. The humor was fun, but Ken disliked the ethnic mockery. In fact, Tina was a good friend of a black family in town. The husband was a dentist, and his son was in Ken's class. Ken, however, never saw the man in his professional capacity, as students were given free care at the student dental clinic that was in the basement of Center Elementary School. However, in his high school years Ken received his dental care (free) from a young dentist in town, John Miller. The two men shared an interest in antique cars and became fast friends, traveling together to antique car events.

FIGURE 13:
Ruby Wheeler, science teacher at Stratford High School and faculty advisor for the Photography Club.

At sixteen, Ken worked after school and all day on Saturday at Howland's Department Store in Bridgeport for $0.30/hr. The giant six-story department store, second only to Read's Department Store, consumed a city block and contained six elevators. Ken started in the display department, although he did not like the assignment. He had to dress models in the display windows, where there were no curtains to prevent people on the street from watching him. Somewhat bashful from the prying eyes of onlookers, Ken requested another position.

He transferred to the shoe department and started working in men's shoes. When the men's shoe department was slow one day, he moved to the women's shoe department. Before long, he went back and forth to cover either department as needed. He loved the work, the people, and the prestige of working at Howland's.

Ken also had the opportunity to manage a counter for the annual "Mill End Sale." The sales events required the setup of small, square booths, about 10' x 10' for each product, with the sales person in the middle. Mill end sales happened twice a year and included a wide array of products, such as sweaters, shoes, rugs, and bolt ends of fabric or upholstery. The goods were the product of New England's industrial output, usually leftover items from the rest of the year. Ken loved the sale frenzy as much as the products.

Since Howland's normally closed at 5:00 p.m., Ken also volunteered as an air spotter with the Aircraft Warning Service (AWS), the civilian service of the United States Army Ground Observer Corps. His father volunteered, too. The wartime organization relied on civilians in coastal areas to observe and report planes from designated lookouts, visually searching the sky for enemy aircraft attempting to penetrate American airspace. One and a half million volunteers staffed 14,000 observation posts along the nation's east and west coasts.[12] Women frequently volunteered, as did men who were unable to serve in the military. Many posts were located on hills or mountaintops to gain the best visibility. Some structures were large towers, while others were the size of small buildings or sheds. Regardless of the exterior infrastructure, the posts were equipped with phones that connected directly to military Information and Filter Centers, which organized the data received from multiple observation posts to track aircraft.

In Stratford, the observation post was a little larger than a phone booth and situated in the front yard of Tom and Elizabeth Small's home on Broadbridge Avenue. Ken, his father, and the other volunteers received training on the different types of planes and wore a button that designated them as official AWS volunteer observers. Always working in pairs, the Stratford volunteers stood outside the small building to scan the skies. When they saw an aircraft, they noted its characteristics and direction and used the phone to quickly report the information. Planes regularly flew overhead in Stratford, sometimes at intervals of only a few minutes, so Ken's shifts were often busy.

Approaching high school graduation, if Ken had dreams for the future, he put them on hold. The wartime draft occupied his near-term thoughts, as young men were asked to serve their country first.

——— Drafted ———

Ken turned eighteen in February of his high school senior year in 1944 and was immediately drafted. Like other boys in school, he had the option to postpone his induction to complete high school or enlist right away. Ken chose to complete his senior year and graduated with the Stratford High School class of 1944. The school conferred degrees on all the seniors, including the students who had left mid-year for military service. Some of those who had left early had already been killed in action, and the graduation ceremony included recognition for the school's fallen heroes. Ken was devastated as the names of his lost classmates were read aloud, and their sacrifice was something that he never forgot throughout his lifetime.

Assigned to the Army Air Corps, Ken traveled by train from Stratford to New Haven, Connecticut. A large building in New Haven provided a temporary facility for medical staff to perform physicals for hundreds of men. Army clothes were issued, with old clothes sealed in a bag and returned by mail to any address the draftee designated. After their physicals, the men traveled by train to the reception center for all New England draftees at Fort Devens in Ayer, Massachusetts.

After a few days at Fort Devens, Ken was assigned to a particular train car for travel to basic training. The train lumbered south, but the soldiers were not informed of their final destination. At various train stations, a car or two detached from the longer train and went in a different direction. During the breaks, several of the men leaned out the train windows and found out where they were stopped from someone on the platform. Most importantly, the soldiers stayed in the car to which they were assigned, as each car was going some place different. Ken rode the train for three days before he reached his final destination, which was finally revealed as Sheppard Field in Wichita Falls, Texas.

Sheppard Field served as a basic training camp for the Army Air Corps. The new soldiers' regimen consisted of exercise, marching, ballistics, and general training specific to the Air Corps. Wichita Falls in July was piping hot and exceeded 100°F every day. Water was scarce and required purification. Lister bags (a canvas bag used to supply purified drinking water[13]) were provided, but the water was so hot and salty that it was nearly unbearable to drink. Eerily, a shower in the salty water turned a soldier's skin white in the sun. The firearms at the firing range also required protection from the heat and were stored in wooden containers. Pistols left in the sun were too hot to handle, burning a soldier's hand if he tried to pick one up.

By chance John Miller, Ken's friend from Stratford, had also been drafted and stationed at Sheppard Field. John's academic credentials meant that he had received an officer's commission and was assigned to the Dental Corps. The two men continued their friendship despite the difference in rank. When Ken and his enlisted friends wanted a watermelon and were not allowed to leave the airfield, John lent Ken his car with an officer's tag to go to town to buy the desired fruit. The car was apparently enough of a distraction for Ken to sneak past the main gate without the guards noticing his rank. He made it back undetected with the watermelon safely in his possession, to the delight of his fellow soldiers. John would later marry his girlfriend, Shirley Mott, at Sheppard Field. Shirley was also from Connecticut and traveled to Texas for a visit when the couple decided to take the plunge into matrimony.

As the new recruits got to know one another, Ken also became friends with a fellow soldier, Richard Whiting. Richard was a civilian instructor pilot from the Northeast. Although civilian pilots were not allowed to fly for the military, Richard was able to rent a private plane from the municipal airport. Richard suggested that the two of them take a ride. Flying a bi-plane, Richard let Ken take a turn at the controls once they were safely in the air. Ken loved the experience so much that Richard began to give Ken regular lessons. Richard signed Ken's logbook as the instructor pilot.

At the conclusion of basic training, Ken was transferred to gunnery school at the Kingman Army Airfield in Kingman, Arizona. He learned the operation of .50 caliber (0.50 inches or 12.7 mm) machine guns that were mounted in B-17 bombers and how to apply sulfur powder to gunshot wounds in various drills that simulated likely injuries. The airmen were also tested in small groups for their tolerance to high altitude in a pressure chamber. If a soldier passed out before 12,000 feet, he washed out of the program. As the trainees lost consciousness, the training staff carried them out of the chamber with an oxygen mask. Ken successfully endured the test to 18,000 feet.

As the men progressed through their training, they were also required to visit the military dentist. The government believed that dental fillings, comprised primarily of silver and mercury, would not survive at altitude. All airmen with fillings were required to have their teeth "lined for high altitude." The dentists drilled out existing fillings, added a cushioned liner, and then re-filled the cavities with the same material as the original filling. For Ken, with a filling in nearly every tooth, the experience was particularly painful. He spent hours in a dentist's chair over the course of several weeks, as his teeth were painfully prepared for flight, one at a time.

FIGURE 14:
Kingman Army Airfield Chapel at Christmas Service December 25, 1944. Ken Jansson sang in the choir.

The least popular aspect of gunnery school was KP (kitchen police or kitchen patrol) duty. The enlisted men worked in the kitchen to complete basic prep work, wash dishes, or scrub floors. They all hated the work. On KP for the first time, Ken was assigned to the potato station with an automatic potato peeler. He was instructed to load the potatoes into the machine and unload it when the potatoes had been sufficiently peeled. Instead, Ken let the machine run too long, and his potatoes were reduced to the size of marbles. Although reprimanded for his lackluster effort, he never had to serve on KP again. His wisdom teeth were pulled as part of his lengthy dental procedures, and he was excused from his second, and last, KP assignment due to the procedure.

After several months of gunnery training, Ken completed engineering school. Before he was shipped out, he was assigned to play the part of a wounded airman with his leg shot off for the drill in emergency aid. With his leg hidden in a hole, Ken wore a prosthesis that faked the serious injury. Groaning loudly, he received compliments for his convincing performance.

Ken was shipped to Drew Army Airfield in Tampa, Florida, for operational training with the 3rd Army Air Force. The OTU (Operational Training Unit) process assigned the new recruits to crews for the newest B-17 bombers. The B-17 "Flying Fortress," in its "G" version by the time Ken arrived in Tampa, had a 103'10" wingspan with four Wright Cyclone 1,200 horsepower propeller engines. The plane was 74'4" long, and 19'1" in height. The B-17G could reach a maximum speed of 300 mph, a cruising speed of 170 mph, and had a range of 1,850 miles. The B-17G had a total of thirteen .50 caliber Browning M-2 machine guns mounted in the chin, cheek, waist, top, ball, and tail turret positions. The plane could carry a bomb load up to 8,000 pounds.[14]

For the first time, Ken met the men that he was assigned to fly with overseas. His B-17 crew was piloted by officer Joseph Fetsco and included three other officers as co-pilot, navigator, and bombardier. The officers had received highly specialized training. The pilot and co-pilots were skilled in flying tactics and bombardment formations, while they were also trained in gunnery and could operate the .50 caliber weapons on board if needed. The bombardier and navigator sat in the nose of the plane. The bombardier sighted the ground targets and called "bombs away" at the appropriate time. The navigator managed the flight paths to and from the targets.[15]

Enlisted men filled the positions of engineer, radio operator, ball turret gunner, waist gunner(s), and tail gunner. The engineer understood the operation of the plane's electrical system, engines, propellers, fuel, and oil systems, and performed airplane inspection. He monitored the condition of the engines in-flight via an instrument board in the mid-section of the plane. The radio operator was stationed near the engineer and managed radio transmissions via Morse code. Both the engineer and radio operator manned guns as necessary. The additional men filled the positions as full-time gunners.[15] Ken was assigned as a tail gunner.

The crew flew regular training missions over Florida, the Atlantic Ocean, and the Gulf of Mexico, as they familiarized themselves with their roles, the aircraft, and the equipment on board. They wore flight jumpsuits, boots, gloves, and a helmet, and communicated via an intercommunication system with an earpiece in their leather helmet and microphones near their throat. They also wore oxygen masks, which were required for use at 10,000-foot altitude and above. Each man also carried a parachute, although the military did not conduct training jumps to avoid unnecessary risk of injury.

FIGURE 15: *Ken Jansson, B-17 tail gunner in U.S. Army Air Corps.*

Instead, the flyers were given on-the-ground training, which mostly consisted of warning them to wait to pull the ripcord until they were at an altitude with sufficient oxygen. Pulling the ripcord too soon meant that soldiers lost consciousness and therefore could not control their descent or landing.

The enlisted men frequently rotated between positions and were also trained to pilot the plane in an emergency. Throughout the war, the allies had learned that enemy fighters often attacked the cockpit to kill the pilot and co-pilot. The other men had to know how to crash-land the plane or keep it out of a spin so that the crew could bail out in a worst-case scenario.

The crew in training flew in formation, dropped dummy bombs, and fired the .50 caliber machine guns in preparation for their overseas duty. They also had a bit of fun and sometimes opened the bomb bay doors when a man walked over a narrow catwalk that exposed him to the ground below while the bomb bay doors were open or turned off a fellow crewman's oxygen until he passed out. The training flights were often long and boring, so the light-hearted atmosphere helped to pass the time. The gunners fired the machine guns at a target flown behind a P-40 pursuit plane for their final ballistics test.

FIGURE 16:
*B-17G Crew at Drew Field, 1945. Back row: Ken Jansson (Tail Gunner),
Simon Higginbotham (Gunner), Rene Sanguily (Gunner),
Melvin Ginsberg (Radio Operator), Front row: Joseph Fetsco (Pilot),
William Blanchard (Navigator), Bart Semeraro (Bombardier).
Missing from photo: Kenneth Chamberlain (Crew Chief / Aerial Engineer).*

The USO (United Service Organization) in Tampa offered some relief from the military regimen. Ken frequented the club, where G.I.'s relaxed to play cards or shoot a game of pool. The club also had a piano. Ken had seen the movie *A Song to Remember*, about the life of Frédéric Chopin, with fellow soldier Peter Gregg in

Tampa. He was shocked when his friend sat down at the USO piano and played the music from the film.

It turned out that Peter had studied music at Julliard and had a great deal of Chopin in his repertoire, including the famous polonaise. Fluent in German, Peter was also able to talk to the cafeteria workers who were German prisoners of war. The U.S. held more than 425,000 Axis prisoners, including 380,00 Germans prisoners of war, on U.S. soil in World War II in 155 installations around the country.[16] 395 were held at Drew Field. [17,18] In the U.S., the prisoners were used to alleviate a domestic labor shortage and mostly worked in agriculture or lumber industries. At Drew Field, "…the POWS worked on the Army Air Force post in quartermaster's workshops, repair shops, kitchens, canteens, and warehouses."[17,19] According to Peter, the POWs were mostly lonely for their families.

Ken sought to continue his private pilot training and ventured to the nearby municipal airport on Davis Island to rent a plane. He had to make his first flight with an instructor pilot, Spike Babcock, before he could rent a plane on his own. Spike was a civilian trained pilot, but did not serve in the military. He had bailed out of an aircraft with a parachute that malfunctioned and landed in a swamp at a high rate of speed. Spike survived, but broke his back in the fall, an injury that later medically disqualified him from military service.

Ken rented a plane a few times and then convinced his father to send him the money to buy his own aircraft in Tampa. He purchased a small, single propeller Piper Cub that had roughly 40 horsepower. The fabric-covered plane could reach a cruising speed of 60 mph and carried one pilot and a single passenger. The Piper Cub had dual controls, so that either person could fly the plane. Sometimes service members would fly several small planes together and use military formations to chase cows a few feet off the ground.

Although six weeks later Ken had to sell the plane in advance of his crew's deployment to Europe, he did not lose any money. His brief ownership had saved him the cost of many rentals.

The weeks spent in Tampa OTU concluded with a two-week furlough before Ken's unit planned to ship overseas. Ken returned to Stratford to visit his family. His sister had become a successful model at the John Robert Powers modeling agency in New York City and had been featured in several notable advertisements, including one for nasal spray. Lawrence Jr. had been deferred from the draft, as he had worked in the defense industry as a sheet metal worker, first at Sikorsky Aircraft in Connecticut, and then at the Republic Aviation Corporation on Long Island, New York. Lawrence Jr. eventually entered the draft approximately one year after Ken. Cousin Donald was still MIA (missing in action) in Europe. Tina sewed her son's 3rd Air Force (3 AF) patch onto his uniform, and Ken returned to Tampa.

The B-17 crew re-assembled but did not deploy for Europe as expected. They stayed in Tampa with few official duties and no communication as to what might lie ahead. A few days went by with nothing to do, followed by a few weeks of the same idleness. The crew was mystified as to the delay in their deployment. Finally, after a few weeks, VE Day (Victory Day in Europe) occurred on May 8, 1945. The World War II allies had secured the unconditional surrender of Nazi Germany.

Although the U.S. was still at war with Japan, the Pacific military operations relied mostly on B-29 planes. The new B-17 crews from Tampa were no longer needed. Ken and his fellow crewman were redeployed to fill other military roles on the ground. Although unhappy to lose a 50% paycheck premium for active flight duty, they were relieved that the European war was over.

Ken's family received the joyous news that cousin Donald was alive and well in a telegram from the War Department. Donald had been in a German Prisoner of War Camp after his plane was shot down over Germany. The B-17 had been hit by enemy fire and lost three engines. The fourth (and last) engine was also compromised. It continued to run, but misfired so much that the plane rapidly lost altitude. While the navigator wanted to trust the plane to reach allied territory, Donald had ordered the crew to bail out while they still had enough altitude to attempt a parachute jump. All members survived except the tail gunner, who was killed by gunfire in the parachute descent.

Ken remained stateside and served as a military air traffic controller at Turner Field in Albany, Georgia, and Enid Air Field in Enid, Oklahoma, for the duration of his service time. At Turner Field, Ken sang in the church choir and explored the surrounding swamp by rowboat with other curious serviceman. The mysterious swamp ecosystem hosted a wealth of southern trees, plants, fish, and other animals that many of the soldiers had never seen before.

The Turner Field chaplain, Father Kimmett, accompanied the men in the rowboats. Everyone looked to kill time, and the men liked the company of Father Kimmett as much as he liked them. To a New England native who had played in the Connecticut lakes and streams as a boy, Ken eagerly joined the excursions into the swamp wilderness. However, when the group passed a hanging snake that looked like an eight-foot tree branch, Ken decided that he had had enough. Even as an adult, he did not like snakes.

The military discharged Ken through Fort Dix in New Jersey in July 1946. At 135 pounds, he weighed one pound less than when he had entered the service. He had served a total of two years and one day on active duty as a World War II draftee.

Ken returned home to a hero's welcome, but all was not well at the Jansson's home: Tina was sick again.

Post-War Home

Tina had discovered a lump in her breast. Shortly after Ken returned from the service, she was hospitalized for a mastectomy. The surgery was extraordinarily successful. However, Tina received contaminated blood in a blood transfusion during the procedure and contracted infectious hepatitis. Ken took his mother for subsequent radiation treatments. She responded well, and the cancer was soon in remission. Unfortunately, there was no remedy for the hepatitis; Tina's liver was permanently damaged. Furthermore, the operation had cost thousands of dollars. Before the advent of modern day health insurance, Larry took out a loan at the bank to cover the thousands of dollars for Tina's medical expenses. It was many years before he paid the money back.

Meanwhile, the Servicemen's Readjustment Act of 1944, known informally as the G.I. bill, provided cash payments for World War II veterans to attend college. As a result, the colleges were overrun with veterans. Ken wanted to attend college, but found that his options were severely limited. The Army had prioritized discharge for soldiers with overseas service or seniority, first in, first out. One of the youngest to have been drafted, Ken was also one of the last soldiers discharged. By the time Ken returned home in July 1946, four-year colleges had stopped accepting applications for the upcoming fall semester.

Ken lived at home in Stratford and took care of his mother, while he also bought his first car, a Model-A Ford. He gained admittance and enrolled in the private Junior College of Connecticut, in Bridgeport, Connecticut, which became the University of Bridgeport at the end of his freshman year. Ken studied biology, an interest that he retained from high school. However, when a friend warned him that the science field might lead to a lab job where he "tested water samples all day," Ken added education to his studies. The idea of teaching biology had a lot more appeal than working at a repetitive job in a lab.

While in college, Ken continued to pursue an interest in antique cars. He sold the Model-A and bought a 1920 Rolls Royce Silver Ghost with a canvas top. Likely, the breezy covering would have made the car cold in winter, but the huge engine managed to keep the interior warm even in the coldest temperatures. The brakes provided more of a challenge. The enormous car was equipped with inadequate rear (only) brakes and demanded a

FIGURE 17:
Ken Jansson in his Rolls Royce.

long distance to stop. Sudden brake application only slightly slowed its momentum. Still, the Silver Ghost served as Ken's primary means of transportation, and he lovingly took care of it.

FIGURE 18:
Ken Jansson's 1911 Cadillac.

By his sophomore year, Ken had added a 1911 Cadillac to his collection. The car was in total disrepair and barely more than a pile of rust. Because he needed a space to work on it, Larry converted the family's chicken coop into a garage to create an auto workshop. With a wood stove to keep them warm in winter,

45

father and son disassembled the vehicle, rebuilt the engine, and refinished the body. The process took years to complete.

An easier restoration came in the form of an 1880s high-wheel bicycle. Ken sanded the bicycle frame and repainted it. He chrome-plated the handlebars and other small parts. When he was finished, Ken used the bicycle to visit friends around Stratford and Bridgeport. Long hills were torturous for his leg muscles, but worth the attention from onlookers. He also rode the bicycle for the annual P.T. Barnum parade, which started at Seaside Park in Bridgeport. With the University of Bridgeport students dressed up in 1800s wardrobe, Ken cycled in full period regalia to the delight of spectators.

FIGURE 19:
Ken Jansson riding his high-wheel bicycle at the P.T. Barnum parade, 1947 or 1948.

Still palling around with John Miller to explore antique car clubs, Ken also developed a passion for Early American antiques and built collections in furniture, musical instruments, watches, fountain pens, books, and oil lamps. At one point, his musical instrument collection included a cylindrical Thomas Edison record player, zither, player piano, music box, melodeon, Estey pump organ, 1880s piano, and Aeolian Orchestrelle. Books included an

1889 Scholar's edition of the *Encyclopedia Britannica* and a collection of leather-bound books by John Burroughs. Still in college, Ken rapidly filled up his parents' house with his new possessions, although he knew that he wanted a house of his own. More specifically, he wanted an old New England colonial to provide a home for his antiques.

FIGURE 20:
John and Shirley Miller in their White Steamer.

Ken completed his practice teaching at Stratford High School under the same teacher, Ruby Wheeler, who had first inspired him in science and finished his undergraduate coursework in the summer of 1950. Without a break, he began graduate level work toward a Master's in administration and supported himself by substitute teaching throughout the 1950-51 school year.

First Job

Having completed his bachelor's degree requirements but not yet his master's, Ken cast around the local area for available teaching positions. He sent letters to all the local school systems, but without success. Among the youngest of the World War II veterans, the men who had completed their four-year degrees ahead of him had filled the vacant teaching slots. To search a wider area, Ken paid to join a teacher's agency, which alerted him to open positions throughout New England.

With visibility to more opportunities, he applied for two available positions in New Hampshire. Offered both jobs, he accepted the science teaching position at Hanover High School in Hanover, New Hampshire. The school kids were principally the sons and daughters of Dartmouth College professors or the Mary Hitchcock Memorial Hospital medical staff. The community valued education, and the students were bright, respectful, and eager to learn. Ken had landed a dream teaching position, although New Hampshire wages were low compared to Connecticut.

The Hanover High School assistant principal, Martin "Bud" E. Heffernan, had served as an officer in the Navy during Word War II and had been on active duty in the Pacific. Bud's ship had been bombed, and he was in the water for several days before he was rescued. Bud was kind to the new member of his teaching staff, a fellow veteran. He went out of his way to help Ken with his transition to New Hampshire and suggested a place to live at the home of a local resident.

FIGURE 21:
Margaret Fogg.

When Ken arrived as a boarder at the small home of elderly Margaret Fogg in Hanover, New Hampshire, he learned that her husband had been a dentist who was associated with Dartmouth College. He had passed away several years earlier. A widow, Margaret earned an income by renting a small upstairs room that had a bed, desk, chair, and closet. Her brother and his wife also lived in a second upstairs bedroom, while Margaret retained the master upstairs bedroom for herself. The downstairs living area served everyone in the house. The arrangement provided Ken with kitchen privileges and access to the dishes and silverware, but only after Margaret and her two family members had finished their meals.

Although somewhat experienced in the kitchen as he had cooked during his mother's bouts of illness, Ken warmed up hash from a can, a dish of chopped meat and vegetables, on his first night as a boarder. When Margaret peered into the kitchen, she was appalled by Ken's efforts. She threw the unfinished meal into the garbage and restarted a "proper" meal for her tenant. Ken never cooked again at Margaret's house. Instead, he assisted Margaret in the kitchen and ate with her family every night. He gained even more technique under the tutelage of a superb culinary talent.

Margaret excelled in the preparation of traditional New England dishes and heavily utilized sugar and cream as prime ingredients. She cooked fresh green peas with a scoop of butter, added a quarter cup of heavy cream, brought the heavy mixture to a boil, and then shut off the stove to serve it. Margaret baked fresh bread almost every day and knew how to prepare sautéed oysters or oyster stew to perfection. She excelled at bread pudding, plum pudding, and a traditional British suet pudding. She had distributed her recipes so widely in the local community that, when the White Church in Hanover published a cookbook, she laughed that many of the contributors had submitted her recipes in their own names. Two of her favorites were scalloped clams or oysters, and pineapple cake.

Margaret Fogg's Scalloped Clams or Oysters

INGREDIENTS:
1/3 cup butter
2 tablespoons flour
1½ cups milk
1/3 cup dry bread crumbs
1 pint clams or oysters
Salt and pepper
Onion juice

INSTRUCTIONS:
- Make white sauce by blending butter, flour, and milk.
- Add dry breadcrumbs.
- Cut clams or oysters into small pieces.
- Season with salt, pepper, and onion juice.
- Pour into well-buttered dish.
- Cover with buttered breadcrumbs and bake 30 minutes or longer in moderate oven.
- Add any liquid from clams or oysters.

While Ken absorbed Margaret's cooking techniques, he also benefited from her connections in the community. Margaret was a great pal to the wife of John Dickey, President of Dartmouth College. As cultural events passed through New Hampshire, the Dickeys frequently received complimentary tickets. They generously passed the extras to Margaret. Margaret romped all over town, sometimes with Ken in tow, to see the travelling attractions to which her free tickets gained admittance. On one occasion, she invited Ken to

Margaret Fogg's Pineapple Cake

INGREDIENTS FOR EGG WHITE MIXTURE:

6 egg whites

¼ teaspoon salt

¾ cup sugar

INGREDIENTS FOR EGG YOLK MIXTURE:

6 egg yolks

¾ cup sugar

1 tablespoon lemon juice

½ cup unsweetened pineapple juice

1½ cup cake flour

1 teaspoon baking powder

INSTRUCTIONS:

- Beat egg whites and salt. Beat to form moist, glossy peak. Add sugar gradually.
- Separately, beat egg yolks. Add sugar gradually. Beat until thick and sugar is dissolved. Add lemon and pineapple juice. Add flour and baking powder. Fold in egg whites.
- Bake one hour in slow oven (not over 325°) in ungreased tube pan.
- Invert on rack and cool.

Boston to see the famous Ezio Pinza in *South Pacific*. While Ken served as chauffeur, he also saw the fabulous performance.

Margaret accompanied Ken on several of his trips home to Connecticut and became great friends with Ken's parents, Larry and Tina. She often carried her own food basket with her and cooked for the Janssons during her visit. If Ken traveled home alone, she packed food for him to take to his parents. When Larry or Tina called Ken on the phone in New Hampshire, they chatted with Margaret, too.

On one occasion, Larry placed an urgent call to his son in New Hampshire. Larry had purchased a V-neck sweater and vest for Ken from a travelling salesman. A friend of the Janssons had heard on the radio that the sweaters were made from a highly flammable chemical that was extremely dangerous, and Larry called Ken to warn him. When the phone rang at Margaret's house, Ken was at school, so Larry gave Margaret the information.

When Ken got home, he found Margaret waiting for him in the driveway, holding his sweater. She informed him about the call from his father and proposed that they light the sweater on fire in the middle of the driveway. Always ready for a science experiment, Ken touched a match to the sweater. Like a firecracker, the garment contorted in every direction before disintegrating into a tiny bit of ash. With the event concluded safely, Margaret thought the whole affair was hilarious. She dashed inside the house to call the Janssons.

"Larry, that was so much fun, send us another one!" she shouted into the phone.

While Ken enjoyed Margaret's company, he also explored Hanover on his own and carried his 16mm camera with him to capture local events on film, such as the Dartmouth College Winter Carnival ski jumping and snow sculpture competitions. He enjoyed a special event with Robert Frost, who read poems aloud, including *Birches*, Ken's favorite. Ken cherished an audio recording from the Dartmouth event.

Still, after two years in New Hampshire, Ken decided to move back to Stratford in 1953. He had the opportunity to more than double his teaching salary if he returned to Connecticut. He could also finish his master's degree at the University of Bridgeport. He accepted a position at the K-8 Grasmere School to teach seventh and eighth grade science in Fairfield, Connecticut. Ken left Margaret's house in New Hampshire two suit sizes larger than when he arrived.

──── Connecticut Teacher ────

Ken moved back in with his parents and passed a pleasant year at Grasmere before another opportunity presented itself. He gained a position at Staples High School in Westport, Connecticut, with an even higher salary in 1954. Staples High School on Riverside Avenue served grades ten through twelve in an affluent community that valued education. By the 1950s, Westport had become a bedroom community for wealthy New York City commuters and even included a few celebrities. Children of the parents with successful careers were held to high standards.

Ken taught biology and physics. He also consulted for the principal, Stanley Lorenzen, on the requirements for a new high school. The two educators met each week to discuss the kind of school needed and visited the construction site once the building was underway. Stanley often invited Ken to dinner after the construction site visits. Stanley's wife, Elena Lorenzen, was an exceptional cook, an Italian food specialist famous for her homemade pasta and stuffed mushrooms. The three adults enjoyed each other's company immensely, and Ken became a frequent dinner guest. Elena's mushroom recipe is shown on the following page.

FIGURE 22:
*Ken Jansson at
Staples High School.*

Elena Lorenzen's Stuffed Mushrooms

INGREDIENTS:
Mushrooms
Olive oil
Marjoram
Thyme
Onion powder
Garlic powder
Salt and pepper

INSTRUCTIONS:
- Wash and dry mushrooms.
- Nudge out mushroom stems and grind them.
- Combine mushroom stems with marjoram, thyme, onion powder, garlic powder, salt, and pepper. Mix with olive oil.
- Stuff mushroom caps with mushroom-stem mixture.
- Place mushrooms in baking dish. Sprinkle heavily with olive oil.
- Bake at 350° for 10-15 minutes.
- Serve in same dish to keep hot. Serve with toothpicks.

The new Staples High School was designed as a "campus school" with seven separate buildings organized by subject area. The students crisscrossed a common area to change classes. The concept had been introduced in the Midwest and achieved acclaim for the reduction of student cliques. The cliques could not sustain themselves when the students were on the move.

The new Staples High School on North Avenue opened its doors in 1958 with eight campus buildings on its sprawling campus: 1. Industrial arts with shops, 2. Gymnasium, 3. Cafeteria, 4. Auditorium, Music, and Art, 5. Business education (typing, shorthand, school store) and Foreign languages, 6. English, Social Studies, and Homemaking, 7. Science and Mathematics, and 8. Administration offices and media center.[20] Due to budget constraints, covered walkways between the buildings were not built. The students and teachers endured cold temperatures during the winter when they moved between the buildings.

In the new Staples school, Ken maintained two classes of biology and gained new responsibilities as the director of instructional media. Educators had begun to recognize that each student learned differently. Teachers no longer relied exclusively on traditional lecture methods but presented the same information using different forms of media. Filmstrips, 16mm films, transparencies, records, and tape recordings, once considered visual aids, were re-introduced as teaching tools. The media department staff facilitated the use of the equipment and helped teachers in all the departments to develop their curriculum materials.

The launch of the Sputnik satellite in 1957 served as a wake-up call for many Americans that the U.S. had fallen behind the Soviet Union, particularly in science. As the Space Age dawned, America aggressively prioritized education funding. Educators were encouraged to continue their own learning and share their knowledge. Honorariums were readily available from the National Education Association for travel to conferences and workshops. Ken traveled to other parts of the country several times a year to demonstrate the techniques that had been developed at Staples. He used a lesson on the digestive system to showcase the different pieces of new media equipment.

The school's media room, where Ken had an office, also included a radio, which connected through a console to the principal's office and each of the classrooms, similar to the announcements system.

Occasionally, teachers coordinated the listening of special programs into their lesson plans. On November 22, 1963, Ken used the radio for a different purpose. Someone informed him of terrible news. Acting quickly, he used the public address system to make an announcement to the entire school.

"Excuse me, I think this is of interest to all of you," he interrupted. With the radio tuned to the local news, he set the media console to "all call," and transmitted the broadcast throughout the entire school. An eerie, hushed silence fell upon the building as teachers, students, and staff heard the live radio coverage that reported shots had been fired on the motorcade of the 35th President of the United States, John F. Kennedy (JFK), in Dallas, Texas, in an assassination attempt.

Stanley Lorenzen opened the door of the media room a few minutes later.

"Thank you," he spoke approvingly to Ken. A school bell rang and pierced the stillness; yet, no one moved. The office staff turned the bells off for the rest of the day; the students simply remained in their seats, transfixed by the newscast and as stunned as the adults. Even as buses lined up in the school's driveway, few people stirred. The school's occupants determinedly waited with their hopes and prayers as they learned that the President had been shot and rushed into surgery at Parkland Hospital. When the news broke that "the President is dead," Ken heard the angry cries of "No!" echoing throughout the school. When Ken finally left the media room, he met one of his colleagues, Karl Decker, in the hallway. The teacher had tears in his eyes. Like the rest of the nation, Ken and Karl had felt an unimaginable, emotional shock. They would never forget where they were when John F. Kennedy was assassinated: Staples High School in Westport, Connecticut.

—— **House Search** ——

While Ken introduced more and more technology at Staples High School, he continued his enthusiasm for antiques, accumulating so many items that he soon exhausted the space available to him in his parents' home. He had always wanted a center-chimney colonial house. Yet, he had looked at many houses in the immediate area and could not find anything that suited his taste or budget. Old houses were often in disrepair and lacked structural integrity. Larry, a construction expert, often vetoed Ken's options due to the cost of restoration.

After years of searching, Ken was referred to a Newtown realtor, Peggy Mason, at the Foster Agency. At the time, Newtown was mostly a rural farming community with approximately 11,000 residents. Peggy understood Ken's requirements immediately and showed him an old 1700s center-chimney farmhouse in the Sandy Hook region of town. The house had not been lived in for some time as the elderly owner, Joanna Farrell, had moved to a different part of town to live with her son. A cow fence surrounded the house, as cows grazed nearby. The realtor had to open the fence to gain access to the house.

The old house had two stories with a full-size attic, which contained a 9' x 6' x 6' loom. The chimney had four stone fireplaces, including the main fireplace that contained iron cranes for cooking and a built-in beehive oven. Each floor of the house had five rooms that surrounded the center chimney. A kitchen and dining room jutted out from the main house. The kitchen contained a soapstone sink and a hand pump. The house rested on a stone foundation with a dirt floor basement approximately five feet in height.

A stone path led to an outhouse about fifty feet away from the house, but an indoor bathroom had been installed on the second floor with an iron claw-foot tub circa 1920. A single electric bulb with a pull chain hung in the center of every room, but no electrical outlets were present. The house contained an indoor woodshed with a mudroom that included a small doorway to the outside of the house. The mudroom was aptly named—the farmers needed a place to knock the mud off their boots.

The property was surrounded by gorgeous century-old maple trees and demarcated by the stone walls of early settlers. Included in the homestead were four large barns: a four-stall horse barn, "middle" barn, chicken coop, and an icehouse. The icehouse contained a second layer of wood on the inside of its frame to create a gap that was filled with hay and corncobs to provide insulation. The old New England farmers harvested ice from the nearby "ice pond" in winter and stored it in the icehouse throughout the year. A cow path allowed the farmers to move the ice by horse and wagon from the pond to the icehouse. Today, the icehouse is one of the few surviving structures of its kind.

Ken liked the property and immediately made an offer. Unfortunately, the transaction grew complicated very quickly. Joanna Farrell's father, Patrick M. Lynch, had purchased the home in 1871. He had raised several children, including Joanna and her older brother Patrick. When Patrick (Sr.) died in 1919, Joanna's brother assumed the head of household status with Joanna, her husband, and her son living with him. With a "Patrick Lynch" managing the farm, and a seventeen-year age difference between Joanna and her brother, it may have been assumed that Joanna's brother was her father and had rightfully owned the property. Outliving her brother and other family members, Joanna was the last survivor of her generation. She had lived in the same house her entire life and long considered herself the owner, even though the deed had never been updated.

The confusion of deed ownership required the assistance of a lawyer. Peggy recommended the attorney Earl Smith, who was also part owner of the local newspaper called the *Newtown Bee*, to handle the matter. Patrick M. Lynch's heirs, if any, were entitled to a share of the property. Indignant at the situation, Joanna Farrell was forced to delay the sale until the attorney sorted out the legal issues.

The house was surrounded by thirty-seven acres of pasture, which was also owned by Joanna Farrell. Ken had wanted to buy more land with the house, but the old woman had already sold the adjacent land to developers. They wanted to buy the old farmhouse, too, but planned to tear it down to make a road.

"No one is going to tear down *my* house," Joanna Farrell stubbornly declared when she learned of the developer's demolition plans. She swiftly removed the original homestead from the larger parcel sale and left two acres of land with the house to meet Newtown's minimum zoning requirements.

Ken was lucky that Mrs. Farrell had saved the house and waited, albeit impatiently, two long years to purchase the property once the legal matters were settled. By the time he had the deed in his possession in 1961, the cows had long since pressed past the cow fence and moved right into the house itself. The iron crane in the fireplace had been stolen, along with the soapstone kitchen sink and hand pump. Of the many 12-over-12 double-hung wooden windows, all the windowpanes that faced the back of the house had been broken. The house needed more work than ever, but Ken was not fazed and hunkered down for a *very* long restoration process. Step one was to get the cows out of the house!

Ken enlisted his father's help, and together they launched the formidable project. At every step, they took great care to preserve the authenticity of the house that had provided a home to some of the earliest Americans, but they had to make some compromises. Urgently, the men replaced the leaking roof, installed sheathing boards, tarpaper, and asphalt shingles. Ken wanted to install wood shingles to maintain historical consistency, but the homeowner's insurance did not allow it. Steve Kovacs was hired to fix the stone foundation, which had collapsed on one side of the house. The men installed stone footings to true up the entire house and did the same for the various barns as needed.

Larry replaced the windowsills and restored the original 12-over-12 wooden windows. The unbroken windowpanes contained hand-blown glass, but modern glass was used as a substitute where the original windowpanes were broken. Larry painstakingly primed and painted each window before it was re-installed to its designated window position on the house. He also outfitted the entire house with custom-made storm windows. The Janssons had replaced their original windows in Stratford with more modern combination windows. The old Stratford windows were rebuilt as storm windows for the Newtown house.

The men removed the interior ceilings to dispose of the corncob insulation. As the old ceilings were torn away, the corncobs rained down in a cloud of dirt, dust, and dead rodents. The men were forced to escape the house for several minutes until the air became breathable again and they could remove the debris with wheelbarrows. They plastered both the ceilings and walls, using two rough coats to match the colonial style. The wood trim was painted to match colonial colors. Steve Kovacs completed the interior plastering.

The wood planks that covered the kitchen walls were removed to add modern insulation. The same wood was then reused to build kitchen cabinets, while the remaining wall area was plastered. The indoor woodshed was converted to a second bathroom and the sagging back porch was shored up and made level. An oil furnace was

FIGURE 23:
The Newtown house and barns during the initial restoration process.

61

FIGURE 23 (CONTINUED):
The Newtown house and barns during the initial restoration process.

installed and the electrical wiring was expanded to include electrical outlets. A telephone with a party line was also added. Harry Clark, a sheep farmer on the same street, shared the phone line with Ken.

A big surprise came to Ken as he tinkered with a small cabinet door above a small fireplace. The wooden door had leather hinges that had stiffened with age. The hinges broke when he touched the door, and the door fell into a space that Ken had assumed was a cabinet. When the door seemingly disappeared, he discovered that it had fallen into a secret room behind the center chimney. The room was large enough to hold several crouching adults and included a small bench at the end of the room. Ken did not know the purpose for the hidden room, but left it intact and used the front part of the space as a cabinet.

After more than a year and a half the house was still a work in progress, but livable. Ken and his father had completed all of the carpentry by themselves. The stonework, plastering, plumbing, and electrical work, had required contractors. With a "rural route" address and an assigned phone number of "GArden6-4120," Ken and his antiques moved in during the fall of 1962. Larry and Tina visited every weekend to continue the long restoration process.

As Ken spent more and more time at the house, he got to know his new neighbors. In typical New England fashion, the neighbors helped one another as needed, swapped vegetables, borrowed tools, and exchanged gossip. While Ken's house was surrounded by farmland, only one neighbor's house was visible from his yard. At the far end of the street lived Don and Edith Tenney with their several children. Don was a truck driver for Curtis Packaging in Sandy Hook, a local company that was originally founded in 1845 to manufacture fancy combs and buttons.[21] Margaret Stehr, a widow and concert pianist, lived next to the Tenneys. Frank and Madeline Keating lived across the street from Margaret. Madeline and Margaret were sisters.

At the other end of the street lived two Beardsley families, Howard Beardsley and his wife, and next door to them, Howard's brother, Ed Beardsley and wife. Howard was the Newtown Road Commissioner. Ed raised chickens and pheasants. Harry Clark, a widower, lived in a farmhouse across from them with many acres of land where he raised sheep. He also drove a truck for the Newtown Public Works Department, with Howard Beardsley as his boss.

Frank and Ellen Orosz lived next to Howard Beardsley. Ellen's family owned a large farm in Southbury where she had acquired a wealth of agricultural knowledge as well as the skill to fix tractors and other equipment. Frank was from New York City, had served in the Marines in World War II, and worked as a machinist.

FIGURE 24:
Ellen and Frank Orosz, 1987.

Both meticulous, Frank and Ellen maintained an impeccably clean house, large yard, fruit trees, blueberry bushes, and a vegetable garden. With Ellen's know-how and Frank's finesse, the garden produced vegetables that were massive in both size and quantity. One secret—sifted soil! The couple raised enough food to supply themselves with vegetables through the winter. Ellen's pickles and pickled beets were famous throughout the neighborhood, as were her Christmas Eve pierogies.

A New Teacher in School

Meanwhile, Ken continued to teach at Staples High School in Westport. He had finished his master's degree in 1955, and commuted to the University of Connecticut's Storrs campus on weekends with his Staples colleagues to complete his Sixth Year Teaching Certificate. He continued to ramp-up the media department and expanded his administrative role at the request of the principal. One of his administrative duties required him to mentor new teachers at the beginning of the school year. One hour a week for six weeks, Ken introduced the new teachers to the facilities available at Staples and the Westport public school system.

Usually, the group was not familiar with either Staples or Westport, but in the fall of 1964, Ruby Kelley joined the Staples High School English Department staff. Ruby had transferred from Long Lots Junior High School in Westport and was also President of the

Westport Education Association, the local teachers' organization. Ken had met Ruby before and excused her from the introductory class, as she obviously knew her way around. Stubbornly, Ruby refused the gesture and attended every one of Ken's sessions.

Ken encountered the new teacher again when she taught an English class with new media to all sophomores in the auditorium. Ken assisted with the creation of materials that extended beyond the traditional lecture. The class was part of a bigger event that had been organized by the Director of Curriculum to teach a large group with the new tools. The event was a success and showcased the possibilities for new technology in the classroom.

While Ken introduced new media to the teachers at Staples, Elena Lorenzen introduced Ken to the dating scene. Elena often hosted dinner parties for small groups of educators. A regular at the Lorenzen's home, he thought nothing of an invitation to a dinner party until Elena added that she "…had also invited Ruby Kelley." Elena suggested that Ken provide a ride for Ruby to the party. Conveniently, Ruby's house in Monroe was located on the way from Ken's house in Newtown to the Lorenzen's house in Westport.

With the dinner party a success; Elena pursued her matchmaking goals with more gusto. A frequent visitor at Staples, she marched into Ken's classroom and jokingly announced that he owed her money. Elena was President of the Westport Woman's Club, and the organization sponsored a dance every year for $50/ticket at the Longshore Country Club. She needed to sell tickets and had kindly obligated Ken for two tickets to take Ruby Kelley to the dance. No one refused Elena, so Ken prepared accordingly. Elena helped Ruby pick out a gown and insisted that they shop at the Fairfield Department Store in the center of Fairfield, an exclusive store for women. As Elena had designed, Ken and Ruby became a couple.

Maternal Roots

—— **Uneducated, Young, and Married** ——

Born on Christmas Day in 1894 to parents William and Nancy "Annie" (Hopkins) Kelley on their farm in Little Rock, Arkansas, Timothy Kelley was the sixth of seven children born from 1880-1898 and one of two boys. His only brother, William Jr., was twelve years older. The family provided for themselves, and life on the farm was probably typical for the era. Timothy attended school and loved the outdoors.

The turn of the century changed the family's fate, however. A bolt of lightning killed one sister, and brother William died suddenly at or around the age of seventeen. Tragedy struck again when John, the head of the household, died a few months after his son William. Timothy, not even ten years old, became the new man of the house. He was taken out of the fourth grade and put to work in a laundry to earn money for the family. He never received further formal education and his childhood was forever behind him.

Annie remarried in 1908. Timothy likely worked in the laundry business until he was drafted in June of 1917 for World War I. Stationed in Louisiana in the service, Timothy met Ruby Bruce, born in 1901, the daughter of Andrew and Hattie (Skaggs) Bruce and one of three sisters. Andrew Bruce was a professional portrait photographer. He played the violin and often shared music with his daughters: Ruby, who sang beautifully, and Marie, who played the piano. Andrew and Hattie opposed the marriage due to the young age of their daughter, but Timothy and Ruby married in 1919 despite their objections. Timothy was twenty-four, while Ruby was not yet eighteen.

FIGURE 25:
Timothy and Ruby (Bruce) Kelley with sons Ernest (left) and George (right), 1926.

Timothy and Ruby made an unlikely couple. Timothy was an extrovert, loved to hunt and fish, and had achieved basic literacy in the few years of his elementary education. Ruby preferred to keep to herself, stayed indoors, and attended school through the eighth grade. She had acquired basic secretarial skills. The couple had two children in Louisiana: Ernest in 1920, and George in 1922. They shuffled between locations in Alexandria, Lake Charles, and Shreveport, Louisiana, before they moved to Port Arthur, Texas, and eventually Houston, Texas, where Ruby (my mother) was born in 1928. Named after her own mother, baby Ruby was delivered at home with a midwife in attendance.

With baby Ruby born at home in September at the beginning of the school year, and Ruby (Sr.) still in recovery, the midwife was sent to take Ernest and George to their first day of school. Ernest was familiar with the school and scampered away to his classroom. A first grader, George had never been to the school before. School officials greeted the new student and asked him for his name, but George refused to speak. The midwife who accompanied him did not know the boy's name either, so the school sent the pair away. The midwife returned to the Kelley home with George to collect the appropriate information from Ruby (Sr.) and then took her charge back to school. George entered first grade a few hours late, although correctly identified as George Kelley.

FIGURE 26:
Ernest (left), Ruby (center), and George Kelley (right).

The strange start to George's school years highlighted the difference between the children's personalities. Ernest was smart, out-going, and a leader among his peers. He played football, collected stamps, and liked to hunt and fish with his father. George was kind, quiet, and painfully shy. He loved astronomy, although disliked the outdoors. He relied solely on Ernest and Ruby for companionship and generally feared interactions with people outside of the family. Ruby made friends quickly, loved horses, read every book in the children's library, and was an outstanding student at school. Like Ernest,

Ruby loved to tag along after her father on his hunting and fishing trips. Ernest, George, and Ruby, however, suffered great misfortune: their childhood aligned with the Great Depression.

Poverty in the Depression

Timothy worked his way from one cleaning job to the next and moved the family from one city in Texas to another as he searched for employment. He acquired more skills in the laundry business as a presser, cleaner, and dyer, with the reputation of being quite proficient, although jobs in the Depression were both low paying and scarce. Timothy's pay could not sustain a family of five. Ruby (Sr.) sewed to supplement their small income while she cared for the children, but it was still not enough to make ends meet.

Ruby recorded her earliest memory from when she awakened from a deep sleep in the back of a jalopy. The family

FIGURE 27:
Timothy Kelley (second from left) working in the laundry.

was on their way to Austin, where her father sought to find work. "The bouncing and jouncing are in my memory. Mother and Daddy were in the front seat, and my two brothers, Ernest, eight years older than me, and George, six years older, were squeezed in the small space behind the driver seat. There was a shelf inside where the back frame came up to meet the rear window. That was my perch. Our daddy had been promised a job in Austin, and our hopes were high. Maybe the job would be steady and pay enough to feed our family of five...Daddy got the job, but it certainly didn't fulfill our dreams. Short of money and always hungry, my mother tried to help. She fried doughnuts and sent my two brothers, then eight and ten, to sell them on the beautiful marble steps of the magnificent State Capitol. A few pennies' profit helped, but the buyers were few."

Timothy hunted to provide food for the family and always had a hunting dog to aid in the task. His trips often led him to wander for many miles. Comfortable speaking with anyone, he gained numerous acquaintances. Ruby was with her father when they met an old man on a farm. Timothy always asked landowners for permission to hunt, but likely the conversation shifted as the horses on the property spellbound Ruby. The farmer noticed the girl's interest and mentioned that he had a horse that "anybody could ride." Impromptu, Ruby was hoisted atop a gentle horse for her very first riding experience. The magic of horseback never left the child. She was in all her glory in the presence of horses. Timothy returned with Ruby to see the farmer and let Ruby ride the big horse a few more times.

Timothy hunted any game that he could find, although Ruby (Sr.) begged him not to hunt rabbit due to her fear of rabbit disease, a dangerous bacterial illness that hunters sometimes contracted in the skinning process. Although Timothy was a fair marksman, the family did not eat when he failed to kill anything. The children were terribly skinny and often hungry. Ruby, the youngest, suffered the most. Once, Timothy returned from a hunting trip with only a small dove. After the bird had been plucked and cleaned, it produced only the tiniest portion of meat. At dinnertime, the entire bite-size morsel was placed in front of Ruby's emaciated frame as her starving brothers looked on with ravenous jealousy.

The insult of poverty never left the children. As school dismissed for lunchtime, Ruby returned home to be with her mother, even though there was no food to eat. Ruby wrote as an adult, "...the endless days of gnawing hunger and lonely, quiet, shame. We were different, I thought, strangers in the midst of a street of many children and a school where others had a nickel for taffy."

On one occasion, her class planned a picnic, and each child was requested to donate a food item to participate. As the date approached, Ruby became more and more desperate to attend with little hope of a solution to meet

FIGURE 28:
Ruby Kelley at age five.

the admission criteria. At the last minute, Ruby (Sr.) had the money to purchase an orange for Ruby to take to school. The elementary school student proudly handed the orange to her teacher and declared that the orange was "for the punch."

If food was scarce, then medical attention was nearly non-existent. Young Ruby had a foldable chair collapse with her hands under the seat. She broke eight fingers and never saw a doctor. More often, she wailed in agony with one ear infection after the next. Ruby wrote as an adult, "I remember being about five or six and screaming with terrible ear aches. To relieve the pain, my mother heated the old-fashioned iron on the stove, wrapped it in a towel, and told me to place my ear against the warm towel to relieve the pain."[22]

At one point, Ruby was so terribly sick with pneumonia that Ruby (Sr.) insisted that Timothy call a doctor despite the fact that the family did not have any money. Timothy finally agreed as his youngest daughter's life hung in the balance. The doctor arrived at the Kelley's apartment, but communicated that he could not help unless Ruby was transported to his private hospital. Ruby had no recollection of the environment change, but clearly remembered that she woke up in an all-white room and was served a full tray of food. She ate!

As the family moved, the children changed schools, which sometimes required them to take a test to determine their class placement. In 1936, the family moved from Fort Worth, where Ruby had attended second grade at the Alexander Hogg Elementary School to San Antonio, where she would finish the school year at Riverside Park Elementary School. Ruby wrote, "The school principal thought I should be advanced to the third grade and directed the second grade teacher to test me orally."[22]

FIGURE 29:
High Third Class of Riverside Park Elementary School on a visit to Stimson Field. Ruby Kelley is the third from the left in front row.

The elementary student probably knew the material, but the exercise led the administrators to detect a different problem. Ruby had asked the teachers several times to repeat the questions. As an adult, Ruby explained, "As the teacher spoke individual words to test my spelling ability, I kept turning my head to listen with my right ear."[22] The school officials did not advance Ruby and suspected a severe hearing loss, likely due to so many ear infections. Ruby (Sr.) chose not to discuss the matter with her daughter. Ruby compensated for the problem on her own and suffered in silence.

Timothy struggled to find employment throughout the Depression. Although he lacked an education, he read chemistry books in the evening and aspired to apply his knowledge of the subject to textiles in the laundry business. Long before colorfast clothing, men's shirts faded in the underarms due to perspiration. The faded garment area was treated at the laundry with a "powder puff" of similarly colored substance to restore the faded area to match that of the original. Timothy developed a chemical formula to produce a substitute solution in the various colors needed.

The entire family worked in the backyard to fill bottles with Timothy's formula. Ruby, still in elementary school, painted the tops of the lids to match the color inside. Timothy completed his first delivery. The product worked well, and he quickly received orders for more. The family was excited and worked to repeat their steps for a new batch of the product. Unfortunately, Timothy was unable to replicate the chemical process and could not achieve the same results. After several failed attempts, the project was abandoned.

As the Depression held the Kelley family firmly in its grasp, Timothy and his wife argued regularly over their financial situation. Timothy was under a lot of pressure to support the family and wanted Ernest to drop out of school to go to work. Years earlier, Timothy had been forced to leave school as a youth for similar reasons and believed strongly that Ernest should do the same. Ruby (Sr.) disagreed and vowed that all of her children would finish high school despite the dire circumstances.

The Kelley family continued to move often. At one point they rented a small apartment that they shared with their landlady. The woman rented one room in her house and shared the kitchen and bathroom with the Kelley family of five. She also gave piano lessons to supplement her tiny rental income. The woman's husband had died years earlier, and times were hard for her, too. Another time, the Kelley family rented an apartment that had been converted from a chicken coop. The arrangements required the family to enter the landlord's house to use the bathroom. Ruby regularly felt the shame of their living situation.

As the conflict over financial matters intensified between Ruby's parents, her father left for days or weeks at a time to search for work on his own. If he found something somewhat permanent, he returned to collect the family in a borrowed jalopy and hastily moved them to the new location. Otherwise, he stayed away, absent more and more as time passed. It is possible that there was some rationale to his behavior. At the time, a mother and her children on their own could gain more sympathy and assistance from the community. If a husband was present, that same generosity was withheld as the man of the house was expected to work.

With Timothy away, Ruby (Sr.), Ernest, George, and Ruby faced rent payments on their own and always feared eviction. In one circumstance, they lived in a duplex apartment that was owned by an older woman in the other side of the house. The woman knew the family's circumstances, but the rental money from the apartment was her only source of income. She could not have afforded for Ruby (Sr.) and her children to stay in the apartment without paying rent. Similarly, she could not have allowed herself to turn a mother and her children out into the streets.

In a gesture of unbelievable kindness, the woman invited the struggling Kelley family to live with her, while she rented out the apartment to new tenants. Ruby (Sr.) and the children moved into the woman's half of the house until they could afford another apartment on their own. Ruby (Sr.) hustled for small office work or sewing jobs at home. The boys were old enough to contribute their small earnings from part-time and weekend jobs, although they both stayed in school.

Timothy dropped in from time to time, but seemed only to argue with Ruby (Sr.) over money and continued to insist that Ernest quit school. The fights between their parents traumatized the boys, particularly George, although they both remained steadfastly loyal to their mother, who had stayed with them. If she wanted them educated, then they applied themselves accordingly. Ernest had shown a remarkable aptitude in school and had a keen interest to study air conditioning, a new technology that promised relief from the hot Texas summers.

The food situation improved for the Kelley family when Annie (Hopkins) Kelley, Timothy's mother, moved to San Antonio and opened a restaurant with one of her daughters. Annie sold the family farm in Arkansas to an aluminum company after bauxite, an aluminum ore, had been discovered on the land. The restaurant opened a couple of blocks off the path that Ruby took to school, and she could visit the restaurant to eat whenever she wanted.

Annie visited Ruby (Sr.) and the children at their home and frequently delighted them with the gift of three pies, one for each child, so that there would not be an argument over the food. During her visits, she also kept a tin can next to a rocking chair to dip snuff. The children were sternly warned, "don't knock over Grandma's tin can," as they played. The restaurant stayed open for only a couple of years, but the support of Timothy's family with restaurant meals was greatly appreciated.

—— High School During World War II ——

Ruby (Sr.) had remained steadfast in her support of an education for Ernest, George, and Ruby. In May of 1938, Ernest graduated from Brackenridge High School in San Antonio, Texas. He was the first person in the family to obtain a high school diploma. Ernest was educated more than most men, but the Depression meant that jobs were hard to find.

FIGURE 30:
Ernest Kelley high school graduation photo, 1938.

After graduation, Ernest bought a car with a friend and drove northwest. The two men attached sheep shears to the engine of the car and sheared sheep for money. They reached Idaho and were able to find odd jobs to support themselves. Ernest wrote home, "I have pitched hay for the last week and boy am I tired." He also reported "topping sugar beets for five days." Ernest explored the surrounding wilderness fur trapping or panning for gold, and experienced ice-skating and snow for the first time. He wrote, "…it is really cold up here," and requested his mother to mail him his winter coat. Worried about the cost of postage, he instructed his mother to send the parcel collect if needed.

In nearly every letter, Ernest apologized for not writing more and inquired about the family's financial situation pleading, "Do not worry about me." Sometimes he sent a few dollars home and asked whether the family received the money. He also requested information on the welfare and school status of George and Ruby, addressing his sister by her nickname of "Snooky." While Ruby was eight years younger than her oldest brother, the two were extremely close.

Midway through 1939, Ernest was likely more aware of his parents' marriage difficulties when he replied to his mother with words of encouragement. He headed south to Phoenix, Arizona, working at a fruit ranch in California along the way. By December, he informed his family that he would not be home for Christmas that year as he had a job all winter. In January of 1940 he wrote "...been working on a ranch the last two months and trying to learn to be a cowboy." He also sheared goats and worked in a mine. In April of 1940 he wrote home on stationery imprinted with "Charles W. Morgan, Tip Top Camp, Phoenix, Arizona."

Ernest may have visited Royalty, Texas, to visit his father's sister Jessie, but then wrote of his plans to travel to California (and probably the northwest). After nearly two years on the road, he was likely tired and found himself desperate again for food. Unexpectedly, his high school education provided him with an opportunity in the military. He learned that the Army was recruiting soldiers to serve in the Philippines under General Douglas MacArthur. With so many men out of work in the Depression, the military had their pick of volunteers. Selective among so many applicants who sought refuge from hunger, the Army required a high school diploma for the Philippines duty. Ernest qualified and enlisted in July 5, 1940 at Fort Lawton, Washington.[23] In a letter to his family he wrote, "...I finally did what I said I'd never do. I joined the army on the condition that they would send me to the P.I....in the Signal Corps. I'm going to take up radio and television....I'm glad that I went through high school, because I had to have a high school education to get in."

Ernest arrived at Fort McDowell on Angel Island, California, in July of 1940 to await transport to the Philippines. By October it was probably clear that his parents had separated. Ernest wrote, "Mother, try hard to keep the house you're in, and if Pop offers you the car, take it. Things will work out somehow." He reached Honolulu, Hawaii, by October 16, 1940 and mentioned that "We were supposed to get paid $5.00 for shore leave, but they didn't do it; so we are all going ashore broke. All I've seen in the last week is water and more water."

Posted to Manila in November of 1940 under Captain Richard M. Bauer, he wrote home and enclosed snapshots of Manila. In a letter dated March 3, 1941, Ernest communicated that he was transferred to the Aircraft Warning Department and explained that it was part of the Signal Corps and G-2 Department. On March 11, 1941, he wrote again and assured his mother that "...in the job that I have now I'll be able to know exactly when the first enemy plane appears or when the first warship enters our waters."

In another letter to the family, dated October 15, 1941, Ernest wrote that he had purchased a 1936 V-8 Tudor Sedan with a friend, Howard Mann. On November 25, 1941, Ruby wrote a letter to her son with the handwritten greeting "A Merry Christmas to One In the Service" printed on the outside of the envelope. The letter was returned to her, stamped "Returned to Sender Service Suspended."

Ruby (Sr.), George, and Ruby lived together in San Antonio and anxiously awaited news from Ernest. Ruby had been watching her mother hem a dress in the living room when they heard President Franklin Roosevelt's voice on the radio. The president addressed a joint session of Congress with his famous words, "Yesterday, December 7, 1941—a date which will live in infamy—the United States of America was suddenly and deliberately attacked by naval and air forces of the Empire of Japan...Last night Japanese forces attacked the Philippine Islands." Ruby never forgot the terror that spread across her mother's face. They all knew that Ernest was in trouble. Indeed, he was declared missing in action on May 7, 1942.

The military spending that accompanied the 1941 declaration of war created job opportunities on the home front. Ruby (Sr.) went to work at Kelly Field in San Antonio, a huge military complex that provided aircraft maintenance and training for airmen, where she was quick to point out that the "Kelly" was spelled wrong. George graduated from high school in 1940 and worked as a bicycle messenger, although he had the bad luck to have been assigned to the Alamo Heights section of San Antonio, the hilliest part of the large city. He was exhausted at the end of each day of bicycling. By 1941, George had started as a mechanic helper at Duncan Field.[24] Records stated his occupation as "Airplane Electrician (Helper)"[25] with duties recorded as "Installed electrical wiring, fixtures and switches in airplanes. Did electrical work on parts of the engine. Assembled aircraft magnetos, generators, and starters."[25] With Ruby's (Sr.) small paycheck and contributions from George, the family finally had some semblance of a small income.

Soon, the U.S. enacted the draft, and George faced immediate conscription. The draft did not allow men to choose their branch of service. George, still a passive and shy person, was terrified at the thought of assignment in the ground forces. A *volunteer* could choose his branch of service, so George went to a recruiting office with plans to join the Navy. He had likely never seen the ocean, but the Navy was ready to accept him. They required him only to have his father's signature on the appropriate paperwork.

George fumed at the paternal signature required for enlistment. He had not seen his father in years. Even if Timothy's whereabouts had been known, George harbored so much anger at his father's abandonment that he refused to ask him for anything. Instead, George switched tactics and enlisted with the Army Air Corps on

October 28, 1942. The different branch of
service did not require his father's signature. Trained as a tail gunner for the B-17
"flying fortress," he was posted to Europe.
Like Ernest, he sent money home to his
mother when he could.

Ruby attended the Thomas Nelson
Page Junior School before entering Brack-
enridge High School in the fall of 1942.
In high school, she excelled in many sub-
jects and gained recognition as a National
Honor, English Honor, and History

FIGURE 31:
*George Kelley in the
U.S. Army Air Corps.*

Honor student. She played on the tennis team, belonged to the
Sigma Epsilon Society, and was selected as a member of the Modern Diana's, which formed in 1943 as "...a club for the purpose of
promoting participation and interest in healthful sports."[26] The
selection process favored girls who "rank high in scholarship, leadership, and charm."[26] The chosen few were known as nymphs
until initiated. Ruby eventually became Sergeant at Arms for the
Modern Diana Club.[26] Denied the opportunity to take shop classes
because she was a girl, the school offered Ruby the opportunity to
take a mechanical drawing class, where she received high praise
for her lettering skill.

More than anything, Ruby continued to read every book that
she could. As librarians picked out books for the eager student, she
rapidly consumed their contents and returned for another. Keen
to learn about the world, she particularly loved Richard Halliburton's *Complete Book of Marvels*. Halliburton, a prolific travel writer,
had published his worldwide journeys that included a visit to Tim-
buktu, Africa, and a swim (no kidding!) through the Panama

Canal. Ruby dreamed of visiting the far-off places herself, particularly the pyramids of Egypt.

Ruby (Sr.) encouraged Ruby to learn music and purchased a violin at a pawnshop for seven dollars. The music teacher accepted the instrument as adequate, but insisted on a new bow. Ruby (Sr.) purchased a replacement bow for two dollars. Ruby played the instrument for several years, but was limited by her crooked fingers and hearing loss such that she never obtained much skill. She had also failed to inherit her mother's beautiful singing voice and lacked vocal talent altogether. Before too long, music was relegated to a matter of appreciation rather than participation.

FIGURE 32:
Ruby Kelley high school graduation photo, 1946.

Amidst so many activities, the war still defined Ruby's high school years. She served as a member of the Junior Women's Army Corps (WAC) and obtained the highest rank in her high school as Colonel of the Girls' Officer Corps. Her striking pictures in uniform reflect a confident young woman, a model of patriotism, leadership, and ability. She may have represented the corps on December 7, 1944, when the high school held a Memorial Assembly. With a program titled "In Memory of The Fallen Heroes of Brackenridge High School," her brother Ernest was recognized as one of more than seventy other graduates among the "The Honored Dead of World War II."

Earlier in the same year, Timothy and Ruby (Sr.) were formally divorced, although the paperwork was a mere formality. Ruby (Sr.) described that she had "grown apart" from her husband. George outwardly despised his father. Ruby sensed her father's many hardships, most significantly his lack of education, and remained more sympa-

FIGURE 33:
Brackenridge High School Girls Officers Corps, 1946.
Ruby Kelley is sixth from left in the front row.

thetic to his memory. At nineteen, Ruby received a final "distribution" from her father. Timothy was legally freed from his obligations as a father when a Bexar Country court upheld a petition for the "removal of her disability as a minor." The court also ruled that, for legal purposes, she was of full age, except as the right to vote.[27]

The Aftermath of War

George returned home in the fall of 1945, soon after the Allied victory in Europe. He had flown twenty-six missions over Germany, participated in the Ardennes, Rhineland, and Central Europe campaigns, and was decorated with an EAME (European-African-Middle Eastern) ribbon with three bronze stars and an Air Medal with three oak leaf clusters.[28] His safe return, however, was greatly overshadowed by the lack of news from Ernest in the Pacific. George held on to the hope that Ernest was alive. He idolized his brother and was emotionally lost in the world without him.

George attended the University of Texas in Austin, Texas, under the G.I. Bill and completed his baccalaureate degree in economics in 1952. He joined his mother as a civil servant at Kelly Air Field in 1955 and remained there until his retirement. He never married and devoted the next forty plus years of his life to the care of his mother. George flew on commercial planes a few times in his life, but generally feared flying. Ruby said of her brother that he never recovered from flying in an airplane "when other people were shooting at him."

As more and more servicemen returned home, the Kelley's unexpectedly received a visit from a G.I., who introduced himself as Howard Mann. The very same person that Ernest had mentioned in his last letter home stood before them. Surviving servicemen frequently visited families of lost service members. Howard had traveled to San Antonio to meet the Kelley family to convey the information he had about Ernest in the Philippines.

Howard and Ernest had been driving the Tudor sedan that they purchased together, south of Manila, when Japanese forces attacked Clark Field in the Philippines on December 7, 1941. They reported back to duty immediately, but the air base could not recover from the damage it incurred.

General MacArthur withdrew American and Philippine forces from several defensive positions to the Bataan peninsula. The plan required them to wait for reinforcements from Hawaii, but the fleet in Pearl Harbor had been destroyed. The troops on the peninsula held out for three months before they surrendered in 1942. 76,000 prisoners of war, including Howard and Ernest, were marched sixty-six miles at gunpoint in the infamous Bataan Death March. Thousands of American and Filipino soldiers died of their wounds or were murdered by the Japanese along the way.[29]

The Japanese "...beat the prisoners as viciously as their ser-
geants and lieutenants beat them—slapped them, punched them,
boxed their ears, bashed their skulls, broke their bones. They beat
them for looking this way or that, for moving or not moving fast
enough, for talking or keeping still—beat them for everything and
for nothing at all."[29] The captives also suffered from the heat, "The
SUN was inescapable. It blistered their skin, baked their shoulders
and backs, beat on their heads."[29] Finally, the marchers were
deprived of water, despite the availability of artesian wells along
the route. The effects of dehydration of the brain caused many of
the men to lose their ability to think clearly as they became "func-
tionally deranged."[29]

According to Howard, he survived the tortuous march with
Ernest and arrived at a POW (prisoner of war) camp where the
Japanese atrocities continued. The American and Filipino soldiers
were already starved before capture, and the Japanese provided little food. Additionally, many of the emaciated American soldiers
were sick from tropical diseases and suffered from their illnesses
without medical care. Some men sought to escape the decrepit conditions of the camp, although the Japanese beheaded any escapees
who were caught and placed the severed heads on posts in full view
of the POWs to deter further escape attempts.

Howard reported that Ernest particularly despised the brutality
of the Japanese and the conditions of the camp. Ernest prepared
to escape with a few other men, undeterred by the consequences
of capture. Howard conspired with the group, too, but was too sick
to join them on the night of the planned escape. Ernest, possibly
with a few others, escaped from the camp into the darkness of the
jungle. Howard was forced to stay behind.

Howard never saw his friend again, but reported to Ruby (Sr.)
that he had never seen Ernest's head on a camp post. Without evi-

dence of capture, Howard assumed that Ernest's escape had been successful. Howard remained in the POW camp due to illness, although, like many other prisoners, he was shipped to Japan to perform forced labor in the salt mines before the war ended. The Empire of Japan surrendered on September 2, 1945.

At a later date, Ruby (Sr.) received a letter from a Filipino family. The family claimed to have hidden Ernest after his escape from the POW camp, but had asked him to leave when the Japanese approached the village for a search. Japanese soldiers killed any Filipinos who harbored Americans. Ruby (Sr.) contacted the War Department with the contents of the letter. The government confirmed the story through their investigators in the Philippines. Ernest had indeed hidden in a Filipino village after his escape, but had never been seen or heard from again. The most likely explanation was that he died of malaria in the jungle. He was declared "presumed dead" as of February 1, 1946.

In May, 1946, Ruby's senior year of high school, Ruby (Sr.) received a letter from the General Headquarters, Army Forces In The Pacific, Office of the Commander in Chief.

May 14, 1946.

Dear Mrs. Kelley:

We have lost a gallant comrade in arms in the death of your son, Corporal Ernest O. Kelley, and I extend my sincere sympathy in your bereavement.

His service under my command in the Pacific was characterized by his complete loyalty to our country. In giving his life in this crusade for liberty, his name takes its place on the roll of our Nation's honored dead.

Very faithfully,

(Signed) Douglas MacArthur

Ruby (Sr.) was overwhelmed with grief over the loss of her son, and the lack of closure added to her pain. While she never gave up hope that Ernest might have survived the war, she also made sure that he was not forgotten. Through his mother's efforts, Ernest's name was imprinted on the World War II plaque at Brackenridge High School and the Memorial Wall at the Witte Museum in San Antonio, Texas.[30],[31] He was posthumously recognized with the Award of the Bronze Star Medal for "Meritorious Achievement in Ground Combat in the South West Pacific Theater of Operations" at the rank of Corporal in the 10th Signal Service Company.[32] Later, Ruby (Sr.) secured a marker for Ernest at both the Manila American Cemetery in Manila, Philippines, as well as the Arlington National Cemetery in Arlington, Virginia. Ruby (Sr.) joined and stayed active in the Gold Star Mothers organization for the rest of her life. Ernest never left her thoughts.

FIGURE 34:
Ernest Kelley (top left) in the Philippines.

Waking Up Without a Brother

In the wake of the news about Ernest, Ruby graduated from high school in 1946 and went to work for Western Union in San Antonio, Texas. Western Union conducted inter-state commerce, and Congress had set the pay rate of $0.40/hour for related jobs. As the G.I.s returned from the war, there were a lot of applicants for any job opening. Ruby had been warned that Western Union would ask whether she planned to attend college in the fall. She answered "no" to get the job, but also knew that her mother did not have the money for college tuition.

Ruby liked the Western Union environment. She was impressed by the fact that the men removed their hats whenever she entered the elevator. Men always wore hats, and it was customary to remove them in the presence of a woman. Even though Ruby was just a telegraph girl, the men treated her with respect.

Ruby excelled at her work and was soon appointed as the weekend supervisor. The managers assumed that there was not much activity on weekends and that a young person could handle the light load. Instead, Ruby's first weekend shift corresponded with a Fort Sam Houston payday, and a long line formed at the counter. Ruby hurried to take in thousands of dollars and stuffed the money in drawers as she ran out of places to put it.

When the supervisor came back from the weekend, he asked why she had not called the central office for help. Ruby never knew that that option was available to her and had only done the best she could. After the supervisor initially questioned that the receipts did not balance, he commended her performance. Ruby had done very well for a new high school graduate.

Ruby continued to work at Western Union through the summer, but Ruby (Sr.) was determined that her daughter would attend college. The University of Texas at Austin was the obvious choice. However, Austin, Texas, was flooded with G.I.s who had returned from the war, and it was difficult to find housing for school. The university even deferred admittance until a prospective student could prove that he or she had secured a place to live. Church associations often helped, and Ruby finally obtained housing through the Methodist Church. She subsequently received acceptance to the University of Texas at Austin.

Although tuition money was still doubtful, Ruby (Sr.) became wary of the Austin option when a friend warned that the city was not safe for a young woman with so many G.I.s. The friend suggested that the Texas State College for Women (TSCW) in Denton, Texas, might offer a better option. Ruby (Sr.) encouraged her daughter to apply. Ruby completed the application and was not only accepted, but received one of fifteen $100 scholarships that were sponsored by the student body. At $25/semester, the scholarship paid for two years of school. Ruby notified Western Union of her new college plans. They were sorry to see her go, but supportive of her decision.

Horse Crazy

Ruby arrived at TSCW and was immediately thrilled with the scenic campus. Sending a picturesque postcard to her mother in September of 1946, she wrote, "The picture on the front is typical of the campus. Trees, trees everywhere, and hills, hills everywhere. It is just like a big park." She also wasted no time in searching for a part-time position to help pay her expenses. Ruby and a friend found a job in the dining hall that served professors, as well as the Denton, Texas, public. The small salary covered her room and board, which relieved her mother of the only expenditure that had not been covered by the scholarship.

Fascinated by chemistry, Ruby planned to major in the subject that had similarly captivated her father. She enrolled in a full course load that included chemistry, English, mathematics, government, German, and other classes. She pursued her college studies with the same vigor by which she distinguished herself with an "A" average in high school.

However, all too soon she was dissuaded from her dream in chemistry. A faculty member warned that no company hired female chemists. Given her poverty-stricken childhood, Ruby must have known that a job was required to put food on the table. She chose not to challenge the status quo and was ultimately confronted with the traditional career options for women of nursing or education. Ruby pursued education and double majored in English and history.

As much as the school may have guided women toward realistic goals, it provided a wealth of opportunities outside the classroom. Ruby attended special events at the school and particularly enjoyed the Concert and Drama Series, which included a performance by Ezio Pinza, Metropolitan Opera Association basso. The school newspaper reported, "One of the fourteen 'most glamorous men in the world,' will sing tonight…'The Frank Sinatra of Long Hair Music,' as his associates call him because of the numerous bobby-soxers attracted to his stage door, has a voice range more than two octaves. For, with a somewhat higher range than the more usual basso profundo and with a cantabile quality which may be difficult for even a baritone to obtain, Mr. Pinza represents a basso cantante and is thus an exponent of the vocal tradition of Edouard de Reszke and Chaliapin." Ruby saved the January 13, 1947, program, as she was so impressed by the performance.

Ruby, still horse-crazy, quickly migrated toward the college's horse stables to join an outgoing group of young women in equestrian. The school's riding facility featured a large barn with an indoor riding arena and twenty-one box stalls that included a tack room, feed room, a classroom for lectures and tests, and an office for the administrator. A large acreage at the north end of campus had two outdoor arenas, one for instruction and one for jumping. The horses were fed hay and grazed in a large area during the winter. Two pastures near the campus allowed for the rotation of "teaching horses," with about twenty horses on campus and around twenty horses resting in the nearby pastures at any given time.[33]

FIGURE 35:
TSCW riding group, circa 1947.

Miss Mary Branche Williams, called "Teacher," provided the riding instruction. Teacher, whose personality and grit were legendary in North Texas, taught the beginners bareback riding and preached, "You must learn to ride first, and then you will be able to ride any style thrown at you in Central Park." Second semester riders were able to choose their preferred style, and the tack room was well equipped with both English and Western saddles, called "stock saddles." Teacher rode both styles with ease.[34]

Although Miss Williams lived on-campus while teaching, about five miles north of town she owned a ranch, referred to as "the big farm," with 640 acres. Miss Williams' father, Will Williams, had bred and raised registered Shetland ponies on the ranch years earlier. At the time of his death in 1956, the ranch was home to the largest herd of registered Shetlands on the North American continent.[34]

Advanced students at the school earned access to "the farm" after a semester. They helped to care for the horses and maintain the ranch, as Teacher masterfully disguised work as fun.[35] The great expanse of land provided a playground for the horse lovers. Ruby described the rides on the Texas plains as a simple pleasure, as a group headed out with just a sweet potato or a few stalks of fresh asparagus in their saddlebags. Presumably, she rode with a Western saddle around the ranch, and converted to the English style for pleasure jumping in the woods or show jumping in competition.

Teacher's fearlessness was often at the center of the riding tales from Ruby's days at the ranch. Ruby described how Teacher killed poisonous rattlesnakes, as the snakes were a threat to the horses. As soon as Teacher heard the ominous rattle, she dismounted from her horse to locate the snake. She used the horse's bridle to prod the snake from its lair and then hit the snake on its head to stun it. Once the snake was sufficiently disoriented, Teacher grabbed the snake by its tail, swung it over her head several times and smashed the snake on a rock to break its back or snapped it overhead like a whip to achieve the same effect.

In swampy areas, Teacher unleashed pigs to clear the area of cottonmouth water moccasins. Pigs were a natural enemy of the venomous creatures, which allowed Teacher to create a safe place for the horses. The water snakes were also detectable by an unmistakable smell. Teacher was the first to sense an undesired snake in her proximity.

"Can you smell it? Can you smell it?" she cautioned her students. None of the young women ever developed their leader's ability to detect the smelly snakes, but admired Teacher's fearlessness as she killed the cottonmouth water moccasins in the same heroic fashion as the rattlesnakes. However, she would *never* hurt a non-poisonous snake, even the Blue Racers that would stand straight up when threatened, very protective of their territory. In general, she felt that people should leave alone anything that was not going to bother them.

Teacher also taught the women not to be afraid of the snakes. When the horses needed to drink from a small pond, Teacher had the student riders splash in the water to frighten the Cotton Mouth Water Moccasins. The snakes swam to the other side of the watering hole, which allowed the students to swim freely while the horses drank. Teacher assured the girls that the snakes would not bother them as long as they continued to splash around in the water.

Teacher successfully managed the threat of poisonous snakes for the safety of the horses and took equal measures to protect the safety of her young riders. She quickly sold horses that kicked or bit anyone, although sometimes ended up with horses that required more skill to handle. Sally Goodin', a stout, gray animal built like a draft horse,

FIGURE 36:
Teacher with a snake.

was one such animal. Sally Goodin' had been chosen by Teacher to serve some of the heavier girls as she kept a few bigger horses around to match horses and riders appropriately. Although Sally Goodin' was a temperamental animal, Teacher maintained that everything a horse did wrong was the rider's fault.[36]

Ruby rode Sally Goodin' one day, along with other riders and their horses, when a train appeared on the nearby tracks. The conductor waved to the Texas women riders and blew the train whistle. Sally Goodin' was spooked by the noise, put down her head, and bucked off Ruby. Ruby was startled, but unhurt. The conductor was clearly surprised, too, and was seen to gesture an apology as the train passed. The event cemented Sally Goodin's difficult reputation among the students.

Teacher, unnaturally protective of Sally Goodin', reassured her students that "...Sally was a good horse and just needed proper handling." Not too long after Ruby had been thrown off, Teacher chose to ride Sally Goodin' herself. She accompanied a few of the girls to catch some horses in the pasture to lead the animals back to the barn. Teacher led two horses with lead ropes, when one of the horses crossed behind her, which caused the lead rope to brush the hindquarters of Sally Goodin'. That was enough to spook the unpredictable gray horse.

Teacher was shot into the air and landed on the ground "still in the saddle" with her legs splayed. The horse had bucked so violently that the saddle girth had been broken. Teacher insisted that she was all right, but the girls feared otherwise and decided to go for help. Someone ran for a jeep, but in the panic of the moment, backed over a roll of barbed wire. The wire wrapped around the jeep's drive shaft and rendered the vehicle unusable. The only other option was for someone to ride a horse to town and get help. Ruby and Teacher's niece, Kay Williams, were dispatched on horseback to find the local doctor. Their horses were both fast, and the emergency created a perfect excuse to "air them out."[37]

Fortunately, Teacher sustained only a severe bruise on her backside. The local doctor, Doc Holland, advised rest for several days to allow the injury to heal, although Teacher did not comply with his recommendation. Sally Goodin' suffered a quiet disappearance from the Williams' ranch soon after.

Ruby loved the horses and spent as much time as possible at the ranch. In order to cover the cost of her participation, she "rode fence" to inspect and repair the many miles of barriers that defined the pastures for horses and cattle. She also worked at the stables feeding horses and ferried horses back and forth between the stables and pastures as needed for the teaching rotation. When one of Teacher's mares gave birth to a foal, Ruby purchased the newborn animal and "broke" the horse herself, which meant that she trained it for riding. The horse, named Sonata, was a source of pride and the object of Ruby's equine affection. When Ruby wrote home to her mother on January 7, 1948, she included the postscript "Sonata sends her love and one of her beautiful locks." Horsehair was neatly tucked inside the envelope.

FIGURE 37:
Ruby Kelley with her horse named Sonata.

Ruby never tired of the Texas plains until Teacher presented her with a new opportunity. A business owner had called the ranch from New England. He was looking for young women with horseback riding skills to serve as camp counselors at a girls' camp in New England. Teacher recommended Ruby.

Ruby left Texas for the first time and made her way by train to the Forest Acres Camp and K-Ranch for Girls in Fryeburg, Maine. The camp boasted a variety of activities that included sports, arts, golf, fishing, drama, dance, music, and a "colorful ranch life program."[38] Ruby served as a riding instructor and helped the girls around the camp. When the summer ended, a child's father walked over to Ruby and handed her a twenty-dollar bill.

"Thank you for being so nice to my daughter," he said. While Ruby had given the girl some extra attention, she had never expected that kind of generosity. That amount of money felt like gold.

Ruby returned to school and finished a four-year degree program in three years to graduate in 1949. Like her brothers, she also faced limited job prospects. Although the national economic situation had improved, jobs for women were extremely hard to find as hiring priority was given to men who returned from the war. After a lengthy job search, Ruby signed a contract to teach at Broadmoor Elementary School in Hobbs, New Mexico. She earned $2,640 for the school year, paid in twelve payments of $220 each.[39] Hobbs had become a boomtown after the discovery of oil and badly needed teachers, including women. The school was brand new and had been built to relieve overcrowding. Ruby lived in Hobbs with several roommates and caught a ride to school with teachers who had a car and passed by her home.

A Texan in Connecticut

After one year in Hobbs, New Mexico, Ruby returned to Texas to work at the Atlantic Refining Company in Dallas as a mapmaker. In a strange coincidence, her skills from the high school mechanical drawing class had provided her with the qualifications to earn the position. Ruby's time at Atlantic Refining Company was uneventful except for an unusual Dallas earthquake that shook the company's building so violently that she was nearly knocked off her feet.

Ruby re-connected with Teacher at TSCW (Texas State College for Women) and boarded two horses at the ranch, one of which was a Tennessee Walker. In 1951, Ruby searched for new living quarters and responded to an advertisement for a roommate placed by Cynthia Smith in the Wynnewood neighborhood of Dallas.

Cynthia lived with three housemates, but one had recently moved out. A replacement roommate, Anne, had been recruited, but did not fit in with the group. The friction caused two housemates to depart, which left Cynthia and Anne to struggle with the household bills. Ruby was interviewed and immediately accepted as the new third roommate to rescue the women from their financial situation. However, the threesome was short-lived. Anne did not blend well with Cynthia and Ruby either.[40]

Ruby and Cynthia quickly became friends. They moved on their own to a smaller, unfinished apartment in the same area of Wynnewood and purchased the barest minimum of furniture to provide the semblance of a home. Both animal lovers, they also acquired a little black cocker spaniel named Jet. Ruby introduced Cynthia to horseback riding, and the women frequently spent evenings and Saturdays at Teacher's ranch. Jet accompanied the ladies on their expeditions, ensconced on Ruby's lap in the saddle.[40]

Cynthia Smith hailed from Connecticut, where she had worked at Chance Vought in Stratford, Connecticut. The company built airplanes and had relocated to Texas in 1949. Cynthia had worked for the superintendent of the experimental department and moved with the company. She badly missed her family in Connecticut, though. Her brother and sister-in-law had three girls, and she wanted to be closer to her nieces in their teenage years. After four years in Dallas, Cynthia decided to return to Connecticut.[40]

FIGURE 38:
Cynthia Smith on a horse named Nutmeg.

After a bit of deliberation, Ruby decided to follow Cynthia to Connecticut. She liked adventure and already had a taste of New England at the K-Ranch in Maine. The women leveraged the camp connection, as the K-Ranch owners re-hired Ruby to be the head riding instructor and hired Cynthia as an assistant riding instructor for the summer of 1953.[40]

FIGURE 39:
*Ruby Kelley show jumping in
North Conway, New Hampshire, 1950.*

At the end of the summer, Ruby and Cynthia moved in with Cynthia's brother and his family in Trumbull, Connecticut. Ward and Nelle Smith were parents to three active girls, Cynthia Lee (CL), Judy, and Betsy. Although a guest in the house, Ruby was loved by the Smiths and treated as a member of the extended family. Because she lacked even the most rudimentary cooking skills, Ruby took charge of dishwashing and endeared herself to the younger crowd who were permanently relieved of the household chore.[41]

Nelle and her three daughters spent summers at their large family cottage on Lake Sunapee in New Hampshire. Ruby, Cynthia, and Jet joined them on weekends. The New Hampshire house was near another cabin that was owned by friends from Trumbull, Stanley and Rowena Jacoby, who had two children, Bobby and Susan. Rowena and Nelle served as Girl Scout leaders together for their daughters' troop in Connecticut. The friendship, food, and fun between the families provided an endless source of entertainment as the large crowd enjoyed swimming, hiking, sailing, and waterskiing.[42]

The Smith's lake house had an aura of grand cuisine, as Nelle's mother, "Grandma Sibley," often joined them. Grandma Sibley was famous for her bread and sticky buns and made the perfect shortcake for strawberry season. Rowena, like Grandma Sibley, also exhibited culinary genius. The Smith/Sibley/Jacoby/Kelley lake crowd was always well fed. Although Ruby was never a cook, she did learn to master Grandma Sibley's shortcake.

FIGURE 40:
*Cynthia Smith (left)
with Ruby Kelley (right) and Jet.*

Grandma Sibley's Shortcake

INGREDIENTS:
1 cup flour
1/3 cup shortening or margarine
1/3 cup milk
2 tablespoons sugar
2 teaspoons baking powder
¼ teaspoon salt

INSTRUCTIONS:
- Mix dry ingredients and shortening. Add milk slowly using a fork to mix.
- When ready to handle, place on a floured board or cloth and form into individual shortcake servings. Results are best if dough is handled as little as possible.
- Bake at 425 degrees for 15-20 minutes.

Grandma Sibley's Sticky Buns[43]

INGREDIENTS FOR BUNS:

1 package dry yeast

¼ cup warm water

1 cup milk, scalded

¼ cup margarine

¼ cup sugar

1 teaspoon salt

3½ to 4 cups flour

1 egg

INGREDIENTS FOR "STICKY":

1 cup brown sugar

½ cup butter or margarine

4 tablespoons light corn syrup

½ cup chopped nuts

1 teaspoon cinnamon

INSTRUCTIONS:

- Divide all ingredients under "sticky" equally between 2 cake pans and melt slowly over medium heat.
- Soften yeast in warm water. Combine milk, margarine, sugar, and salt. Cool to lukewarm. Add half the flour and beat until dough is soft. Add egg and softened yeast. Add the remaining flour until dough is soft and smooth. Cover and let rise in a well-greased bowl. Put in warm place (82°F) until doubled in size.
- Turn out on floured board and divide in half. Make 2 rectangles about 12" x 8".
- Brush ¼ cup melted butter over each rectangle and sprinkle them with brown sugar, cinnamon, and nuts, as desired.
- Roll lengthwise and seal the edges.
- Cut the two rolls into ½" slices and place cut side down in cake pans. Let rise for ½ to ¾ hour.
- Bake at 375°F for 20-25 minutes until golden brown.
- Invert on rack and serve warm.

Although Ruby and Cynthia lived comfortably with the Smith family, Ward suggested that there might be a chance for them to build a house on some land that was for sale in Monroe. They immediately liked the idea and purchased 7½ acres of land in Monroe with

FIGURE 41:
The Monroe, Connecticut, house.

Ward's help to negotiate a price. Ruby wanted the extra land to build a barn and have a horse. The ladies found a contractor and proceeded to build a small three-room house. To save money, the interior was left unfinished and the exterior shingles were left unstained; the new owners completed the work themselves. The tiny house was ready for move-in on Labor Day, 1954, one year after they had moved in with Ward Smith and his family.[40]

Growing New England Roots

Settled in Connecticut, Ruby found employment in the reading lab at the University of Bridgeport, while she pursued a Master of Science degree in guidance from the school's College of Education, finishing in 1956. The reading lab served the surrounding towns of Stratford, Fairfield, and Bridgeport, as the local public school systems outsourced their need for the resource. At the time, reading instruction was a totally new educational field. The lab provided one-to-one instruction and utilized new techniques and equipment, including a film projector that scrolled across lines of text at varying speeds.

Ruby worked for several years as a reading specialist and then moved to teach math, history, and English at Long Lots Junior High School in Westport, Connecticut. The school system had hired her specifically because she had the versatility to teach three subjects. At Long Lots, Ruby met Ella Williams, a fellow math teacher. Ella had an apartment in Bridgeport, but had also inherited her family's large home in scenic Washington Depot, Connecticut. Ella was passionate about golf and the outdoors and invited Ruby and Cynthia to spend weekends in Washington Depot. The three women played golf, explored the beauty of the Shepaug River, or planned other adventures. Ella was an excellent cook, which allowed Ruby to happily support the group's meals in her well-established role as the dishwasher.

Meanwhile, Ruby had started to build a barn in the backyard of the Monroe house that she shared with Cynthia. She had almost finished, but could not figure out how to raise the center beam for the roof. Perplexed by the challenge, she generously accepted the help of her colleague, John Day. John was the industrial arts teacher in woodworking at Long Lots, and immediately understood the problem with the barn. On a Saturday morning, under John's direction, a small group that included Ruby, Cynthia, and their Monroe neighbors, raised the center beam for the horse barn by the same technique used by the early New England settlers.

With the barn built, Ruby acquired a horse that had been part of a circus. The horse was perfect for riding, while also gentle enough for the neighborhood children. Ruby was a favorite on the street as the surrounding kids loved to visit for a ride. Ruby obliged to trot them around the neighborhood. Cynthia's nieces also boarded a horse and pony. When the three girls visited, CL and Judy rode the horses, while Betsy rode the pony.[44]

As a teacher, Ruby had summers available to travel. The two friends acquired camping equipment that included a tent, stove, ice chest, lantern, sleeping bags, and other essential items to support the cheap mode of travel. Ruby had an old Ford, and with the car loaded, the ladies took trips through New England, New York, and Canada. Ruby's mother and brother George visited Connecticut a few times. They drove the nearly 2,000 miles from Texas because George still feared flying.

When Cynthia's oldest niece, CL, gradu-ated from high school in 1958, Ruby planned a cross-country camping adventure and took CL with her on the trip. The trav-ellers explored the southern route to Texas and camped in state and national parks along the way. They cooked over a Coleman stove and went horseback riding as much as possible. They reached San Antonio and stayed with Ruby's mother and brother for a few days.

FIGURE 42:
Ruby Kelley hiking.

Ruby (Sr.) and George joined them on the road to travel to the Grand Canyon. The group explored the canyon rim together. Ruby and CL rode to the bottom of the canyon on mules, while Ruby (Sr.) and George returned to Texas.[45]

The mule trip was not without incident. The original Bright Angel Trail was quite steep, and inexpe-rienced riders could fall forward over the head of their mules if they were not careful. Ruby and CL found themselves in a group with equestrian novices. The beginners did not fall off their mules, but

FIGURE 43:
Grand Canyon mule trip July 20, 1958. Ruby Kelley is third from top. CL Smith is center.

dismounted voluntarily to walk. The tourists were not "saddle-ready" and could not take the long hours atop a mule. Ruby assisted the guides and led the abandoned mules back to the stables as the group split between walkers and riders.[46]

Ruby and CL continued west and traveled through the desert to the Hoover Dam, where they camped near a man who had helped to engineer the huge project. They visited Las Vegas, Nevada, and made their way to California, where they camped at the beautiful Muir Woods, near San Francisco. Cynthia flew to San Francisco for a business trip, and the threesome enjoyed a dinner together at the campground before Cynthia returned to Connecticut the next day by plane.[45]

Ruby and CL visited Yosemite National Park in California and headed north to Portland, Oregon, and Yellowstone National Park in Wyoming, where they observed an abundance of bears and raccoons that visibly foraged for food in the campground. Bears at the Yellowstone campground were everywhere, and all campers had to be on the lookout. Ruby and CL made their way back east through Montana and the Black Hills of South Dakota. They reached the Smith cabin in New Hampshire in time for CL's mid-August birthday.[45]

FIGURE 44:
Bears making a pest of themselves with tourists at Yellowstone National Park.

Three years later, in 1961, another adventure ensued as Ruby headed west again with Judy Smith, Cynthia Smith's second niece, on a similar trip. Ruby and Judy traveled through Pennsylvania and Kentucky, across the Midwest, and met Cynthia in

Denver, Colorado. The threesome continued on to visit the Rocky Mountain National Park, Dinosaur National Monument, The Great Salt Lake, Yellowstone National Park, Glacier National Park, Grand Teton National Park, Mount Rushmore, and the Badlands National Park. At Yellowstone, the bears remained a danger in the campground. When a small girl from an adjacent campsite walked into the woods with a plate full of food and called, "Here bear, here bear!" Ruby rushed to the girl's side and took the food away.

"Don't you ever let your child do that again! She could have been seriously injured!" Ruby admonished the girl's mother.[47]

In the summer of 1964, Ruby and Cynthia traveled by themselves. The ladies flew to Shannon Airport in Ireland, rented a car equipped to drive on the left side of the road, and successfully navigated their way to Dublin without understanding the Gaelic street signs. They flew from Dublin to Edinburgh, Scotland, visited John Day's aunt in Carnoustie, and reached London by a train that traveled at over a hundred miles per hour.[48]

After they visited the popular London tourist destinations, they took an overnight boat to the Hook of Holland. They toured the sites for several days and viewed the works of Rembrandt at the Rijksmuseum. The pair returned to London by boat with little time to spare before their flight home. As a late cab raced to pick them up, the vehicle brushed a pedestrian and knocked him down. Fortunately, the man was unhurt and able to get up. The cab driver collected his passengers and sped to Heathrow Airport with just enough time for Ruby and Cynthia to catch their plane for New York.[48]

Also in 1964, Ruby and Cynthia decided to expand their cramped home and build an addition that included two additional bedrooms, a second bath, and a full cellar. John Day from Long Lots performed most of the work while Ruby and Cynthia were in Europe. The new rooms were furnished with handmade furniture that the women had built themselves with the knowledge acquired in adult woodworking classes that John taught at Long Lots.[48]

Linguistics and New Media

Ruby enjoyed her peers at work and was successful at Long Lots. She was elected to the presidency of the Westport Education Association, the local teachers' organization that advocated for improvement in education, new methods in teaching, and assisted teachers with their navigation of local and state educational authorities. She also served on the National Council of Teachers in English for the Commission on the English Language.

Ruby began her Ph.D. studies in linguistics at New York University with Professor Neil Postman as her advisor. Linguistics had entered the public's awareness through Noam Chomsky's introduction of transformational generative grammar through the publication of *Syntactic Structures* in 1957. The 1961 creation of the Peace Corps by President John F. Kennedy also encouraged worldwide participation through the study of languages.[49] With Neil's guidance, Ruby led and published the results of a classroom study titled *A Study to Teach the Context of Linguistically Based Grammar Instruction of a Junior High School*.

FIGURE 45:
Ruby Kelley in the classroom.

While her hearing loss remained a significant handicap, Ruby was captivated by language. She often marveled that the human vocal tract was capable of more than a hundred distinct sounds, of which English used roughly forty phonemes. Similarly, she cited that the English language contained hundreds of thousands of words, but that an educated person may never know more than a few tens of thousands of them. More humorously, she noted that a linguist could identify a person's geographical roots through the recitation of a special list of words that revealed dialect. Ruby knew that she never lost her Texas accent. Her pronunciation of "pen" and "pin" sounded the same.

By the time principal Stanley Lorenzen hired Ruby to join the English Department faculty at Staples High School in Westport, Connecticut, he was fully aware of her accomplishments and out-standing reputation. Stanley's high standards for Staples reflected the strong academic expectations of an affluent community. Ruby fit right in with her talented colleagues Doris Raymaley and Karl Decker in the English Department. Ruby and Doris bonded immediately and ate lunch together everyday.[50] Already familiar with the Westport school system, Ruby also gravitated toward the inductive teaching methods at Staples, as well as the opportunity to use new media.

FIGURE 46:
Stanley Lorenzen on his sailboat.

Ruby developed a new method to teach grammar, so that students could become better readers. She embraced the new technology from the media department and used transparencies with an overhead project to demonstrate her technique. In one lesson, she replaced the traditional lesson that defined a noun as a person, place, or thing, and guided the students to recognize nouns even if they did not know the word. For example, nouns were preceded by determiners such as 'the', or signaled by a possessive form with an 's. The grammar lessons extended to all parts of speech. When Ruby substituted Swahili for English, the students did just as well.

Soon, Ruby was invited to demonstrate her newly devised grammar lessons to a national audience of educators in Washington, D.C. The offer allowed her to take one class from Staples to make the day trip. All their expenses were paid.

Upon consideration of which class to take, Ruby chose an average-level class, rather than the highest-level class. She feared that the use of above-average students would bias the audience against her techniques. Generally, most people believed that outstanding students were not hard to teach; the challenge was teaching the masses.

When Ruby informed the chosen class of her decision, the kids were thrilled beyond words. The average class had not expected for Ruby to pick them over their higher-performing peers. For many of the students, it was the first time that they had achieved academic recognition of any kind. As Ruby talked the proud students through the expectations for the lesson, the class insisted that she did *not* reveal the material to them ahead of time.

"It would not be fair," they protested. They intended to prove themselves as honest students.

Ruby prepared the lesson content and utilized transparencies for use with an overhead projector from the new media department. Ken Jansson, the media director, assisted with the creation of the materials. Since the presentation required the school's equipment, Ken accompanied Ruby and her class on the trip.

With an audience full of linguistics teachers from various secondary schools and colleges throughout the country, Ruby and the class demonstrated the prepared lesson. The students discovered and recognized the various language patterns, as the audience witnessed the inductive process. The lesson was a success; and while there were a few naysayers who resisted any change to the traditional lecture method, Ruby received an award for her demonstration.

After the successful trip, Ruby chatted with Ken Jansson at Staples and invited him to stop at her house in Monroe for a drink of lemonade. Ken's house in Newtown was only a few miles away from where Ruby lived with Cynthia. To Ruby's surprise, Ken showed up on her Monroe doorstep soon after. Ruby was dressed in work clothes and had been writing her Ph.D. dissertation. She did not expect her colleague to accept the offer, but he was obviously smitten.

As the two teachers got to know each other, Ken was surprised when Ruby offered to help him with the restoration of his Newtown house. Never afraid to get dirty, Ruby tackled any task at hand. She painted a room and drove the tractor. At work, Ken spent more and more time "hanging around the English Department at Staples,"[51] as Ruby and Ken had become a couple. Ruby confided her relationship with Ken to fellow teacher and friend, Doris Raymaley. Doris was dating, too. She had recently met a local physician, Dr. Thomas Bucky.

FIGURE 47:
Ruby Kelley driving the tractor with a load of hay. Lawrence and Tina Jansson watching.

As Ruby neared the completion of her dissertation, she was stressed over the foreign language requirement for her Ph.D. Doctoral candidates in linguistics had to demonstrate proficiency in a second language. Ruby had studied German as an undergraduate in Texas and chose German for her Ph.D., but her grasp of the language remained limited. Physically, she could not *hear* another language well enough to learn it.

To improve in her second language, Ruby enrolled in night classes and convinced Cynthia to join her in the endeavor. The classes were heavily grammar based, and whereas Cynthia excelled, Ruby struggled. A mutual friend recommended a tutor, an Austrian, Karl Knaur, who agreed to help Ruby. Ruby worked with Karl for the year before her exam at New York University, but her German remained shaky at best, and she constantly worried about the impending examination. Ruby wrote, "I *had* to pass a reading test on five hundred pages, I had two books approved; one a book in German on linguistics and another a series of short essays on major English writers, one of whom was Thomas Hardy. The linguistics book was so difficult that my tutor had trouble...I never finished reading either book; I translated, with his (Karl's) help, the first five or six pages of each chapter. Because of time constraints, I never learned what the author's intended message was since I never read the end of the chapters for the summary or summation."[52]

On the day of the test, Ruby was uncharacteristically nervous. Jittery with stomach pains, she sat uneasily for her examination. She described the experience: "I was terribly frightened on the day of the exam. About one hundred candidates were in the lecture hall, divided by languages. We placed our books on our writing desk arm. The professor stopped at each student, picked up a book, opened it, and said 'begin here'...he chose the linguistics book, third chapter on Walt Whitman, and I had actually done about four pages...old German sentences are *very* long. The first sentence was half a page. It cannot be done in English, so I devised several English sentences and added a note that English could not handle this construction in one sentence.

I then continued for two more pages, struggling, of course. In two hours, I had translated just over two pages. I was sure I would fail."[52]

Ruby had to wait to find out whether she passed the test. She described the moment when she learned her score, "Two weeks later the letter came; I was almost too frightened to open it; I had a form letter which merely said 'passed. Come, pick up your books'."[52]

Relieved, she set German aside and went on to defend and publish her dissertation titled *A Study to Identify the Content of Linguistically Based Grammar Instruction of a Junior High School*. She graduated from New York University with a Ph.D. in 1966.

Marriage

Ruby and Ken decided to get married at the end of the 1965-1966 school year. Ruby rushed to share the news with Doris in the English Department and asked for her friend's help to pick out a wedding dress. When Doris relayed the shopping plans to her boyfriend, Thomas, he replied simply, "Why don't you pick one out, too?"[53] The women had separate weddings, but the shared milestones cemented a lifelong friendship.

Meanwhile, Ken had shared the engagement news with the Lorenzens and communicated the couple's plans for a small wedding with only family in attendance due to financial constraints. When Elena, who had been so instrumental in the match-matching process, learned of the small-scale plans from Stanley, she was heard to exclaim loudly, *"NO, they're not!"* Not to be excluded, Elena appointed herself wedding planner of approximately seventy guests and, together with Ken's neighbor, Ellen Orosz, coordinated a potluck wedding reception in which the guests contributed the food.

The wedding ceremony was held at the St. Rose of Lima Church in Newtown, followed by an informal wedding reception in the backyard of the Newtown house with a three-layer wedding cake from the local bakery. Ellen had also cleaned the house from top to bottom and made curtains for every room as a personal gift to the new couple. Ken and Ruby planned to share the home as a married couple.

Ruby's mother and brother drove from Texas for the big event, while Ken's mother, father, and local relatives also attended. The Newtown neighbors were invited, as well as close friends from Long Lots Junior High School and Staples High School, including the Lorenzens, Ella Williams, and Doris Raymaley with Dr. Thomas Bucky. Doris served as the maid of honor. John Miller served as the best man, while his wife Shirley, a semi-professional singer, sang at the wedding.

FIGURE 48:
Ruby Kelley (bride),
Ken Jansson (groom),
Doris Raymaley (maid of honor),
and Dr. Thomas Bucky, 1966.

The married couple honeymooned for two days in Kennebunkport, Maine, and returned home to the house in Newtown that was still a work in progress. At the beginning of their marriage, Ken owned two donkeys, a cat named Zipper, and chickens. Ken affectionately referred to the donkeys, named Rose and Fannie, who were mother and foal, as "ass" and "little ass." Ken had tried to adopt a female baby goat, but the animal cried so pitifully for company that Ken felt compelled to sleep outside with it. After enduring a cold night on the ground, Ken gave the goat back to the original owner the next day. Ruby's horse was sold to neighbors in Monroe.

Married, Ruby dutifully assumed the wife's role as cook, but still lacked the skills to execute even the most basic meal. After a few days, Ken could no longer stand to watch his bride struggle. He banished

Ruby from the kitchen and assumed control of the cooking, freeing Ruby to return to her preferred role as dishwasher. Ken invoked the lessons he learned from both his mother and Margaret. He prepared one delicious meal after the next and made it look effortless.

As Ruby and Ken settled in to married life together, Larry and Tina continued to visit on weekends throughout the summer to help with the house restoration. Ken went back to teach at Staples. Ruby had resigned from her position in the Staples English Department due to a state law that prevented a husband and wife from teaching at the same school. She began to write a series of English textbooks for Haydn Publishing with co-authors Robert Boynton and Ruth Reeves, which were published several years later.

FIGURE 49:
Mom, Dad, and me!

By January, 1967, the couple was expecting their first baby—me! I entered the world, classified as Generation X. My parents belonged to the World War II generation, although in many ways, I perceived Mom and Dad as young parents. They had the gumption and fortitude to build a family life with limited financial means, but unlimited will. They built what they could, grew what they could, and saved what they could. While the Depression and war never left their thoughts, they forged ahead with a sense of responsibility and optimism. I inherited their sense of appreciation and hopefulness to find my own way in the world. It all started with a wild childhood.

Doting Grandparents

———— Papa the Protector ————

Larry and Tina were both ecstatic over the anticipation of their fourth grandbaby. Lawrence Jr. had two children, a girl and a boy, and Bernice had one son. Both grandparents applied themselves to prepare for my arrival. Larry worked to complete a baby room across the hall from Ken and Ruby's bedroom. Tina enthusiastically sewed baby clothes and stuffed animals.

As my birthdate approached, the festive mood was darkened as Tina fell ill again. After a long stay in the hospital, Tina died in June of 1967, three months before my birth. After living more than twenty years with hepatitis, her liver finally failed. Larry was heartbroken; he had been married to Tina for forty-five years. His misery overwhelmed him...until I was born. As soon as he saw his new granddaughter, he was magically transformed. All the affection that he had held for Tina he transferred to me. I was the living replacement for the love that he

FIGURE 50:
Papa with his pipe, 1970.

115

had lost upon my grandmother's death. To him, I was precious beyond words.

My grandfather, whom I called "Papa," was at the Newtown house when I arrived home from the hospital with my parents.

"When do I get to hold her?" asked Papa shyly. In a blink, I was handed into his loving arms. For the next seven years, until he passed away, he never wavered in his affection for me.

Papa built me a wagon for the summer and a sled for the winter. If he was not pulling me around the yard, he held my hand or let me "help" him with his carpentry. I played with his tools as my own toys, and Papa told my father not to interfere. If I wanted to bang on the piano with a hammer, Papa told Dad to leave me alone. If I wanted to walk around with Papa's pipe in my mouth, then I could do that, too. Toddler boundaries simply did not exist with Papa as my protector.

FIGURE 51:
Papa pulling me in the sled, 1971.

To celebrate my first winter snowstorm, my mother skied with me down the slight hill in the side yard. I was only a few months old. Mom held me around the waist and pointed me downhill as she snowplowed to the bottom of the hill. My feet dangled in the air, several feet above the snow. I expect that I giggled in delight as the cold winter air blew against my face in our descent.

While I may have been entertained, Papa had other thoughts about the mother-daughter stunt and bawled out my mother for her reckless behavior. He had witnessed my hill descent and feared for my safety. Mom easily shrugged off the insults. Papa used Swedish when he was mad, and Mom had not understood a single word of his tongue-lashing. Mom always told me what fun she had with me on that occasion. The pictures that document this downhill excursion are among my favorites today.

When Papa thought that I was in danger, Dad caught his share of abuse, too. I fell down the cellar stairs and scraped off a good portion of skin from my face. Papa blasted Dad for the lack of a railing, but took matters into his own hands and put up two railings the very next day, one for adults, and one at a lower height for me. I never fell down the cellar stairs again and, fortunately, neither did anyone else.

FIGURE 52:
*Skiing with my mother
in the side yard.*

Papa drank Tang in the morning and chuckled when I took his teeth (dentures) out. When he slept at our house, he wore a maroon and white flannel nightshirt to bed and let me climb on the covers to wish him goodnight. Papa also spoke my special language of "eh." Before I could talk, I simply said "eh" when I wanted something. There was no need to use actual words as Papa always understood me and attended to my needs.

Papa had lots of funny little sayings for things. He saw a group of people on church steps after a wedding and grunted, "Somebody's making a mistake." He saw an ambulance drive by and remarked, "There goes the meat wagon." If he burped at the dinner table, he was likely to say, "Sorry, the other end is plugged up" or "If it comes up again we'll vote on it." A very old person had "one foot in the grave and the other on a banana peel." If Dad painted something and missed a spot, Papa called the unpainted area a "holiday" and proceeded to insult Dad as a "stumblebum."

Papa referred to a boat pulled behind a car on a trailer as a "dry land sailer." If someone acted out, he warned, "Keep that up and the wagon will be coming." If he wanted to confuse someone, he said, "My mother and father are twins, but I don't look alike." If a person needed a bit of a pick-me-up, he suggested that he or she go outside the house and "chew on nails" or "put your thumb on a block and hit it with a hammer." He was sure people would feel better about whatever was bothering them after they followed his advice.

Papa also liked to invent his own words. A chamber pot, which he may have used as a boy, Papa referred to as a "thunder mug." Papa used the word "thunder" to express the sound of gas. Papa also had an aversion to shoveling "sh-t" in the chicken coop. To avoid profanity, he devised the slang "kaka-laka," and declared its definition as "something on the bottom of the chicken coop." The humor did nothing to motivate his desire for chicken maintenance, though. My mother did the shoveling.

I was two years old when my sister was due to be born in December amidst a huge snowstorm. My father and Papa outfitted the tractor with a plow and worked day and night to keep the driveway clear of snow, so that they could get the car out when it was time to take Mom to the hospital. When Mom sensed it was time to leave, Dad left with Mom, while I stayed at home with Papa as my babysitter.

After a harrowing trip to Danbury on I-84 in the middle of a snowstorm, Doris was born safely at the hospital. Dad returned home many hours later and found me happily running around the house in Papa's care. However, my diaper was full. Papa had not changed my diaper the whole time that Dad had been gone.

"Pa, why didn't you change her diaper?" asked my father in disbelief.

"I don't do that kind of work," replied Papa with a shrug.

That was that; Dad learned that Papa was not cut out for diaper duty.

When Mom showed up a few days later with baby Doris (named for my mother's friend at Staples High School), I apparently inquired as to where the small bundle had come from. I do not remember the answer given, but I quickly admonished them to "take her back." I guess there's a "no return" policy on babies, so I became a sister in 1969.

When I was old enough to walk around the yard on my own, Papa watched me play in an empty shed that matched the style of the main house. The shed had originally been a three-seater out-house that had served the farmhouse residents for hundreds of years. Dad and Papa had cleaned it out and removed the bench to convert the structure to a usable toolshed. The small building served as my playhouse, although I was often in competition for the space with my father's tools.

Dad frequently referred to the outhouse as the "Chic Sales," a reference to the author Charles "Chic" Sale whose name became a euphemism for an outhouse after he wrote a book titled *The Specialist* in 1929 about a carpenter who specialized in the building of "privies." Charles Sale apparently explained important things, such as why a door should open in and not out. An inward opening door allowed occupants to brace their legs against the door as a means to protect their privacy.

As an adult, I learned that the merits of indoor plumbing had once been debated in our family. Papa started his education at the Lincoln School in Bridgeport, Connecticut, in 1902. The school had just been built and featured indoor plumbing. All the bathrooms were in the basement. The boiler room provided separation between the boys' and girls' restrooms. Papa's father was horrified by the thought of *indoor* plumbing. Johannes was certain that the bathrooms would smell.

"Disgraceful," he said. "The kids will never learn anything." Not everyone gets to claim that they played in an outhouse as a kid, but I am sure glad that forward progress meant that I never had to use one!

Papa arrived on Saturday mornings to stay the weekend, and I looked forward to every visit. As he climbed out of his big blue Cadillac, he always carried gifts; but what I cherished the most was the quarter he gave me each week. I had a big metal savings bank that was stored on a top kitchen shelf. Papa and I, ceremoniously, put the quarter in the bank's coin slot as soon as he got settled.

FIGURE 53:
Papa pulling me in the wagon. The outhouse is in the background.

By sheer coincidence, the metal bank looked very similar to an actual bank in the center of town. With every quarter that we dropped in the metal bank, I assumed that the deposit was made directly to the real bank. It took me a few years to figure out that there was no connection. Still, I love that metal bank, as it reminds me of Papa's visits on Saturdays. I have not opened it in years, even though I know that there are a few quarters in it. Those quarters are special. They came from Papa.

Papa died in 1975 when I was in the second grade.

——— Proud Grandma ———

Ruby (Sr.), my maternal grandmother, was elated by the news of my arrival. Since Ernest had died in the war and George never married, I was her first grandchild. To prepare for my arrival, she collected news clippings of my parents' marriage and accomplishments to start a scrapbook for me.

When I was a few months old, my parents planned to take me to San Antonio, Texas, to visit Ruby (Sr.) for the first time. We had tickets to fly out of John F. Kennedy Airport (JFK) on Long Island where the runway ended at the edge of the water. My parents may have admired the ocean view as the plane gained speed for takeoff, but the plane never left the ground. The landing gear collapsed during takeoff and the plane skidded to a stop on its belly, narrowly avoiding a disastrous

FIGURE 54:
Ruby (Bruce) Kelley, 1979.

"water landing." The passengers safely exited the plane onto the runway. As the emergency vehicles swarmed the scene, my mother and I were the first ones rescued, while my father was left in the winter cold with the rest of the people for a more orderly pickup.

We spent several hours in the airport where I received all sorts of special attention as a newborn before we started out again on a different plane that eventually took us to Texas. When my grandmother saw me for the first time, she made sure that all the strangers knew who had arrived.

"That's *my* grandbaby!" she exclaimed loudly for all to hear. She did, however, question my brown eye color.

"All *my* babies had blue eyes," she commented to my father. Obviously, my father, with brown eyes himself, had contributed the dominant gene that determined my eye color. Grandma also declared that all New York City airports were unsafe, not just JFK.

My grandmother and Uncle George visited us in Connecticut several times during my youth. They drove or took the bus. A leisurely five-day road trip allowed them to sightsee along the way. Both of them liked to travel, and Grandma liked to conduct genealogy research along the way, stopping at various places inhabited by our ancestors. Grandma carried her "Polaroid" with her at all times to document her research and took pictures at every historic site. She was one person I knew who never had trouble identifying a picture after-the-fact, as she always took pictures of signs. She stopped at majestic landmarks, took pictures of the various signs, and sometimes skipped a picture of the landmark itself. Her only explanation was that she "wanted to remember where she had been."

Grandma often visited in August to escape the hottest part of the Texas summer. She loved card games, and we frequently sat at a card table to play Pitch, Crazy Eights, or Hearts. We took day trips to sightsee in New England or otherwise just relaxed in the backyard. By evening time, Grandma wrapped herself in a shawl to keep warm, as the temperature usually dipped into the 60s or 70s. She made a "*brrrrr*" sound that made me laugh and told me that it was so cold in Connecticut that she had to wear wool socks to bed. I can confirm that she really did wear the wool socks. Grandma also carried a "compact" in her big, black pocketbook and escaped to the bathroom to "powder her nose." She coated her face in the substance, and the ritual left her smelling of powder.

Grandma always picked out "travel clothes" for her long trips, which usually meant that a real dress substituted for her usual housecoat and stockings. I never understood the need for special clothes to board a bus or plane. Mom tried to explain that "women used to have travel clothes," and that Grandma maintained traditions from an earlier era. I found out much later that Grandma wore a corset, too. She was in her golden years when she wore a corset to a doctor's appointment. Grandma undressed in the examination room and laid her clothes and corset on a chair. When the doctor entered the room, he saw the corset as well as the impressions from the garment on my grandmother's back.

"Mrs. Kelley, you don't need to wear a corset to come to my office," said the doctor.

"I don't?" said Grandma in southern disbelief. Grandma abandoned the corset. The doctor may have freed her from a silly tradition, but the travel clothes remained significant.

I took two trips to Texas with Mom and Doris when I was older. Grandma showed us the Texas sights. I vividly remember our trip to the Alamo, Natural Bridge Caverns, and the San Antonio Zoo when I was in the second grade. During our trip to the zoo, an announcement came over the speaker system that elephant rides were available. My mother had no sooner heard the announcement than she rushed us to the elephant area. Before my grandmother knew it, my mother, sister, and I were riding an elephant. As we dismounted, Mom caught an earful from Grandma for "...putting her grandbabies in danger."

FIGURE 55:
My mother, sister, and me on an elephant at the zoo.

"They could have been hurt!" Grandma scolded. Once again, Mom turned a deaf ear to criticism from an overprotective grandparent. At least for the elephant ride incident, she had been chewed out in English!

As Texas history and landmarks were a big part of our trips, so was the food. Mom loved the fresh pecan pies, but I was hooked on the watermelon. Farmers sold watermelons on the side of the road in Texas, just like they sold corn in New England. Mom quickly extended an unlimited watermelon policy. I could eat all I wanted, and I did! I only stopped when Uncle George took us to eat Mexican food. He fed us something called a taco and a sugary candy, called a praline, for dessert. I had never seen anyone eat a taco in Connecticut, but it was apparently quite common in Texas. To a kid from Connecticut, Mexican food was an adventure.

I romped around the San Antonio house and explored the trees and fields that were full of bugs, big, *Texas-size* bugs. Before too long, I had accumulated a cicada collection worthy of a junior ento-mologist and expanded my search beyond the yard. I wandered into an overgrown area at the end of the street as I continued my quest into a large pile of soft dirt. The dirt contained more insects, and I sat down to study them. The bugs did not interest me for very long. Before I knew what happened, I was covered in bugs. The bugs stung me over and over again, as I ran back to the house. To my Yankee surprise, I had discovered fire ants. As Grandma said when something went wrong, "cuss words!"

Grandma photographed my San Antonio bug collection for pos-terity before Mom took Doris and me north to Denton to visit Teacher on "the big farm." Teacher provided horses for us, and we all went bareback riding in the pastures. The terrain was flat, and grasshoppers buzzed loudly in the grass and jumped in every direc-tion. They frequently landed on the horses and rode along with us for a few steps before they hopped off again. I am not sure whether I was more fascinated by the grasshoppers, horses, or Texas terrain.

Regardless, I knew Denton, TSCW (Texas State College for Women) and especially Teacher were all very special to my mother.

Each year, Grandma asked Doris and me what we wanted for Christmas. I was more than happy to oblige with the annual requests and selected choice gifts for delivery by mail from Grandma and Uncle George in Texas. My list was lengthy. I reasoned that a well-prepared wish list increased the number of gifts that I would receive. My homemade three-foot stocking also encouraged Santa's generosity, or so I thought!

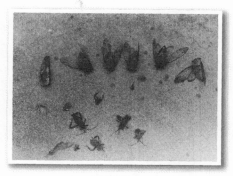

FIGURE 56:
My bug collection from San Antonio, Texas.

Doris, however, never provided a hint to her desires. Grandma repeatedly asked my sister over the phone what she wanted for Christmas, but Doris responded only that she would be happy with anything that Grandma sent. I never understood my sister's indifference to gifts. She was not able to make decisions easily, so I attributed her lack of a response to the fact that she simply had not yet made up her mind. Of course, Christmas Day rolled around on schedule every year, whether Doris had ever compiled a wish list or not.

It was tradition that we opened Grandma's package last on Christmas morning. Grandma and Uncle George shipped their gifts by U.S. mail and covered them with brown paper for shipping. Because the gifts were also wrapped individually inside the shipping box, there was an extra element of surprise.

Elatedly, I unwrapped my packages one Christmas and received exactly what I had expected. Doris, however, unwrapped a plastic bronze-colored moose head that was about ten inches tall. We all froze in bewilderment at the sight of the unusual gift. Clearly, Grandma had made the best choice that she could in the absence of my sister's input, but a moose head was surely odd. Doris loved animals and had just received a miniature plastic re-creation of a hunter's trophy! It was a lesson to all of us. *If you do not say what you want for Christmas, then you may get a moose head.* (The antithesis of this anecdote may have been when my father threatened that all I would get for Christmas was "a spider in a cage." Dad delivered, and I received a homemade wooden cage with a stuffed spider animal that he had purchased from a craftsman at a local mall. He was never so proud of himself as at the moment I opened his special gift.)

FIGURE 57:
*My sister's
moose head.*

About the time I was in middle school, Grandma and Uncle George visited us in Connecticut, and we planned to drive them to Maine to see the progress on the cabin. We had added a bathroom with a standing shower and hot water. Grandma was not at all one to rough-it in the outdoors and needed the comfort of the basic amenities. She had also been sick and was instructed by her doctor to follow a sensible diet and drink skim milk for health reasons. I took the advice to mean that her life was in danger if she did not strictly follow the medical advice. I insisted that the family switch to skim milk to set a good example. My parents agreed.

However, when Grandma arrived, she quickly shared her knowledge of milk options. She explained that stores offered whole milk, 2%, 1.5%, 1%, 0.5%, and skim milk options. Since Dad had done the bulk of grocery shopping for our family, I had no idea that so many milk choices were available. Grandma announced her preference for the 2 % option, although I was not convinced that there was much of a difference between whole milk and 2 % milk. I urged the family to stick to the skim-only plan.

On the way to Maine, we stopped at a restaurant that offered standard American fare at reasonable prices. As a rule, we never ate at restaurants due to Dad's good cooking. We usually packed picnic lunches for road trips, but travelling with Grandma and Uncle George was a special occasion. The six of us sat down at a large round table and ordered our drinks and meals. Aware of my sensitivity to the milk issue, Grandma carefully inquired about the milk options that were available.

"Do you have skim milk?" asked my grandmother.

"No," said the waitress.

"Do you have 0.5 % milk?" she asked again.

"No," said the waitress.

"Do you have 1 % " milk?" she asked a third time.

"No," said the waitress.

"Do you have 2 % milk?" she asked once more.

"No," said the waitress.

"Do you have whole milk?" she finally asked.

"Yes!" said the waitress, relieved.

"That'll be *fine*," said Grandma in her Texas accent. I could not believe it, but could not argue that there was another milk option, either.

Grandma enjoyed the cabin, although clearly she preferred to be closer to civilization. Moreover, the brook in the backyard petrified her. Floods were a real threat in Texas, where the land was flat and could not absorb a heavy rainfall. However, our house in Maine was at an elevation quite safe from flooding. Like most New Englanders, we suffered the annoyance of water in the basement, but laughed off the threat of flooding. If floodwaters ever reached the cabin, most of the Eastern seaboard would already have been wiped out. Still, the facts did little to allay Grandma's fears.

Grandma was not in Maine very long before she had written postcards and asked us to take her to the post office to mail them. The post office in Acton, Maine, was in an old house with a fence around the front yard. Customers were required to enter through the front gate where sheep grazed in the yard, close the gate behind them, and navigate through the sheep to enter the house where the post office was located.

When the family station wagon pulled up to the yard with sheep, my grandmother was aghast.

"I want a *U.S.* Post Office!" she announced, as she emphasized that we were in the United States. We all laughed and knew that my city Grandma did not understand rural New England.

"But Grandma, that is the only kind there is in this country!" joked my father. My grandmother overcame her initial reservation and eventually became good friends with the postmistress. In memory of the occasion, the family still refers to every American post office as a *U.S.* Post Office!

When I was in high school, my mother was both surprised and pleased when I expressed an interest to visit Grandma and Uncle George in Texas on my own. They had moved to Richardson, Texas, which was north of Dallas, and part of a massive suburban construction boom in the 1970s. I had been to their Richardson home once before, but the trip by myself was special, as I had Grandma and Uncle George all to myself. We traveled around the area, played cards, hit golf balls at the golf range, walked around shopping malls, visited the International Wildlife Park in Grand Prairie, saw a pre-season Dallas Cowboys game, and toured the Southfork Ranch where scenes from the popular *Dallas* television series had been filmed.

I loved Grandma's eccentricities, Texan sweetness, and silly traditions. She frequently called me "Sugar," in her southern accent. "Did you have a good night's sleep, Sugar?" "Can I get you anything, Sugar?" "Ready to play cards again, Sugar?"

As I write the story of my grandmother, I owe her a tremendous debt of gratitude. She was an avid genealogist and traced our ancestors from the 1700s in Virginia, across the U.S. to Mississippi where she had been born, and to Louisiana where she had met and married my grandfather. She had written away for court records, visited and photographed gravesites, drawn maps, and corresponded with people who had memories of our ancestors. The depth of her research was extraordinary, and we reviewed her notes and pictures during my solo trip to Richardson. Her organization and filing was impeccable, and she made sure that everything was written down, so that I would have it one day.

Grandma—thank you!

FIGURE 58:
*My grandmother, Ruby (Bruce) Kelley,
and my uncle, George Kelley.*

Newtown Childhood

Anachronous Living

By the time Doris and I were born, Mom, Dad, and Papa had restored the Newtown farmhouse to provide a comfortable home that was filled with anachronisms. The homestead's exterior had been returned to its dignified 18th century colonial appearance, while the interior resembled a

FIGURE 59:
Our Newtown center chimney colonial house.

19th century household due to Dad's antiques. The 20th century conveniences included only electricity, telephone, indoor plumbing, and an oil furnace.

Dad repurposed the barns for his own needs. The old horse barn housed Dad's Silver Ghost and Cadillac, tools, and most of the lawn equipment. Half of the middle barn was used for the tractor and gardening supplies, while the other half, designated the "paint

131

barn," held paint and related supplies. The chicken coop retained its original purpose. Dad populated the structure with both chickens and pheasants, which were separated in different runs. The icehouse served as a stable to the two donkeys. A hitching post and granite carriage step remained in the front yard. Other than two cars parked in the driveway, little revealed the 20th century to a passer-by.

FIGURE 60:

The donkeys named Rose and Fannie.
The icehouse (unfinished) is in the background
with the chicken coop and house in the distance.

Dad's antiques filled the 19th century interior of our home, either for everyday use, or to complete his desired aesthetics. A variety of tables, including tavern table, fireside table, and gate leg table served our living needs, along with wingback chairs, rope beds (converted for modern frames), Governor Winthrop desk, dough box, wooden trunks, and a cobbler's bench. Oriental rugs covered the wood floors, while candle molds hung from the walls. Dad displayed his strawberry china, old maps, old books, and musical instruments, with a collector's pride. As a baby, my mother rocked me in an antique wooden baby rocker that sat beside the large colonial fireplace adorned with pewter plates, pewter candlesticks, railroad lanterns, whale oil lamps, and a Civil War Kentucky rifle that rested on the mantel.

The antiques were so integrated into our daily lives that I never knew we lived differently until I visited Old Sturbridge Village on a Girl Scout field trip. The wonderful living history museum in Massachusetts depicted early American life. An appointed tour guide, dressed in colonial costume, led the troop through the facility as she tested our knowledge of the various antiques.

Like a brat, I spoke up to answer each question that the tour guide asked. Ruffled by my knowledge of the colonial period, the docent politely acknowledged my correct responses and proceeded with the full explanations for the rest of the girls. As the tour continued, I observed that my Girl Scout troop leader quietly explained my odd behavior to our museum host.

FIGURE 61:
Sleeping in an antique baby rocker by the fireplace with my mother watching me.

"Kelley's house has a lot of antiques," she whispered. The docent nodded in acknowledgement, but probably had no idea as to the extent of the comment.

Dad filled up the house, attic, and the four barns with his possessions. He also never threw anything away. Relatives teased Dad that there was a box labeled "string too short to save," somewhere in the house. Mom claimed very little space, but managed to keep a dresser full of clothes, several bookcases of reference books with her notes scribbled in the margins, and a small Christmas ornament of a dog named "Cleff," that she had received as a child. If Dad was a packrat, then Mom made sure that she never accumulated "stuff."

"If you buy a new pair of shoes, then throw an old pair away," she cautioned Doris and me.

Over time, as Mom grew more involved with town politics, she claimed additional space for an office. Mom catalogued every piece of paper in numerous filing cabinets around the house: agendas,

133

meeting minutes, committee reports, letters to the editor, and personal correspondence on political issues. She also had a propensity to cut out articles from various newspapers and magazines that served her voracious appetite for data. Mom fought her political battles with the cold, hard facts.

"Those who cannot remember the past are condemned to repeat it," she claimed, citing the philosopher George Santayana.

Dad's pride in his antiques extended to Christmas decorations, too. A huge section in the attic was reserved for storage of antique lights, ornaments, and other decorations. Dad had inherited many generations of Christmas treasures from his family and knew the origin of every ornament. He cradled the objects in his hands to admire them, as he affectionately retold the history of each one. Only our homemade stockings were relatively new items, perhaps indicative of our own ages.

Dad's spirit for Christmas was insatiable. The family worked together to decorate the house and set up as many as three trees a year. We completed the work over several weekends as Bing Crosby's voice crooned to us from Dad's old record collection. We purchased a fresh wreath for the door each year. Otherwise, everything else came from the Christmas stores in the attic.

Dad took special pride in the display of a miniature Santa's sleigh with nine reindeer on the fireplace mantel. The reindeer, cast from lead, were a favorite with the older generation. Dad also set up an antique manger scene underneath the largest Christmas tree. A miniature colonial village replica made of paper sat next to a smaller tree in the dining room. Antique sleigh bells adorned the walls. We lit electric candles in the windows each evening.

Taking the decorations down took longer, and Dad did not like to be rushed after the holidays. Slowly and lovingly, he repacked the various items for return to storage in the attic. The winter season could easily have passed before all the Christmas decorations disappeared entirely from view. When I was dropped off by the school bus one day in April, the bus driver caught my arm as I moved toward the door.

"You can tell your father to take down the wreath," he grinned. "It's Easter!"

Instigator and Protector

I was an early riser. If Mom and Dad were still asleep by the time I woke up in the morning, I made my way into their room to climb up the railing of their antique cannonball bed. Much higher than a normal bed, I really had to *climb*. Once in the bed, I wiggled my way between them and shook them with the encouragement to wake up. If they did not respond, I used my fingers to force their eyelids open with the command of "open eyes!" When Doris got big enough, she accompanied me on my trips into the big bedroom. Mom said many years later that she could still visualize our "…little heads appearing at the foot of the bed." Dad only remembered that my early morning visits had all the tenderness of an eye poke.

I often led Doris into games, fun, and trouble, but Mom and Dad kept a close eye on me due to my propensity for fast-paced action. One day, I chased Doris around the inside of the house. The center-chimney colonial allowed us to run from room to room as we circled the chimney. The home's four fireplaces originally provided the only source of heat at the time the house was built, so all the rooms were small. The early New Englanders knew what they were doing to stay warm in winter.

Mom and Dad yelled for us to *stop running*, but we kept going to make a full one and half laps before Doris slipped and fell in the front hallway. She hit her head on the door jam and opened a small gash on the back of her head that gushed blood. My parents dashed to the rescue and carried Doris to the bathroom to try to stop the bleeding with towels. With no success, they pushed Doris and me into the car and sped to the local pediatrician.

By the time we reached the doctor's office, the towels were soaked through with blood. With several people waiting in the reception area, the first person to see Doris incited the staff to "Please, take this child next!" Mom and Dad rushed Doris into the examination room, while a nurse cleaned up the blood that had dripped from the towels in the waiting room. Doris received only a few stitches from the doctor, but collected much more in sympathy.

We returned home to find Papa at the house for his usual weekend visit. White as a ghost, he sat trembling in a chair. He had entered the unlocked house to find the bathroom full of blood. Terrified as to what might have happened, he sat down to wait for us with no idea where we were or how long we would be gone. Relieved to see us, Mom and Dad explained to him what had happened. Papa finally relaxed as he heard the full story. To me, it was just Doris' head that had been cracked open. Otherwise, we were all okay.

Doris may have suffered punishment through participation in my ideas for fun, but she also received my protection. The Labor Day Parade was (and still is) an annual event in Newtown, Connecticut. The whole family loved to watch the parade and assembled at the same place each year to watch it. The parade was a veritable "who's who" in town that included local politicians, the high school marching band, firemen, police, local organizations, and businesses. Doris and I had a keen interest in the groups that threw candy to children. As these special groups passed by, kids ran into the street to grab the candy.

At elementary age, I was fast enough to compete against the other kids and collected a formidable stash of sweets. However, at one parade, I encountered head-to-head competition with a boy my age. He gathered the candy thrown near him and then unabashedly intruded into Doris' space to collect the candy near her before she had time to pick it up herself.

My parents observed that I was clearly irritated by the boy's actions. As another batch of candy was thrown into the street, I swooped up the pieces nearest to me and then raced to get the candy next to Doris. Beating my male competitor, I turned to face him and brashly declared, "That piece is for Doris!" According to my parents, the boy was so dumbstruck by my rebuke that he retreated to collect candy in his own area thereafter. *There are always bullies at the parade; they just have to be put in their place when your younger sister's candy is at stake.*

Apparently, I had no trouble standing up to adults, either, and was quick to instruct them to suit my pleasures. My parents arranged for me to visit Ella Williams, my mother's teaching colleague, for my first overnight stay away from home. Ella's Bridgeport, Connecticut, apartment had sidewalks on the street. I looked forward to riding my tricycle on the smooth surface.

As my clothes and tricycle were packed into Ella's car, my parents worried about my leaving home for the first time, anticipating an emotional meltdown. Instead, I simply hopped into Ella's car and waved goodbye. My parents chuckled in surprise and waved back at me as Ella backed her car out of our driveway.

FIGURE 62:
Easily the most memorable parade event for a young child– Mae Schmidle (Town Clerk and later State Representative) riding a baby elephant in the town's Labor Day Parade.

When we arrived at Ella's apartment in Bridgeport, she hastened to unpack everything so that I could immediately ride my tricycle. Ella's apartment was on a hill, and I zoomed down the hill again and again. At high speed for a tricycle, I passed an empty pool behind a fence that belonged to another apartment complex. I had never seen an empty pool before and thought it looked both strange and sad.

After awhile, I did not want to ride alone and insisted that Ella stand on the back of my tricycle to ride with me. Decades later, we reminisced.

"You made me ride on the *back* of the tricycle," Ella recalled, laughing. It may not have been fun for an adult, but it sure was fun for me at the age of five.

I still think empty pools look funny.

Charlotte Knaur, Karl's (Mom's German tutor) wife, also entertained my young demands and indulged me by baking homemade apple pies for our family. Charlotte loved to bake, and I loved to consume the output. She also delighted in my lavish compliments of every pie. I reasoned, correctly, that more praise meant more pies!

Charlotte often called us on the phone after she had delivered a pie to us to ask if we liked it. Very young, I happened to answer the phone to hear Charlotte's voice inquiring as to whether there had been anything wrong with the most recent pie. I could tell my father had overheard the question, as he glared at me from across the room. I am sure he worried that his young daughter might answer inappropriately.

"Yes, there was something wrong with the pie," I spoke evenly. My father froze, as I paused for effect.

"It was too small!" I quipped. My father broke out into a large smile and took the phone from me.

Charlotte was thrilled with my humor and used bigger pie plates to bake bigger pies. Still, I taunted her that the pies were "Not big enough!" After several progressively larger-sized pies, Charlotte finally resorted to baking her delicacies on cookie sheets.

"I can't make them any bigger," she finally declared. I was satisfied, too. All those pies were delicious!

Kindergarten

Before I ever started school, I had gained a head start on my education. Mom and Dad had read to me nearly every day. I sat on Mom or Dad's lap as they turned the pages. However, they no sooner finished the book than I wanted them to read it again.

"Read it again, read it again!" I begged. Mom and Dad usually complied, but Dad often liked to skip pages on the second or third reading. Despite his attempts at trickery, I called out his shenanigans.

"You skipped a page Daddy," I corrected. Many times, Dad was forced to go back to read a page in a book that I had already memorized. Mom happily read to me until I fell asleep. Some of my all-time favorite titles included *Good Night Moon, Blueberries for Sal, The Little Engine that Could*, and especially *Corduroy*. I imagined my own teddy bear in the stories of *Corduroy*.

In the fall of 1972, I started kindergarten assigned to Mrs. Rafferty's afternoon class at Sandy Hook Elementary School. Mrs. Rafferty, a Newtowner herself, had long acquired the reputation as a standout teacher at the school. She was a favorite with students and their parents alike. I was lucky to have been assigned to her class. My mother was thrilled with the match as well.

Mom chatted with Mrs. Rafferty frequently. The two women discussed all kinds of subjects that not only included my academic progress, but also Mrs. Rafferty's daughter in the Peace Corps, local news, and world affairs. With so many common interests, I could only watch as the pair stood in the classroom doorway for what I considered much too long a time, and wait for one of them to break free.

Mom sometimes picked me up at the end of school day so that I could accompany her on errands around town. Otherwise, I rode Mr. Wilson's bus back and forth to school and had a placard hung around my neck that spelled my name, my street, and a green square that identified "Wilson 1," a required signage for all kinder-

FIGURE 63:
My kindergarten photo at Sandy Hook Elementary School, 1973.

garteners. In Newtown, the buses were owned and operated by town residents. Mr. Wilson lived nearby and was a much-loved member of the community. His smiling face and warm greeting each day made the trips to school fun.

I also had the security of my stuffed animal "doggie" that I carried to kindergarten with me each day. My grandmother, Tina Jansson, who had died before I was born, had sewed the animal for me. I kept it with me at all times up until a friend referred to it as a "dish rag." I had clung to the animal for so long that only a few scraps of material remained. After the insult, I abandoned my beloved "doggie."

The school's two kindergarten classrooms were at the end of a hallway, near a large blacktop area with an adjacent playground. At recess, we favored a large cement block, about the size of a refrigerator, to the traditional playground equipment. The cement object contained a few steps that led to a flat area on top. We competed to climb the steps to jump off the top and yell "king of the mountain" midair.

While I held my own on the playground, at one point Mom expressed concern about my organizational skills to Mrs. Rafferty. The veteran kindergarten teacher chuckled and reported with confidence that I managed much better than most of the other students. To prove her point, she invited Mom to visit during the next show-and-tell session. It was my turn to share something, but I had also been selected to lead the class discussion. I was excited. Show-and-tell was a big deal for a kindergarten student, and I wanted to take a chicken to class for my presentation.

My unusual choice did not faze Mom, who even offered to transport one of the chickens to school for me. A less remarkable mother would have discouraged me, but not *my* Mom! However, she seized the opportunity to provide my first lesson in public speaking. The day before my presentation Mom insisted on a dry run. She had me stand at the edge of the living room, while she crossed the room to the opposite side and entered the kitchen. Two rooms away, she turned to face me.

"Now," she commanded, "tell me what you are going to say." I had barely begun to speak before Mom interrupted me.

"What? I can't hear you!" she shouted across the room. I began again; but as quickly as I had started, she stopped me again.

"You need to speak up!" she instructed forcefully. "Project your voice, *enunciate* your words!" I started again and again, and gradually built my confidence in a louder voice. Slowly and distinctly I described my chicken, what it was—a chicken, what it ate—corn, what it drank– water, and that it did not fly. Almost satisfied, Mom offered her final words of encouragement.

"You need to speak loudly and clearly so that someone who is hard of hearing, like me, can hear you in the back row."

It was a powerful lesson, and one that I never forgot. If Mom could not hear, then someone else might have the same problem. Any presenter needed to speak to the full audience, including the back row, and to anyone with a hearing problem.

On the day of my big presentation, Mom arrived at school with one of the chickens from the chicken coop. I took the bird out of the carrier and described how I held it (Mom had taught me how to handle chickens). I walked around the class to give each child a closer view as I delivered my rehearsed comments about the animal. After my turn with the chicken, and it is hard to beat a chicken for show-and-tell, I led the rest of the discussion. I called on various children to speak as I held Mrs. Rafferty's long wooden pointer. Mom proudly observed me from the back of the classroom and filmed the whole episode with a 16mm camera!

FIGURE 64:

My kindergarten class at Sandy Hook Elementary School. I am in the striped shirt carrying the chicken.

Mom surely must have shared my show-and-tell experience with her brother in Texas. To further advance my public speaking skills, Uncle George sent me a copy of *Robert's Rules of Order* for Christmas. The title, which was originally published in 1876, provided rules for parliamentary procedure, meetings, and assemblies. The gift likely required college-level reading. Mom laughed as she conveyed to George that a kindergartener "might be too young for Robert's." I kept the book on my shelf, though, and thumbed through it from time to time in an attempt to understand its mysterious text.

Kindergarten was special, and my mother filmed other activities throughout the year. She captured Mr. Wilson as he unloaded his bus full of kids at the front of the school. With the camera running, Mom also situated herself on the playground to observe "king of mountain." When Mrs. Rafferty silently raised her hand to indicate the end of recess, the class ran to her immediately. Mom filmed that, too.

Thowing Balls and Kicking Balls

Before kindergarten, my mother had taught me how to throw a ball in the backyard. She was determined that I would not "throw like a girl," and moved my arm back and forth to demonstrate the correct technique. Again and again we practiced how to throw a ball. We practiced batting, too, and by the time I was in kindergarten I had one of the best throwing arms in school. The blacktop outside of our classroom proved the perfect distance to challenge a five-year old. I stood on one side of the blacktop and chucked a tennis ball back and forth to whoever could come the closest to matching my distance.

Recess was always fun, but it changed the day a classmate showed up with a big, round black and white ball. We all kicked the ball around and could barely wait, day after day, to do it again. I did not know it at the time, but I had been introduced to the game of soccer, which was a relatively new sport in the U.S. The soccer ball likely belonged to a son of European immigrants. Before too long, soccer dominated my kindergarten world.

I joined a group of kids to play soccer every day at recess. No one ever said that I should not participate, although at some point I realized that I was the only girl on the field. Furthermore, I sensed that I was at a disadvantage for having to wear dresses and saddle shoes. The soccer ball did not respond to my buckled shoes in the same way as it did to the boys' sneakers. I resented that my wardrobe held me back and begged my parents to let me wear sneakers to school. Mom and Dad refused to give in to my demands. To them, I had sneakers at home and that was good enough.

The battle over my footwear dragged on until I took the risk to defy my parents. Secretly, I carried my sneakers to school in my book bag. I took off my shoes and changed to my sneakers for recess. Wow—what a difference! I left my sneakers on for the rest of the day and rode the bus home in the afternoon with my shoes in my book bag.

The bus dropped me off at the end of my street. I had planned to switch back to my shoes on the walk home; but it had started to rain, so I must have forgotten. Much worse, one shoe fell out of my bag on the short walk from the bus stop. When I arrived home in sneakers, my mother was furious. I was also forced to confess that I had lost a shoe, although I had no idea where I had lost it. The shoes were fairly new, and Mom impressed on me how much they had cost.

Angry, Mom put me in the car and drove me up and down our street to look for my shoe. She must have sensed that it had fallen out somewhere on my walk home. Remarkably, we found the missing shoe on the side of the road in the rain.

As punishment, Mom put me in a room by myself and warned that I should wait there alone "until Dad got home." For the next several hours I contemplated my fate. My imagination ran wild as I contemplated a terrible beating. Not that I had ever experienced a beating, but Mom sometimes threatened that Dad would "take off his belt." I sat and stared at the walls as the minutes and hours ticked away. In the end, my father opened the door and let me out without a word. That was it; I was freed from confinement, without further rebuke.

The event must have reinforced to Mom and Dad that they had a strong-willed child in their midst. They gave in to my sneaker demands and the dresses disappeared soon, too. I played soccer daily, and that was all that I desired.

Everybody Knows Mom

Mom became a regular at Sandy Hook Elementary and was elected to serve as Treasurer for the PTA (Parent Teacher Association). She moved freely between the administrative office and my classrooms. She was welcomed in the school wherever she went. She knew the principal, secretaries, teachers, janitors, and pretty much every one else. Energetic greetings of "Hi, Ruby!" resounded up and down the school hallways, and soon it was the same everywhere else in town. My mother was on her way to finding her voice in town politics, too. When Mom was elected to the Board of Education in 1974[54], my school identity became as much "Ruby's daughter" as it was "Kelley."

Everyone seemed to know my mother; and while she knew a lot of people, too, more people knew her than the other way around. Mom had difficulty remembering names, which provided for some awkward moments around town when she met people out of context. When the familiar "Hi, Ruby!" greeting sounded, Mom hesitated to personalize

FIGURE 65:
Mom on the phone discussing Board of Education topics, 1975.

her response unless she was sure of someone's name. I learned to detect when my mother was in trouble, and she trained me to come to her aid. If I knew a person's name when Mom failed to recall it, I interrupted the initial flurry of conversation, gently extended my hand, and pronounced "Hello, Mr. or Mrs. So & So," loudly enough so that Mom could hear me.

Mom was recognized and greeted in the strangest places. She used to take Doris and me to a Haunted House for Halloween each year. A local charity converted an old Victorian house in Newtown to a haunted house as a fundraiser. The abandoned structure fit the image of a haunted house perfectly. The event was a local favorite, as long lines of anxious children and their parents waited to gain admittance.

Each room of the house was decorated in ghoulish fashion. Local townspeople dressed up as monsters and hid in dark corners to scare the visitors. As my mother, sister, and I crept along, we screamed as one monster after the next sprang from the darkness.

As we neared the end of the haunted house experience, one final monster leapt from its hiding place and landed right in front of us with a gigantic "BOO!" Startled, we had no sooner reacted than the creature's expression changed to a look of surprise. The actor straightened up to face us, broke character, and spoke in a cheerful voice, "Oh, Hi, Ruby!" Without further remark, the costumed man turned around and disappeared into a dark room. Even to this day, the identity of the "Hi, Ruby!" monster remains unknown.

Mom was a favorite among my classmates, too. As the school offered numerous field trips, the kids always wanted my mother along as chaperone. Most kids did not want their own mothers to attend the trips, but I also wanted my mom to chaperone. She never passed up an opportunity to visit an interesting place, either, and had as much fun on the trips as the kids.

Mom had a passion for education that did not stop at the school's borders. Besides frequent trips to the local library, which was a favorite activity, Mom was continually searching for places to take Doris and me to expand our knowledge of the world. I was often taken out of school for a day to visit significant travelling exhibits, such as the King Tut or Pompeii exhibitions in New York City.

Mom also noted in my childhood scrapbook that I particularly enjoyed the "Arms & Armor" exhibit at the Metropolitan Museum of Art. We also made several trips to Franklin D. Roosevelt's home in Hyde Park, New York. Mom admired the 32nd President of the United States and could never see enough of his Springwood estate, although she could not help herself to comment that it was "a lot of rooms to vacuum" every time the big house came into view.

Otherwise, we spent the summers romping around the local museums and attractions, such as Putnam Memorial State Park in Redding, which was the site of Major General Putnam's winter camp during the American Revolutionary War, the Dinosaur State Park, Mystic Seaport, the Connecticut State Capital, the Yale University Art Gallery, or my favorite, the Peabody Museum of Natural History at Yale University that included the Great Hall of Dinosaurs as well as the Hall of Minerals, Earth and Space.

FIGURE 66:
*Dinosaur tracks delivered to
Sandy Hook Elementary School, 1974.*

I expect that every little kid likes dinosaurs, so Mom worked with the PTA to make sure that the Sandy Hook Elementary students had real dinosaur footprints to admire. In 1974, the Sandy Hook PTA obtained negative-positive prints of the Dilophosaurus from the Rocky Hill State Park.[55] The rock slabs were placed in the Sandy Hook Elementary courtyard. I attended the installation as the rock swung in chains from a giant yellow bucket loader. To little fanfare, workmen guided the slab to the designated location on the ground.

A year later, a local Newtown artist, Betty Christensen, donated a large, wall-size painting of a Dilophosaurus to the school's library. My mother had recruited Betty for the special assignment and provided the artist with a small picture to serve as a model.[55] Many of the school class pictures, thereafter, were taken with the dinosaur painting on the wall in the background.

While the Dilophosaurus may have wandered through Connecticut in the early Jurassic period, other large footprints were seen at Sandy Hook Elementary. The prints belonged to a large, imaginary green creature that celebrated the annual arrival of the Jolly Green Giant Fair. The weekend event offered a tag sale that contained mostly children's clothes and toys, as well as an array of crafts and games to entertain elementary age kids. The fair attracted most of the student body and served as an annual fundraiser for the PTA.

As the date of the fair approached, volunteers spray-painted giant green footprints on the long quarter-mile driveway that led to the school from the main road. As soon as the prints appeared, I made sure to have a window seat on the bus so that I could follow the large footsteps to the front of the school. Imagining the creature that could have left the magnificent prints far surpassed any activity at the fair. Green footprints adorned our Sandy Hook Elementary book bags, and we had fun with the jolly green giant theme throughout the school year.

Third Grade Politics

The year of America's bicentennial, 1976, I was in the third grade, and the whole school celebrated by dressing up as early colonists for a period of time. Mothers busily sewed costumes for both boys and girls. I dressed up as an Indian, which bucked the trend a bit; but the real reason was that I already had an Indian dress, and that my mother could not sew very well. Mom would not be outdone, however. She took Doris and me to see the Tall Ships that sailed to Boston for the bicentennial celebration. That beat a silly ole costume any day!

FIGURE 67:
My third grade teacher, Mrs. Holmes, dressed up for the bicentennial celebration at Sandy Hook Elementary School, 1976.

By third grade, I had been playing soccer at recess for three full years and wanted to play on a team. With no soccer teams for my age group available in Newtown, Mom suggested that I write a letter to the Head of the Parks and Recreation Department to suggest that the town organize a soccer team for elementary age players.

"If you want something done, then you'll have to take action," encouraged my mother. She introduced me to the concept of a petition, which meant that I would write a letter in support of a youth soccer team and have all my classmates sign it. The collective voice of many students had a better chance to influence the town officials than just mine alone.

With my mother's optimism as inspiration, I sat down and wrote what I wanted to say. Mom helped me to perfect the language. I printed the final draft on a clean sheet of paper and left space at the bottom for the signatures that I planned to collect. The next day, I took the petition to my third grade class, explained my initiative, and asked them to sign it in support of a youth soccer team. Nearly everyone signed.

A few days had passed, when I received a phone call from the head of the Newtown Parks and Recreation Department. He had received my letter and wanted to discuss it with me. I felt very grown up to speak to an adult that I did not know on the phone.

With conviction, I reviewed my request for a team and explained that my classmates and I played soccer every day at recess. He listened politely and sounded very agreeable. In the spring, I was informed of a new youth team's first practice. Mom had been right: action paid off!

Mom drove me to the practice field and stayed on the sidelines with the other parents. It was a dreary day, and the field was wet with rain. I recognized a few boys from my elementary school, but most of the kids were from another part of town. I practiced with the team for about an hour and then waited around while my mother talked to the coach. I was used to waiting for Mom as she knew so many people, but on this occasion she seemed quite agitated. That was not at all like Mom.

As we walked to the car, we passed another coach with a number of middle-school boys ready to use the field. Impromptu, my mother stopped to talk to him. Again, she seemed agitated by the conversation. As the discussion concluded, the coach turned to me and asked how long I had been playing soccer. When I responded that I had played for four years (Kindergarten, first grade, second grade, third grade), he gestured to the older boys and remarked that *they* had played for more than six years. He suggested that it would be better for me to wait to play soccer until I was older. I failed to see his point, and my mother had a look of disgust on her face. She pushed me into the car and quickly revealed the source of her frustration. Newtown did not want a *girl* to play on the newly formed soccer team for which I petitioned. I had been invited to practice by mistake because the coach thought "Kelley" was the name of a boy.

Since Mom had argued my case, the coach agreed to accept me on the team after he observed my skill-level, but he adamantly refused to let any other girls participate. The lack of equal opportunity infuriated my mother. If other girls could not play in Newtown, then I would not play, either. Without hesitation, Mom's solution was to enroll me in the youth soccer program in the neighboring town of Monroe, Connecticut. Monroe welcomed both boys and girls equally, and I joined as one of two girls from Newtown.

In Monroe, I was assigned to a team with a terrific coach, Julius Szalay. Mr. Szalay had emigrated from Hungary and knew the sport of soccer well. He organized the team masterfully and made sure that every kid knew his or her position. Mr. Szalay accentuated the positive with incessant compliments of "you do good" in his halting English. He refused to let any player speak disparagingly to another player. Only his mischievous son Stephen dared to challenge his authority. When Stephen occasionally stepped out of line, Julius bellowed *S-T-E-E-E-V-I-I-I-E-E-E* across the field to return his son's attention to the game.

The Monroe team was part of the national AYSO (American Youth Soccer Organization), which had a strict uniform code. Each player was inspected before a game to ensure that shirts, shorts, socks, and cleats were worn properly. Clothing substitutes were unacceptable. The shirt was a reversible red and white that represented Monroe's town colors, with a number on the back. The shorts were plain white cotton. Each player also received an AYSO patch. I still have mine!

FIGURE 68:
My first organized soccer experience with AYSO, 1976.

The jerseys were usually numbered by size, but that did not matter to my teammates or me. We all wanted to wear #10, the same number that our soccer hero, Pelé, wore for the New York Cosmos in the North American Soccer League. I never got closer than #9, but took consolation in the fact that I had a Pelé lunchbox to take to school every day.

I did get to see the Connecticut Bicentennials play, however. The team competed in the same league as the Cosmos, but played at the Yale Bowl. The team held a public outreach event at the Newtown High School stadium. Any child who kicked a ball through a small hole in a wooden structure received two free tickets to the game. The challenge was clearly designed for kids older than me, and once again I was likely the only female player on the field. Not yet ten years old, I made the shot on the first try. Mom took me to the game in New Haven, where I received a souvenir banner as a keepsake.

Playing in uniform every week, my white cotton shorts accumulated grass stains. Technically, my uniform was not out of compliance, but my father was determined to rid my shorts of grass stains using an old-fashioned New England method. To my horror, I found Dad boiling my shorts in a big pot on the kitchen stove. With a big wooden spoon, he stirred in a concoction of homemade soap to make the shorts white again. I was dumb-founded by the effort, as the grass stains had not bothered me a bit. Dad's Yankee method did not work, however, and my shorts disintegrated into a white soup.

With my shorts gone, I presented myself on the next game day wearing a substitute pair of white shorts that were not the standard AYSO issue. During the pre-game inspection, the referee spotted my non-regulation shorts and told me that he would not allow me to play. The referee simply could not bend the rules for an elementary age child!

I left the team and walked back to the parking lot with my father; but, as luck would have it, a league organizer had just pulled his car into the parking lot. The man had a whole trunkful of shirts, shorts, and socks. He generously handed me the regulation item that I needed. I changed instantly and bolted back to the field to play. Fortunately, I never had to explain to anyone that my father had boiled my shorts into oblivion.

The team won our division, handily, several years in a row. Mr. Szalay gets all the credit.

Perpetual Motion

By my third grade, Newtown's population had grown enough so that Sandy Hook Elementary required expansion. Caught in the lurch, without enough time to construct permanent infrastructure, the town expanded the school to include the use of trailers as temporary classrooms, where I spent my third, fourth, and fifth grade years. My mother may have been annoyed by the town's lack of foresight and planning, but I did not mind the makeshift structures. We had windows that opened to provide fresh air and surrounding blacktop to ride our skateboards. More importantly, the "portable crowd" was cool.

If there was a downside to the portables, it may have been that the ice and snow built up around the buildings in winter. When I slipped and hit my head on the ice, my mother was called to take me home. I had suffered my first concussion, and Mom observed that I was not my normal self. The nurse issued strict instructions to keep me awake, but I fell asleep almost immediately despite my mother's best efforts to the contrary.

In hindsight, Mom should have been relieved for the few hours of downtime. The teachers had observed my energetic behavior and concluded that I was bored in class. They recommended that I should have more activities with which to occupy myself. Mom worried about taking me out of class, but the teachers readily dismissed her concerns. Soon, I left class regularly to attend violin lessons and Junior Great Books discussions during the day, while I also started piano lessons and Girl Scouts after school.

Both piano and violin came easily. When I pounded out the *Indian War Dance* on the piano at a recital, the instructor conveyed amusingly to my mother that I would "never have a problem with speed." I learned the Suzuki violin method at school and played in the Sandy Hook Elementary orchestra. Mom and Dad designated one room in the house as the "music room," where Mom insisted that I practice each instrument for thirty minutes each night. Equipped with a square grand piano that we kept tuned and in working condition, I was otherwise surrounded by Dad's collection of antique instruments that were rarely touched.

The school orchestra performed two concerts a year, as proud parents took pictures and admired their children. Beginning string players sawed away at *Mississippi Hotdog* and *Twinkle, Twinkle, Little Star*. During my fourth grade performance, as the auditory dissonance filled the auditorium, my father glanced at a family friend, Arthur Forcht. The two men had obviously been thinking the same thing: the string players were pretty atrocious. Both men snickered and were soon laughing uncontrollably. Unable to regain their composure, the two fathers escaped the auditorium to avoid further humiliation. Mrs. Forcht sternly admonished her husband's behavior, but my mother thought the whole episode funny. As for me, Dad made sure to praise my performance.

I continued with Girl Scouts and loved the camping trips most of all. We learned how to pack our clothes in a duffle bag, make a fire, and pitch a tent. The camping trips were fun, although I was chastised for always being the first to fall sleep. I suppose that I had a farmer's genes, as I grew sleepy as soon as the sun went down and was wide awake at sunrise. I also had the reputation as a sound sleeper and apparently slept through a raccoon walking on my head, a fact that so delighted my fellow troop members that they teased me about it endlessly.

The troop proceeded to tackle the challenges to complete the requirements for the various badges. Besides camping, we cooked, sewed, learned photography, and played sports. We took trips, too, with one of the most memorable excursions to the Ringling Brothers and Barnum and Bailey Circus at the New Haven Coliseum. Excited to see the human cannonball that had been advertised on television, we screamed and chanted from our seats, desperate for the promised performance. With the show nearly over, an usher approached our section to inform us that the "human cannonball was sick" and would not perform that evening. Deflated, we stayed silent for the rest of the show.

By fifth grade, I added the trumpet and band to my musical repertoire. I had always liked brass instruments and owned a record of a Mexican brass band that I played over and over again. I had wanted to start the trumpet much earlier; but Mom had taken me to a music school in Danbury when I was younger, and an instructor concluded that I did not yet have the strength to blow the instrument.

I picked up the trumpet easily and became the only student who played in both the orchestra and band, which likely distinguished me as one of the more musical kids in the school system. Indeed, a special hearing test identified me as a candidate for the gifted music program. Subjected to further tests, I played a snare drum for the first time and sang a song with a piano accompaniment to measure my musical ability. Despite a good chance to join the program, I was not accepted.

Since I did not know what the program offered, I was not as crushed as I suppose I might otherwise have been. The music teachers who knew me at school, though, were irked by the rejection. Their investigation revealed an unexpected answer. While the testing had concluded that I had substantial talent for musical instruments, I could not sing a note. I had failed to qualify by a less than rousing rendition of *America, The Beautiful*. The choral director led the gifted music program and did not accept anyone who could not sing. My case was closed.

I may have been disheartened by the gifted music outcome, but was soon vindicated by another test that showed I was an above-average speller. I joined the top ten spellers at Sandy Hook Elementary and represented the school at the town-level spelling contest that included about forty kids.

I passed several rounds of competition and felt supremely lucky on one round when the girl in front of me spelled "parakeet" correctly. I had misspelled the word "mosquito" on the Sandy Hook Elementary test and was determined not to lose on an animal. I had no idea how to spell parakeet. As the competition whittled down to just a few of us, I received the word "Wednesday." Confident, I spelled phonetically W-E-N-D-S-D-A-Y. Nope, wrong.

Deflated, I left the line of remaining spellers to join my parents in the audience and waited for the contest to finish. A friend's mother joked that I did not know how to spell WED-NES-DAY. I was not so amused by the humor, but felt better when the Sandy Hook Elementary principal came over to me and congratulated me on my success. I had been the last student standing from Sandy Hook Elementary. That had to count for something.

Newtown was on-track to reach 19,000 residents by 1980. The town's growth meant that a fourth elementary school was added at the start of my fifth grade year. While I stayed at Sandy Hook Elementary, the redistricting meant that the teacher I had hoped to have, who was keen on science, was transferred to the new school across town. Dejectedly, I received notification of my fifth-grade placement to a two-room cluster in the portables with teachers Mrs. P. and Mr. M.; Mrs. P. was straight-laced, while Mr. M. was a bit crazy with an odd sense of humor. If Mrs. P. left me uninspired, Mr. M. confounded me.

Mr. M. forced kids to sit in a chalk-drawn circle on the floor as punishment, while miscreants received a printed "Dead Rat Award ~ 1978 ~ " certificate. The text read, "This award is special and is given only to those children who have managed in the course of the year to drive their teacher crazy. This certificate is given to < name > making < him/her > a member of the Dead Rat Club." A picture of a dead rat, upside down with its feet in the air, adorned the bottom of the paper. Fortunately, I received only one such award and was never forced to sit in the chalk circle.

To me, Mr. M.'s personality was strange and his interests stranger. He spoke of J.R.R. Tolkien's *The Hobbit* as if it contained the secrets to the universe. Every day, we heard something about Mr. M.'s favorite book. When *The Hobbit* movie premiered on television in 1977, Mr. M. could hardly contain his enthusiasm, and the build-up spilled over to the class. My parents let me watch the animated film, which premiered on a Sunday night; although cartoons bored me, and I considered the television special equally uninteresting. I am not even sure that I watched it to the end.

The day after the movie, I returned to school to find Mr. M. thrilled beyond belief. *The Hobbit* movie had exceeded his expectations, but he was curious about the monsters.

"What color were the monsters?" he eagerly inquired of the class. He had apparently watched the movie on a black and white television and wanted to know whether the monsters were green. The class stayed silent as he probed individual students about the quality of their television sets at home. Finally, one student offered that the monsters in the movie had indeed been green.

"I knew it!" gasped Mr. M. I did not know whether the monsters were really green or not, but I sure was sick of hearing about *The Hobbit.*

Mr. M. continued to amuse the class by making stilts for all of us to use at recess. With many pairs assembled by springtime, a good portion of the class was on stilts any time we were outside. He also led us in the creation of a gigantic balloon that we ironed together out of large plastic trash bags on the floor of the classroom. Whenever we thought class was over, we found ourselves ironing again, and the project never seemed to end. On the day of the flight, the local newspaper, the *Newtown Bee*, reported on the balloon's short flight with the caption "It Wasn't a UFO." In my mind, it was a teacher's folly.[56]

A Snowstorm and an Ankle

I delighted in an idyllic elementary existence. I played soccer, basketball, and softball, learned the piano, violin, and trumpet, and consumed books as fast as we could make trips to the library. Mom ensured that I had plenty of challenges to occupy my mind. If I expressed boredom, Mom suggested that I try to "take something apart to learn how it works." I needed to look no further than my own treasure trove of books on the great inventors or scientists, Leonardo da Vinci, Louis Pasteur, Benjamin Franklin, Thomas Edison, and Albert Einstein, to find inspiration. Yet, my perfect young life temporarily shattered on a snowy winter evening on December 18, 1977.

The family had been driving across town when a surprise snowstorm suddenly blanketed the area. We were in a hurry to get home, but Dad drove the rear-wheel station wagon slowly because of the slippery roads and poor visibility. Several inches of snow had accumulated by the time we reached our house. With a sloped driveway about a hundred feet long, my father parked the car near the road. It was easier to dig out after a snowstorm when there was less distance between the car and the road, so we usually took this precaution in advance of a major snowfall.

I was ready for the warm house and collected my things in the car. Doris whined that she did not want to get her feet wet in the snow. I ignored my sister's complaints. She was always bothered by the slightest inconvenience, and my parents catered to her needs with special attention, which always annoyed me. To avoid the situation, I hopped out of the car and ran up the driveway to the back entrance, where I waited for my parents to unlock the door. As I shivered on the porch for several minutes, it seemed that much too much time had passed. No one was behind me, and I was cold. In frustration, I stepped off the porch to run back down the driveway to find the source of the delay. I had barely accelerated when Mom appeared around the corner of the house. Her fearful expression froze me in my tracks.

"Dad's hurt," she murmured as she hurried past me to enter the house. I raced around the corner to see my father sprawled awkwardly on the ground, midway up the long driveway. I slid to a stop beside him, ready to provide aid and rescue.

"Are you ok, Dad?" I panted. Dad winced and answered in a strained voice.

"No," he moaned. The honesty of his answer ruined my perfect world. My parents were my heroes and supposed to be invincible.

I stared at the unexpected scene. My father was lying in several inches of snow. His head was uphill, while his legs extended perfectly in the tire tracks of the straight driveway. He kept glancing toward the back corner of the house as if to will his body to move toward it. Writhing, he made no progress.

"I can't move, Kelley, maybe you'd better pull me in the sled," he suggested. The words had no sooner passed his lips, than I flew back to the house to grab a plastic red sled off the porch. The cheap child's sled was flat except for a shallow rim around the edge. It was my favorite design for hill speed, but we also used it to carry things to and from the house when there was snow on the ground. It received heavy use to transport groceries from the car and haul firewood from the woodpile.

Dad rolled uncomfortably onto the sled. With Mom still in the house, I threw my weight behind the sled's rope to pull Dad to safety. Mightily, I pulled, and pulled, and pulled, but the sled, with Dad in it, did not budge. Realizing the futility of my effort, Dad looked at me with concern.

"Maybe you'd better go get help," he urged. Without waiting for further instruction, I took off running across the field to the house of the nearest neighbor. The beautiful pastures that had once surrounded our house had slowly been developed into large houses. The nearest house was now within sight and had been occupied for only a few months.

I rang the doorbell at our new neighbor's home. (Our 1770s colonial did not have a doorbell!) The door opened to the home of Bruce and Jo Griffiths. I shouted that my father was hurt. Mr. Griffiths had barely heard my frightened speech before he grabbed his coat and followed me out the door. In a heartbeat, we were on our way back to Dad in the driveway.

Mom was kneeling in the snow by Dad. She had called the volunteer ambulance corps, and the EMTs (emergency medical technicians) were on their way. We lived approximately six miles from the center of town. In the middle of a snowstorm, it was anybody's guess as to how long it would take the ambulance team to reach us. In the meantime, Mr. Griffiths assessed the situation. Dad had severely injured his leg and required a splint.

"Kelley, we need a piece of flat wood about this long," said Mr. Griffiths as he held up his hands to express the desired length. I bolted away to complete my new assignment.

In a house full of on-going restoration projects, wood was not hard to find. I located what was needed and rushed back to the scene. Mr. Griffiths splinted Dad's leg with the wood. Mom tried to keep Dad comfortable, but he shivered in the cold. Mom asked me to get blankets for him, so I darted back into the house yet again, to retrieve as many blankets as I could find. We covered Dad to keep him warm.

While Mom and Mr. Griffiths attended to Dad, I ran down to the end of the driveway to wait for the ambulance. I had learned at school that someone needed to watch for first responders to guide them to the correct address. The snowstorm had increased in intensity, and the poor visibility meant that they would have trouble finding us.

Before too long, the ambulance arrived. Its headlights illuminated the mass of snowflakes that were falling all around us. The EMTs lifted Dad off the ground onto a stretcher and placed him in the back of the ambulance. Mom rode in the ambulance with Dad to Danbury Hospital. Doris and I stayed at home with the Griffiths.

The next day, I learned the details of Dad's fall. Doris was a week away from her eighth birthday, and Dad had tried to carry her up the driveway because she had not wanted to get her feet wet. Halfway up the driveway, he slipped on ice beneath the snow. He tossed Doris to the side as he fell, but broke his ankle under his own weight.

The experience at the hospital was unpleasant. X-rays confirmed Dad's broken ankle, but the orthopedic surgeon had joked, "That's what you get for skiing." Mom and Dad were both taken aback by the remark, since the doctor had never asked how Dad's injury occurred. The doctor used his hands to push Dad's bones back in place and casted Dad's left leg below the knee.

With Dad back from the hospital, Mom prepared the sofa bed downstairs to accommodate Dad for his recovery. He mostly stayed in bed and was able to get to the bathroom on crutches. We took his meals to him, although he ate very little. In constant pain, he grew quite irritable. His acute sensitivity to motion in our old house kept us on high alert. He grimaced when the furnace turned on with a clunk and yelled if he felt someone walking in another room.

"You're shaking the house!" he shouted. Even tiptoeing, Dad claimed that he could feel the vibrations of our footsteps. On Christmas Eve, a week after the accident, Dad was in so much pain that Mom took him back to the hospital to have his ankle X-rayed again. The doctor reported that nothing was wrong and suggested that Dad take "more Percodan" for the pain.

After several weeks, Mom was desperate to find something to keep Dad's mind off his ankle. She suggested that he read a book that her students had liked, Jack Schaefer's *Shane* from 1949. Unfortunately, the popular Western did not hold his attention, and his dyslexia made it hard for him to read whether sitting up or lying down.

Eventually Dad began to create macramé. He had learned the various knots required for the art in an adult education class and applied his knowledge of the craft to pass the time. He tied the starting point of his creations to a hook on the fireplace mantel and sat in an antique wooden chair with his casted leg elevated to the side. Soon, plant hangers appeared all around the house and in such abundance that every family friend received one as a gift.

Dad continued to suffer, though. He steadily increased his dose of Percodan as recommended by the orthopedic doctor, but the drug's side effects became unbearable. Confused, he could not find his way to the bathroom or how to open a door. At one point he left his bed but could not remember where he was going. The painkiller had failed in its purpose. Instead, it made Dad nutty.

Roughly six weeks after Dad's fall in the driveway, Dad was still in the same excruciating pain when his cast was removed at Danbury Hospital.

"Your bone is not healing and I don't know why," the doctor commented unapologetically. "You'll have to accept the fact that you'll be a cripple all your life."

The callous remark did not sit well with my parents. Dad struggled to get to the car on crutches in an icy parking lot. Without a cast, his injured ankle flopped to the side. His pain was as severe as ever.

Solemnly, Mom and Dad returned home, although both sensed that something was wrong. They called their friend and physician, Dr. Thomas Bucky for advice. Without hesitation, Dr. Bucky referred Dad to an orthopedic surgeon at Norwalk Hospital, Dr. Jens Hermann. Mom drove to Danbury to collect Dad's X-rays and then drove both Dad and the X-rays to Dr. Hermann's office.

Dr. Hermann viewed the images and immediately saw the problem.

"There's nothing wrong with the X-rays, but it's what's *not* there that's the problem." The Danbury doctors had treated only broken bones, but Dad's deltoid ligament was not where it should have been. "The idiots don't know how to read an X-ray," he stormed. "Didn't it hurt? Didn't you see a doctor?" he probed further. Dad had been in great pain, but at last the root cause was known. Without a ligament to hold the bones in place, Dad's bones had knit and broken at least six times and shifted nearly one centimeter away from where they should have been.

"You need surgery," stated Dr. Hermann.

"When?" asked Dad. Dr. Hermann wanted to admit Dad to Norwalk Hospital immediately. However, the hospital's nurses and staff were on strike, and admissions were allowed only if the physician in charge of admittance approved the case. As luck would have it, Dr. Thomas Bucky had that authority at the time Dr. Jens Hermann called him with Dad's diagnosis.

"NO PROBLEM!" Dad overheard Dr. Bucky's voice on the phone. Mom drove Dad to the emergency room for admittance. Dad expected that Dr. Hermann would operate the next morning, but instead my father was in a hospital bed for several days with his leg raised in the air.

"I need to get the swelling down before I can operate," explained Dr. Hermann. The doctor finally performed the operation to repair Dad's ligament and used a metal plate and four screws to hold Dad's ankle together. Dad also received an implant of pig bones, no bigger than toothpicks, to allow his broken bones to knit correctly.

Dad woke up from surgery to find that his leg was sore, but found the excruciating pain that he had endured for so long had finally disappeared. He stayed at home for a few days and was soon well enough to return to his teaching job for the first time since his accident. At school, he used a big demonstration table at the front of the classroom so that he did not have to move around much. The students were extremely helpful. One kid even jumped out of his chair to retrieve a pencil after Dad had dropped it. Dad had the support of his fellow teachers, too. They helped him as needed and encouraged the kids to do the same.

Dad's recovery also meant that he joined us in the dining room for meals. He sat askew at the table to accommodate his new cast. Mom had managed the meal responsibilities adequately. With all our concern focused on Dad's health, none of us had thought to complain about the simplicity of Mom's cooking. Dad was still on crutches when we ate dinner at the historic Yankee Drover Inn in Newtown to celebrate his recovery. I cannot recall another occasion when the family indulged to eat at a fancy restaurant, but the visit to the Newtown landmark proved fortuitous as the building burned in 1981.

Dad avoided a second surgery to take out the pig bone. His body had not rejected the foreign matter as Dr. Hermann had predicted. When his second cast was finally removed, he happily returned to the kitchen as the cook. Life returned to normal, but the incident lived in our memories as a horrible experience. "The year Dad broke his leg," became synonymous with misery.

More than thirty years later, the pig bone worked its way to the surface of Dad's skin,

FIGURE 69:
Dad lying on the sofa bed with his broken ankle, 1978.

where he unknowingly whisked off the tiny bones with a swipe of his hand. The metal parts remained inside his ankle, while an unsightly scar proved a permanent reminder of the incident. Furthermore, Dad had to endure our insults of being "part pig."

Throughout Dad's ordeal, snowstorms had pounded Connecticut and the rest of New England. Many feet of snow filled the yard, and the path to the driveway looked like a tunnel as the snow on each side of it was well above my head. While Doris was declared too young to help, Mom assigned me extra responsibilities. I set and cleared the dinner table each night and also fed and watered the chickens!

Mom fretted all winter long that she might get injured herself. If anything happened to her, then she worried that Doris and I had no one to take care for us. Convinced of the danger, she insisted on extra precautions when any of us had to go outside. In particular, she policed our footwear to ensure that we were outfitted with rubber-soled shoes. Dad's leather-soled shoes were replaced, too. Mom did not want anyone to fall again and was certain that leather-soled shoes had contributed to Dad's accident.

"Let me see the bottoms of your shoes," she demanded as we left the house. Mom was determined that there would not be another broken ankle in the family.

Caring for the chickens presented a challenge. The chicken coop was about one hundred fifty feet away from the back door, but seemed far off in the distance behind the snowdrifts in the yard. Mom devised a plan for me to reach the chicken coop with fresh water each day. We walked halfway down the shoveled path, where Mom hoisted me onto the snow bank that faced the yard. As soon as I gained my footing, she handed me snowshoes and a pail of water. On snowshoes, I carried the water to the chicken coop.

The snow had drifted away from the structure, so I never had any trouble opening the door. I emptied the ice in the chickens' water dish and re-filled it with the hot water from my pail. The chicken feed was stored in the coop, so that part was easy as I just scooped out what was needed. I returned to the house on snow-shoes with the empty pail.

The snowshoe routine to feed the chickens continued throughout the deep snow season. I never minded the chore and continued with "chicken duty" even after Dad recovered from his broken ankle. The spring thaw made the walking easier, and I had fun collecting eggs when the chickens started laying again in the warmer weather.

One summer, we received a gift from a friend that contained Christmas ornaments packed in cracked corn. The ornaments had been sent to us from Alfred "Tommy" Thompson, an educator at Staples High School. Tommy had started at Staples in the guidance office and eventually became the Assistant Principal under Stanley Lorenzen. Tommy was a bachelor and traveled the world on com-mercial freighters during his summer vacations. A former Lieutenant Commander in the Navy during World War II, he had the connections to gain access to the unusual mode of travel, which allowed him cheap access to far-away destinations.

Each summer, Tommy mailed Christmas ornaments to us from whichever country he had visited. The box with the corn had been shipped from Greece, but we never knew the origin of his gifts until we opened them. Mom and Dad carefully took the ornaments out of the box and told me to take the corn to the chickens. I went to the chicken coop and dumped out the corn in the outside run. The chickens flocked to the food.

A few days after Tommy's package had arrived with the cracked corn, I spied a similar ornament lying in the middle of the chicken run. It had been scratched badly, although clearly matched the oth-ers that Tommy had sent. Mom and Dad must have missed it when they unpacked the other ornaments. Similarly, I had not seen the ornament when I fed the corn to the chickens.

I rescued the ornament from the chickens and took it inside to show Mom and Dad. We all laughed, but were also very sorry for the mistake. The ornament continues to be in the family's collection, although it has not always made it onto the tree over the years. Still, every time I see the scratched ornament, I remember how it looked lying in the middle of the chicken coop when I found it. Thereafter, we unpacked Tommy's yearly packages with considerably more care.

Ice Paradise

It may have snowed endlessly the year that Dad broke his leg, but other winters were just cold. Freezing temperatures *without* snow provided for optimal skating conditions on local ponds. Shovel-bearing volunteers could clear the public ice of a few inches of snow, but more snowfall than that generally prevented skating. The frozen water was a magnet for winter recreation, and whole families trekked to the ponds to enjoy the outdoors together.

Mom and Dad skated with Doris and me. A few miles away from our house there was a small pond in front of the high school that was usually cleared of snow for the public to enjoy. We skated there regularly until the construction of Exit 11 for I-84 destroyed the pond and consumed the land.

A large skating center near the Town Park filled the gap and included a warming hut with benches to sit down. The swampy area was considerably larger than the pond by the high school and provided fearful parents with an element of safety due to the shallow depth. The adults removed the trees, twigs, and plants that poked through the ice.

In kindergarten, my ultimate skating environment created itself in the backyard. A fluke ice storm covered the entire yard in ice. I donned my skates on the porch and had two acres of yard to skate through in all directions. In the evening time when it was dark, Mom put on the porch light to illuminate enough of the yard so that I could continue to skate. Amazed at the icy scenery, Mom insisted that I stay out as long as I wanted. The winter wonderland was likely a once-in-a-lifetime experience. Mom was right because that type of ice storm has yet to recur.

By the winter of 1975-1976, in my third grade year, I advertised to teach $0.25 skating lessons to other children. I created a flyer that read, "Dear Parents *deliv* your child ages 4, 5, 6, to Kelley Jansson to learn how to ice skate *refreachments* will be served after ice *skateing* lessons will be 25¢ each parents will not be allowed *ofter* the first lesson, the first lesson will be free." To my knowledge, I had no customers.

As I got older, Mom and Dad let me hike into the woods with a friend to find a pond or swampy area for skating. Sometimes we went to the ice pond behind our house, but its size restricted our skating to small circles. We needed more ice if we wanted to race. With a larger swamp identified behind a friend's house, my friend and I hiked into the woods with our skates, hot chocolate to drink, peanuts to eat, and a shovel to clear the ice of snow if needed. At the beginning of the skating season, we also hauled wood clippers to cut small trees or branches. We wanted to clear the biggest area possible.

In 1980, the Winter Olympics were held in Lake Placid, New York, where American Eric Heiden won an unprecedented five gold medals in speed skating, including both short and long distances.[57] His performance was thrilling and, like a lot of kids, I tried to emulate his technique on the ice. I swung my hands back and forth to look like my hero, to race faster and faster. I also discovered that, if I got going fast enough, I leaned forward and tripped over the toe picks on my figure skates. I painfully suffered one face plant after another.

Enough was enough, and I pleaded with my father to get me a pair of hockey skates that did not have a toe pick. It never occurred to me that Eric Heiden might have had special skates, but I sure knew that he was not encumbered by the toe picks on figure skates. Hockey skates were the only other type of skate in the stores. Dad was firm, though, "Girls do not wear hockey skates."

My falls continued, and I whined even more loudly about my need for hockey skates. Dad refused to give in and finally solved the problem with his own ingenuity. He disappeared to his workbench with my white figure skates and sawed off the toe picks! He had a big grin on his face when he handed them back to me. I no longer tripped over my skates, so the solution worked for both of us. I still think that figure skates are for sissies but remember that, for the winter of 1980, I raced on one-of-a-kind "custom" skates. Eric Heiden may have been jealous.

Rocking Horses and Real Horses

I may have discovered ice-skating on my own due to my New England surroundings, but felt Mom's influence with horses at a young age. As a toddler, my first riding experience was a new rocking horse. Unfortunately for my father, mine arrived disassembled. As soon as I had seen the spotted plastic horse amidst a box of parts, I shrieked with delirious anticipation. Dad studied the instructions, while I expressed at the highest volume possible my desire to ride. Eventually, Mom led me away from the scene so that Dad could work in peace. Assembled at last, the horse hung more than a foot off the ground, connected to a metal frame by springs that allowed it to rock back and forth.

I loved that horse! I rocked away while I watched *Sesame Street,* and sometimes with such rigor that the entire contraption tilted on the front or rear edge of the frame. I stressed the limit of the springs, too. One day I rocked so hard that I launched right off the front of my horse.

Catapulted into the air, my mother observed her ultimate horror, as her first-born child seemed destined to collide headfirst with the furniture. In what must have seemed like slow motion, Mom witnessed that I tucked my head just before I hit the floor and completed a forward somersault worthy of a circus acrobat. Dazed and unhurt, I paused only for a moment before I climbed back on my horse. Mom was aghast, and surely must have sighed in relief that I had avoided serious injury. She vowed

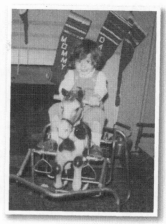

FIGURE 70:
Riding my rocking horse in 1969. My face is bruised from my having fallen down the cellar stairs.

to more closely supervise my rodeo habit thereafter.

A few years later, Mom wanted to teach me to ride for real. Mom and Dad sold the donkeys and replaced them with three Shetland ponies. The icehouse continued to serve as a barn, with hay stored in the second floor above the stalls. The ponies included Cotton Candy, a striking black animal with a gentle personality, and Bim Bam Boom, a beautiful tan pony with a blonde mane. Cotton Candy had a

FIGURE 71:
Wearing my cowboy boots and mounted on our Shetland pony named Cotton Candy under Mom's watchful eye.

big belly and was easy to ride. Bim Bam Boom was frisky and required a bit more handling. She had recently delivered a foal that we named Omega Dandy.

The two adult ponies allowed Mom to commence my pre-school riding instruction. Mom led me around on the ponies as I rode bareback. Surely, she repeated the same training that she had learned herself from Teacher. I was outfitted with cowboy boots and a western hat. The boots were a gift from Teacher in Texas. Mom had traced my feet and sent the outline to her former mentor who sized and ordered the boots. I fell off only once, when Bim Bam Boom reared. I tumbled backwards off the pony into a pile of manure. In hindsight, I am sure that the pony's hooves never left the ground, although she did make a sudden movement. Regardless, my memory is sound as to where I landed. It stunk.

When I was old enough to ride horses, Mom and Dad sold the ponies. They required a lot of work, and it was easier to take riding lessons at nearby farms. I took lessons in both English and Western styles, but much preferred Western. My Western lessons were in Southbury, Connecticut, with a seasoned horseman, Mr. William McAllister. Mr. McAllister owned a horse farm with an outdoor riding ring. I am sure that my mother had arranged for the more practical lessons of horsemanship. Mr. McAllister taught me how to take care of the horses, as well as how to ride them. I learned how to clean and pick a horse's hoof in the barn and then raced around barrels in the ring.

My English riding lessons were across town in Newtown at an indoor riding ring called Open Gate Farm. The facility had a large stable and boarded many horses, some of which were used for classes. My group contained only a handful of students. We had the chance to request a particular horse if we desired, but the instructors made the final decision as to which horse we rode for each lesson. The gentlest horses were always in the highest demand. I felt a sense of relief when I received one of the dependable favorites to ride.

Compared to Western, though, I considered the English riding style too uptight. I had to swap my Western cowboy boots and hat from Texas for English boots and a helmet. English style also required a rider to post for a trot, where a rider rises out of the saddle for every other stride of the horse's forelegs. The formality seemed like a lot of nonsense. Nevertheless, my mother insisted that I learn the English style because it was "the only way to jump." To Mom, jumping was the ultimate goal.

Mom had won several show-jumping championships before I was born and was passionate about the sport. My lessons at the farm progressed from walking over a rail on the ground to jumping very low rails. I never quite understood Mom's enthusiasm, however. A rider was so jarred upon landing after a jump that it took a tremendous effort to stay atop the horse. I fell off plenty of times.

Horses rotated in and out of our class, and I soon had a new horse assigned to me named Rufus. No one in the class had ridden Rufus before, so no one knew whether to be envious of the assignment. As I rode around the ring and jumped the small rails, Rufus felt like a special horse. He obeyed my commands and landed so gracefully that I did not fall off. If I could continue to ride Rufus, I decided that jumping might be fun after all.

I requested Rufus for the next several lessons and jumped rails with confidence, amazed at the sensation of feeling so connected with my horse. However, the experience was short-lived. I showed up for my next lesson and heard the terrible news that "Rufus was sold."

I stood motionless as the reins of another horse were handed to me. I am sure that I managed the new horse adequately, but at the end of class I missed Rufus even more. I felt handicapped without

Rufus and questioned the value of a sport where an animal, as much as a human, could make the difference in success.

Before too long, the farm held an indoor horse-jumping show for all the students who had been taking lessons. The older youth riders competed on horseback, but the riders my age ran the course on foot, without their horses. Both groups competed for show ribbons. As I raced around the course in sneakers to jump over low rails, for once I thought the course was easy. I placed near the top of the division, which convinced me more than ever that I preferred sports that relied on my own athletic ability. A horse was only holding me back.

I gave up riding for the rest of the school year until my mother enrolled me in a Girl Scout horseback riding camp during the summer. I had just finished the fourth grade and joined a small group of girls, including a friend of mine, in the camp for two weeks. The camp provided instruction in English riding and horse care.

I was excited about horses again, but was still only an average rider. By the end of the two weeks, I had worked my way back up to the low jumps that I had completed in Newtown. I had been assigned to a gray horse that I liked very much for most of the camp. She was a bit smaller than the other horses and had much more spunk. It was not quite like riding Rufus, but my gray horse understood what we were doing. She did not just follow in the line of the other animals.

On the last day of camp, the counselors prepared us for a relay race on horseback. They planned for teams to ride from one side of the ring to the other to collect soda cans that had been placed on the far-side railing. The first team to collect all their cans would win the relay.

I started for my team and immediately pulled ahead of the competition to get to the opposite side of the ring first. I held the reins in my left hand, while I leaned forward in my stirrups to reach for the nearest soda can on the railing. I grabbed the can with my right hand in a giant sweeping motion as my arm ended up over my head. The horse flinched, and I felt my weight shift uneasily as I fought to maintain my balance. I realized my mistake, but it was already too late.

My arm movement with the shiny can had spooked my horse. She took a few sudden steps sideways and started running at breakneck speed, headed directly for the biggest jump in the middle of the ring. Only strides away from the jump, it appeared bigger than ever. It was many rails taller than anything I had ever attempted. I tugged on the reins in a sheer state of panic.

Miraculously, with only steps to spare, I steered the horse away from the terrifying jump. My relief was short-lived, however, as the horse continued to run wildly. She bolted to the end of the ring and stopped abruptly; I was thrown into the railing with force. I screamed hysterically as the counselors and scouts ran to my aid. My leg was hurt and I could not comprehend what had just happened. The counselors called for the ambulance and ordered me to lie still.

I had calmed down by the time I reached the hospital. My leg still hurt, but I had recovered from the trauma of the bizarre episode. The doctors and nurses treated my leg injury, but I was alone in the emergency room for several hours. The hospital had not been able to reach my parents by phone. Mom and Dad had been working in the garden and not heard the phone ring until they entered the house for lunch. They rushed to the hospital without any knowledge of the severity of my injury, worried beyond belief.

When I finally saw their faces in the emergency room, I popped up with a jubilant, "HI, MOM!" Stunned, my parents almost fell over in their tracks. They had not known how badly I was hurt, but knew immediately that I would be okay, judging by my cheerful reaction. My leg was badly bruised, not broken. I spent a few weeks on crutches and was as good as new.

Mom had hoped for me to obtain some level of equestrian skill. Unfortunately, as I graduated from rocking horses to real horses, I discovered talent only for a spectacular dismount.

Life Without Pavement

The horseback riding camp incident probably discouraged Mom from pushing me further in equestrian. I preferred to pick up a soccer ball and run to the backyard than drive to a farm thirty minutes away to ride a horse. However, I liked to try new sports. Some blended well with my natural athleticism, country life, and middle-class existence; others did not.

Roller skating hearkened as a new activity for experimentation. Mom had talked about roller skating on the sidewalks of San Antonio, Texas, when she was a child. Since ice skating was one of my favorite winter activities, I envisioned roller skating as a spectacular summer equivalent. I did not know anyone in Newtown with roller skates and had not even seen a pair in real life. Still, I imagined gliding on the road as smoothly as on a frozen pond.

After I nagged Mom and Dad about wanting to try roller skates for enough time, they gave in and found a used pair for me to try. The skates consisted of a flat metal plate with four metal wheels. A small metal toe hook kept the front of my shoe in place, while several straps crossed over each shoe and tied to the metal plate. A rubber stopper on the front of the skates provided a brake.

Mom accompanied me to the road for my first test run. She helped me put on my skates and held my hand as I stepped off the gravel driveway onto the paved road for the first time. I shuffled for a few steps to get a feeling for the skates and then pushed off with one foot to glide. I coasted a couple of feet and then slowed to a stop. I tried again and the same thing happened. I pushed harder and harder, but never gained much momentum. The friction from the rough asphalt road in front of our house offered no speed whatsoever. Disappointed, I abandoned the roller skates rather quickly. Mom apologized and tried to explain that kids in the city had smooth sidewalks for roller skating. Our street did not have sidewalks, so it did not take much for me to conclude that roller skates were useless in Newtown.

Other odd inequalities persisted to frustrate my sports interests. I had always been fascinated by tennis, glued to the U.S. Open broadcast from Flushing Meadows long before I had any knowledge of the game. My mother had even written in my baby book that I liked to watch tennis on television. When I was old enough to hold a racquet, Mom enrolled me in a group lesson for kids at Dickinson Park. The park was in the center of town, and the courts were in high demand. Written sign-up sheets allowed adults to make court reservations on the honor system. Mom played in a women's league, but the distance to sign up and then drive back to play presented challenging logistics.

I never gave up my interest in tennis, though, even without much playing time. Mom signed me up for tennis camp at the home of a teaching colleague, who lived on the other side of Newtown. The woman had a tennis court in her backyard, as well as a pool. She ran a weeklong summer camp for local kids. I spent one week at the camp and thoroughly enjoyed it.

With very little background in tennis, the instructor informed my mother that I "showed promise." Mom never shared the news with me, though. We did not live near the town courts, and it would have been impossible for me to play on a regular basis. Lessons were expensive, too. Mom worried that I would never be able to compete fairly against kids with greater access to the courts and paid lessons. She managed my on-going disappointment as gracefully as she could and explained, albeit uncomfortably, that "tennis was for the kids on the other side of town."

"You can play team sports," she consoled me. "They're cheaper." Fortunately, I liked my options. Soccer remained my primary interest, although I also played basketball in the winter and softball in the spring. I threw a ball 76' 9" to win the 7/8-year old division softball throw at a Newtown Jaycees event in 1976. My superior throwing arm meant that I was almost automatically assigned to third base for all the years that I played youth softball. I never liked the position, though, as few runners ever made it to third base. In my mind, first and second basemen saw all the action, and I would have much preferred to play either of those positions.

I played basketball regularly and made a decent point guard in the youth recreational league. Basketball presented a challenge, though, as I never developed good shooting technique and heaved the ball toward the basket in an awkward two-handed motion. With my mother's encouragement that I "needed to practice to get better," country life presented yet another dilemma. The nearest basketball courts were in the same park as the tennis courts.

My frustration led Dad to install a basketball hoop in the backyard. He had found a large utility pole that was discarded by a gas station and purchased a basketball backboard, rim, and net. The setup was a success, but it did not have the desired effect to increase my practice time. I threw the ball toward the basket to hit the backboard or rim, and it descended to land with a thump in the soft grass. Without a hard surface for the ball to bounce, I got tired of picking up the basketball again and again. The revelation that my practice court needed a paved surface led Mom to explain once again that paved city streets and court availability led city kids to have an advantage in the sport. I dribbled fairly well, but never developed a good shot.

Although focused on soccer, I still played basketball by the time I reached high school. I had grown to approximately 5'7". I was taller than half the girls on the team, which meant that I could no longer play guard, but was really too short to play forward effectively. With poor shooting skills, my greatest contribution to the team was defensive re-bounding. I had an impressive vertical leap and loved the aggression under the basket as both teams vied for the ball. If I won possession, then I dribbled to the side a few steps and hummed the ball in an overhead throw to a speedy point guard who had sprinted to the opposite court to execute a fast break.

The strategy worked often, and the coach even had us execute the play a few times during practice where the team lined up at the opposite end of the court to receive my throws. I did not need any practice to throw the basketball like a softball, but the rest of the team needed practice to catch it. Without realizing it, I learned that I threw the ball pretty hard when I broke a teammate's finger during the drill. Later on, I broke a different girl's finger throwing a football to her in gym class and broke a goalie's finger with a soccer kick.

"You don't know how strong you are," Mom warned. I was lucky that no one at school ever figured out that I was behind all the finger injuries.

I never played softball in high school, but decided to try out for the women's softball team in college. When the coach asked me what position I played, I started to ramble on about my youth league experience and that I was always "stuck" on third base, because I could throw. I readily expressed my interest to play first base.

"You can throw?" the coach said with piqued interest. "We already have a third baseman; try outfield." I collected my gear and made my way to the outfield. Before too long, the coach was hitting balls to me in center field, and I was throwing them to home, again, and again, and again. I won a starting position in the outfield and discovered that I absolutely loved it. As a bit of a bonus, the coach trained me as the backup first baseman. I covered the position when the starter had batting practice.

With my combined throwing skills and soccer speed, the outfield was a thrill. There was not a ball in the air that I thought I could not catch. However, my unique talent did nothing to help me behind the plate. Because I had not played softball in high school, I missed the transition from soft, underhanded throws to fast, windmill pitches. The college pitchers threw the ball with such speed that I could not swing fast enough before I heard the "thud" the ball made in the catcher's glove. I was late on nearly every pitch. Simply put, I could not hit worth a darn.

Swim, Run, Putt

Mom and Dad recognized that many kids have a fear of water, and they were determined that I should learn to swim at a few years of age. Mom had not learned to swim until she was an adult. Dad had flopped around in Lake Zoar at Boy Scout camp and accompanied his brother on fishing trips where he preferred splashing around to fishing. Neither one of them had learned the basic strokes, although they did well enough to enjoy the water. They were determined to introduce me to swimming via proper instruction so that I could learn the right way.

As a toddler, Mom took me to the Danbury YMCA (Young Men's Christian Association). I dog-paddled around the big pool with a Styrofoam bubble on my back for flotation. On the last day of class, the instructors dangled me off the end of the diving board, dropped me gently into the water and swam beside me as I dog-paddled to the far end of the pool. My parents enabled me to reach an important milestone early; I always felt comfortable in the water.

Mom enthusiastically took Doris and me to Dickinson Park in Newtown on hot days in summer. The park offered an enormous pool with water that was fed naturally from a nearby stream and resembled a small pond. The pool had been well designed with a shallow bottom in one area and a progressively deeper section that led to a diving board. A white wooden dock was anchored in the middle of the pool, a popular hangout for teenage swimmers.

Originally, the pool had a muddy bottom, but it was paved and painted blue when I was very young. The blue paint never quite stuck, though, and frequently peeled away. The water was crystal clear for several feet, although murky at greater depth. We did not mind, though, as the fresh water provided a similar experience to swimming in the natural outdoors. There were always rumors of snapping turtles, but I never saw a turtle, fish, or any other animal in the pool. I can only presume that the myth was perpetuated by teenagers who wanted to scare the younger kids and did not know any better. If we ever tired of the water, we moved a short distance to the playground with swings, seesaws, and jungle gym.

I gained most of my formal swim instruction at the Green Knoll Camp in Brookfield, Connecticut. The rustic camp had three pools, a softball diamond, archery range, woodshop, and crafts workshop. Every camper participated in swim classes twice a day. I learned most of the major strokes and advanced to the top swim class, where I also learned water safety. We were challenged to tread water with our hands out of the water for thirty minutes, retrieve objects in the deep end, and swim two lengths of the pool underwater in one breath. We even learned how to survive in the water with our clothes on, although the first part of the lesson stressed the importance of getting our shoes and pants off! Despite all the swim lessons, I never officially passed a swim test. I always had an ear infection before the end of camp.

As the whole family enjoyed swimming, we were frequently invited to the home of Dr. Thomas and Doris (Raymaley) Bucky for a swim. They had a beautiful in-ground pool in their backyard with a surrounding patio to relax out of the water and eat a picnic lunch. Dr. Tom also had a number of rubber snakes and frogs that he kept around the pool as a joke. Dad liked the frogs, but shied away from the snakes even though he knew that they were only rubber. Doris Bucky noted that I devised competitions as soon as I arrived at the pool. I challenged her to race or asked for objects to be thrown in the pool so that I see how many I could retrieve in a single breath.

Doris may have observed my competitive spirit around the pool, but Mom and Dad had to deal with my overabundance of energy all the time. Whether diving for objects in the water, kicking a ball, or running a race, I preferred to beat someone in the task and constantly challenged my parents and their adult friends.

If I lacked a competitor, then I begged Mom or Dad to devise a dare just for me.

"Ugh," Dad groaned. "Not again."

"You were hatched," declared Mom.

"They had to crack the egg open with a sledge hammer," Dad chipped in. Obviously, I had more than the average amount of energy for a child and was not of this earth, hatched from an alien egg instead of born like a normal child. Still, if for no reason other than to tire me out, Mom and Dad obliged my requests and kept me occupied as they feigned surprise at my extraordinary feats.

If Mom and Dad wanted me to burn off energy, they acted as though they were interested to learn how fast I could run. Dad had only to look at his watch, which I took as a cue for a challenge. I hopped up from whatever I was doing, flew out the door and raced the length of the yard and back. When I returned to the house, Mom and Dad invented a reason why I needed to repeat the effort and encouraged me to do better. Inspired, I always ran a second or third time.

When I finally tired, Dad usually declared that I had "beaten the record." Mom and Dad amused themselves with this scheme on numerous occasions, but eventually the jig was up for my parents. They had too much fun, and I caught on to the family conspiracy to drain me of my energy.

Sometimes it did not take anyone to construct a challenge at all, as some games, such as miniature golf, inherently presented obstacles to conquer. Mom was a great sport to take Doris and me to putt-putt courses that we happened upon in our travels. The more complex the course, the more I liked it. Purely flat courses did not measure up to moving windmills or 360° loops that were more challenging. I also liked water holes, where a good shot "jumped" a water hazard. If a ball got stuck under an obstacle or fell into the water, we laughed ourselves silly.

Mom took us to play at one course that had overhead lights for nighttime play. We frequently found that fighting off mosquitos was as much a challenge as the golf, but we still loved it. We were regular visitors and liked the course design, although the 18th hole zigged and zagged with a steep ramp that led to a flat green proved particularly daunting. The green was located directly outside the small check-in stand so that an attendant could observe golf play and award a free game to anyone who hit a hole-in-one. I coveted that prize!

After many visits to the same course, I was frustrated. No matter what I did on the 18th hole, my ball never had enough momentum to

Hatched in Newtown

make it up the ramp. If I could not find a solution, I could never get a hole-in-one and win the free game. After much thought on the subject, I concluded that I needed to swing the club with more power.

I faced the 18th hole one more time after many failed attempts on my seasonal record. Without hesitation, I pulled the club back over my head and brought it down on the ball as hard as I could. The ball launched into the air with force. The attendant who watched us from the small check-in stand ducked for cover as the ball sailed over the structure to land in the woods well beyond the course limits. I stood astonished. Who knew that a putter could launch a ball thirty feet into the air? The attendant popped his head up and looked at our surprised threesome. After a brief pause, I heard my mother snicker.

"Well, you better go get it," she said. I ran around the course into the woods and found my colored ball in the periphery of the bright lights. I returned to the 18th hole with my ball to try again and used more restraint the second time. I never won the hole-in-one challenge, but never gave up trying.

Dad Cooks, Not Mom

Although competitive in sports, I never had the slightest inclination to develop cooking skills. Dad ruled the kitchen, and his culinary skill was legendary. He prepared a hearty New England meal every night. The family ate together in the dining room at 5 p.m. sharp, except for Sundays when we ate at noon in the Swedish tradition. Dad insisted on cooking alone in the kitchen. As soon as Mom, Doris, or I stepped over the dining room threshold to collect plates, glasses, and silverware to set the table, he insisted that we got in his way. Cleanup was an entirely different matter. Dad left his plate on the table after dinner and escaped to his many proj-

184

ects around the house. I usually loaded the dishwasher and cleaned the pots and pans, while Mom managed the leftovers.

Dad also did the food shopping at the famous family-owned *Stew Leonard's* supermarket in Norwalk, Connecticut. The large store had opened with live farm animals in front of it to attract customers. It also maintained an unusual floor plan that required each customer to zigzag through the whole store rather than shortcut through a traditional layout of parallel aisles. The store sold its own brand of milk and had an enormous number of checkouts compared to other local grocery stores at the time. (Note: Dad later boycotted the store after Stew Leonard Sr. was convicted of tax fraud in an elaborate scheme to manipulate cash register receipts.)

Dad calculated our daily food needs precisely from an ingredient standpoint, but overindulged on the quantity. The pantry adjacent to the kitchen held Dad's excess of dry goods, while the freezer in the cellar was stuffed to the brim. Dad built shelves in the cellar, too, as he stashed more and more canned goods for "when he needed them." Dad liked to shop the sales and never missed an opportunity to save money.

Dad cooked in such abundance that leftovers were commonplace. We got used to many choices at the dinner table, whether the meal du jour or the previous night's feast. Mom made sure she never had to put a small portion of something back in the refrigerator more than once.

"Eat that last little bit," she pleaded. Her job with leftovers was simplified if we each did our part to finish off the meal portions from the previous nights.

I have always said that the dark days of my childhood corresponded to when Dad was not available to cook. Each semester for a few days, he was taken away from us at dinnertime to conduct parent-teacher conferences wherever he taught. Without the cook in the house, Mom, Doris, and I were left to fend for ourselves. We joked that Mom had the cooking versatility to prepare three types of sandwiches: cheese, tuna fish, or peanut butter with banana. To soften the blow of Dad's absence, Mom sometimes treated us to "TV dinners," which were actually sort of fun, but certainly did not measure up to the daily culinary extravagance to which we had grown accustomed.

Feeling sorry for us one year, Dad organized a meal in advance and left instructions for us as to how to cook it. He conjectured that we should be capable of managing a simple meal and chose ham as our first test.

"*Anyone* can cook a ham," he declared.

Dad left in the morning on the day of his parent-teacher conferences with a ham on the countertop and written instructions for Mom to put the ham in the oven at a particular time. He planned to prepare the rest of the meal when he got home, so that we could eat together, albeit later than usual.

Mom carefully followed his orders and put the ham in the oven at the assigned time. The meat had been cooking awhile by the time Dad arrived home and took over in the kitchen. The very first thing Dad did was to check the ham in the oven. Very quickly, he discovered that the meat still had the plastic on it. The ham was obviously ruined and he could not believe that Mom had made such a simple mistake. He was absolutely incensed by the error and stormed around the kitchen in a state of incredulity until he could whip up a substitute dinner. Sheepishly, we ate the alternative as Dad fumed shame on all of us.

Despite the failure, Dad believed that the ham idea still had merit and wanted to try it again. He decided to repeat the experiment during the following semester's parent-teacher conference week. However, the next time he placed his faith in me. My mother had obviously failed at the first go-around, and the next in line for this great responsibility was his eldest daughter. Dad left in the morning after he provided me with both verbal and written instructions and commanded me to remember to "take the plastic off the ham." Goodness, how could I forget after the first incident? I would not fail!

Dutifully, I executed his instructions in the afternoon, took the plastic off the ham, set the oven to the right temperature, and put the ham in the oven to cook. I proudly stood at the doorway upon my father's late return and explained that dinner was on track. Before too long, we all heard Dad yell from the kitchen. The ham, once again, had been cooked with plastic on it. Another ham was ruined! I immediately professed my innocence and offered the removed plastic as evidence that I had followed his instructions.

"There are many layers of plastic on a ham!" barked my father. I had made the same mistake as my mother. In disbelief, Dad sent us all out of the room and mumbled under his breath that he could not trust us to do anything in the kitchen. After that, it was back to "TV dinners" at parent-teacher time. They were a lot safer bet than a ham wrapped in multiple layers of plastic.

Dad's daily New England fare was fairly consistent with meat, potatoes, and a vegetable almost every night. Otherwise he made a terrific beef stew, spaghetti, or a turkey tetrazzini, as different menu options. He also supplemented our diet with his seasonal specialties. In early spring, he tapped the maple trees and hung buckets on them to collect the sap and make maple syrup. In summer, he pickled peaches. On warm days he made fresh oatmeal bread and allowed me to turn the crank of the antique bread maker. In fall, Dad made homemade applesauce. We peeled most of the apples with an old-fashioned apple peeler that Dad set up in the kitchen. One year Dad even made dandelion wine, but the results did not warrant repetition. For Thanksgiving and Christmas, he made cranberry sauce with fresh cranberries. The family laughed amongst ourselves if we ever saw cranberry sauce from a can. The wiggly, jellylike cranberry substitute looked ridiculous to us.

Dad prepared an extraordinary Thanksgiving Day feast every year. Good cooks can often exceed the capacity of their kitchen,

FIGURE 72:
Picking apples with Papa.

but Dad took holiday cooking to a whole new level. He plugged in electric burners all over the house and shuttled back and forth between the rooms in the house as he stirred, mashed, seasoned, and tasted.

An extreme culinary event required advance preparation, which led Dad to stuff our Thanksgiving turkey the night before the holiday. He lacked space in the refrigerator for a large bird, so he substituted the porch for overnight storage. The cool New England air provided natural refrigeration.

One night, a raccoon discovered the Thanksgiving turkey on the porch and took a visible bite out of the turkey breast. The rest of the bird remained untouched, which likely meant that something had scared the scavenger away. Dad was surprised to discover the damage on Thanksgiving morning, but cut off the turkey section that had been visibly chewed and cooked the rest of the bird to perfection.

As it happened, Dad's aunt and uncle, Grace and Harold Peer, joined us for the holiday that year.

"Don't you *dare* tell Aunt Grace that a raccoon chewed the turkey," Dad warned me sternly. My father and I both knew that Aunt Grace would never eat a bite if she knew that a raccoon had been served first. Despite the temptation, I kept my mouth shut. Dad carved the turkey before Aunt Grace saw it, and she enjoyed every morsel.

Many years later after Harold had passed away, Grace and her sister Elva joined us regularly for Christmas dinners. Elva was in her nineties and more than ten years older than Grace, but Elva took care of her younger sister in their Milford, Connecticut, home. Grace had begun to suffer from dementia, but somehow the two women were able to manage together. Mom and Dad made weekly trips to take care of their grocery, household, banking, and other needs.

As the two older ladies were no longer able to drive, Dad asked me to pick up Grace and Elva in Milford on a particular Christmas Day and drive them to our house in Newtown for our usual feast. This allowed my father more time in the kitchen, and I was always happy to help the cook!

When I arrived at the Milford house, I picked up the morning newspaper, which had been left on the sidewalk, and rang the doorbell. Grace opened the door.

"Kelley! What are you doing here?" I was surprised because certainly my father had told her that I would pick them up.

"It's Christmas, Aunt Grace. I'm here to take you to Newtown for dinner," I answered.

"Christmas! Nobody told *me* it was Christmas!" rebutted Aunt Grace in a huff. She took the newspaper from my hand and walked into the living room to spread it out on the table.

"Well," she said, "the newspaper says it's Christmas, so it *must* be Christmas!"

It took a little while to get Grace and Elva ready for the drive to Newtown. Grace sorted through a dozen shoeboxes to look for the "right pair," but I finally got them in the car and safely to Newtown. We all enjoyed Dad's usual feast, but knew that Grace and Elva could not live by themselves for much longer.

That was our last Christmas together, although we remembered the event many times by restating Grace's now famous words, "Christmas! Nobody told *me* it was Christmas!"

The Quadruple Mow

Dad's propensity to collect things extended to useful items that he needed to maintain the Newtown house and yard. To add to his barns full of carpentry tools, garden tools, and yard equipment, Dad also accumulated a small fleet of used tractors and lawnmowers, including an International Harvester Cub Highboy from the 1960s.

Dad tinkered with the old equipment endlessly and was determined to keep the machines running. He insisted that the "old stuff" was better than anything he could have bought new. I very much doubted the argument as there were never more than a few lawnmowers in working condition at any given time.

Unfortunately, Dad's enthusiasm to keep the old equipment operational did not match his skills as a small engine mechanic. His lack of success was a continued source of frustration for him. Several different neighbors often helped Dad out with the mower problems. The men had more experience with engines and could detect and fix the problems in a few hours. Dad received the gift of engine repairs like a kid with a new toy and used the equipment in a sheer state of delight until it broke again.

With two acres of land that included two fields, mowing the lawn consumed an entire day for one person. We used the Cub tractor for the fields, while the smaller riding mowers or push mowers were more suitable for navigating around the numerous trees, bushes, and stone walls to mow the shorter grass.

Dad and I performed the bulk of lawn maintenance. Mom mowed occasionally, but Doris rarely touched a lawnmower. Yet, the yard was too much for any one person to manage on a regular basis. We cut the lawn on no particular schedule, just whenever it needed attention. During a rainy spring, the grass sometimes grew so fast that we needed to mow it more than once a week. Sometimes, we could hardly keep up with the chore.

One summer day, I fired up a lawn tractor and made my way to the far end of the backyard to mow. Shortly, Mom and Dad were both mowing, too, and even Doris had

FIGURE 73:
Dad on his International Harvester Cub Highboy tractor. I'm helping to drive.

ventured outside to help. I was still in the back part of the yard when I heard someone call my name. Mr. Griffiths, our next-door neighbor, had walked over to our yard with a camera.

"Four Janssons mowing at the same time!" he exclaimed. "That's worth a picture." He had us line up with our respective lawn equipment and snapped the photo. A few weeks later, he delivered a print to our family with a big grin on his face. In his mind, the moment was simply worthy of a "Kodak moment." It was unusual for a family to have so many lawn mowers, let alone putting them to use all at the same time.

I always completed the various chores that my parents assigned to me. During my teenage years before I had a part-time job, Mom

left written lists of chores for Doris and me on the kitchen countertop each morning in the summertime. Like my father's mother,
Tina (Bissonnette) Jansson, my mother also did not believe in idle
children. Both the lists were short, but my list assigned tasks such
as "mow the (gigantic) lawn," or "paint the barn." Doris received
simple chores such as "unload the dishwasher" or "take the trash
out." Obviously, my tasks could take the whole day, while Doris
could complete her chores in a few minutes. The disparity was the
source of a running joke between Mom and me, as I chided her
about the assignments. She never felt guilty, though.

"I knew that you would get the big tasks done," she confided
with a grin.

The lawn may have consumed a good deal of time, but the house
and barns also required regular maintenance. Painting the various
structures often seemed as endless as the yard work. Dad knew all
about house painting from Papa, but had been relegated to paint cellar windows and lally columns whenever he worked on his father's
crew. As a result, he avoided all painting tasks like the plague. Fortunately, I did not mind it. I liked the smell of oil and turpentine
and appreciated how much better the house and barns looked with
a fresh coat of paint. I did not much care for the preparation or
cleanup, though, so Dad and I made a good team. He mixed the
paint and cleaned the brushes, while I did the actual painting.

Mom supervised to make sure that Dad provided me with a safe
environment. Dad liked to use Papa's equipment, and some of it
had deteriorated to the point where it was no longer safe. No matter the tool, Dad insisted that the old stuff was better. Once he
jumped on the lowest rung of an old wooden ladder to prove its
sturdiness, and the ladder split halfway up the side. Never defeated,
Dad sawed off the broken part, which made it shorter, but kept it
in use. Mom and I knew to be suspicious of Dad's cavalier attitude

toward ladders. We made sure that each one held my weight and was firmly placed on level ground.

If Dad criticized my work in any way, then Mom was quick to remind him that he could do the painting himself. His derogatory remarks that I missed a spot, used the wrong paint stroke, or had not adequately worked the paint into the shingles never went unnoticed. It was too much fun to josh Dad when these exchanges occurred. Like Mark Twain's fictional Tom Sawyer, I was more than happy to share the privilege of hard work.

"Wanna paint, Dad?" I called from the ladder. Mom smiled, and Dad walked briskly away before either of us could hand him a paintbrush.

Mad Scientist

As a scientist and teacher, Dad made sure that I had plenty of opportunity to explore nature. When I first learned of protozoa in biology class, Dad set up a microscope in the dining room for me to discover as many living microscopic creatures as I could find. When I could not find anything else to put under the microscope, Dad put some straw in water for a few days. I watched in amazement as tiny paramecium appeared and prepared my scientific equipment for examination of the new creatures.

"It's easy to get paramecium from good Timothy hay," Dad declared, as if to state the obvious.

My biology class also studied slime mold, and the teacher challenged us to find it at home. Excited about the hunt, I shared my plans with Dad. Without saying a word, he got up from his chair and walked to an indoor woodpile that was stored next to the fireplace. He picked up a piece of wood, turned it over, and pointed to the middle of the wood.

"There's your slime mold," he remarked smugly. I looked at the stringy white substance with surprise, but was disappointed that Dad had spoiled my search. Still, I could not believe that slime mold had been in the house all along and I had never known about it.

I often conducted experiments from books and liked the discovery process. In a study of the visible light spectrum, I wanted to experiment with refraction. I planned to shine a light through a jar of milk to see the spectral colors. I filled the jar and left it in the refrigerator for a month to sour. Mom and Dad asked me nearly every day when they could get rid of the milk, but after many failed attempts at the experiment, I insisted that it was not yet sour enough.

Finally, Dad looked over the instructions that I had followed and recognized my mistake. I was supposed to have used "diluted" milk, and had not understood the word "diluted." Dad filled up a new jar with water and added only a teaspoon of milk. The experiment still did not work, so he dumped out a portion of the mixture to add more water. By the time we saw the spectrum with the light source, the jar must have contained only a few drops of milk. I had learned both a science and vocabulary lesson at the same time.

Dad liked to hear what I was doing in science classes. He explained electrons and protons to me with salt and pepper shakers. When I studied human anatomy, he described the function of each organ at the dinner table and impressed me with his ability to name the bones in the body. When I studied plants, he set up a small greenhouse in my bedroom under a plant light. When I studied animals and learned the taxonomic rank, he challenged me to define and understand the definition of each species.

Fascinated by the animal kingdom, I took a special high school class in oceanography. Enthralled by a final project that allowed for independent research, I poured over Dad's college textbooks and collected stacks of reference books from the library. While a good portion of the class presented papers titled "The Shark," I produced a personal masterpiece on invertebrate locomotion. Needless to say, I received an A +.

Dad also nurtured my scientific interest in geology and shepherded a huge rock collection that the two of us amassed in the basement, along with a rock tumbler that we kept running to polish various specimens. We joined the Danbury Mineralogical Society together and attended the monthly meetings, lectures, and annual Gem, Jewelry, and Mineral Show. A few times during the year, the club organized field trips for active exploration. With a small rock pick, I clamored on the rugged terrain next to Dad, but never found much more than a quartz crystal. The few rocks that I took home with me paled in comparison to the rocks we had purchased. I learned the hard way that the stunning specimens at the rock shows were mined all over the world. I had only scratched the surface of the Earth in Connecticut.

Dad catered to my new interests and added a tropical fish tank next to the plants in my bedroom. The fish tank captivated my attention, as Dad built an elaborate ecosystem that more closely resembled the bottom of an ocean than a kid's fish tank. Each week, he added something to the tank including more fish, water plants, and a tiny frog that was no bigger than the size of a dime. He explained that one fish had to be a plecostomus to eat algae and keep the tank clean. The other fish were chosen only for their hardy survival rate and random color patterns.

The frog provided entertainment, as "find the frog" became a check-off item each morning and night. When the frog disappeared for a while, I assumed that it had found a hiding place among the plants. Instead, I found the tiny frog's skeleton in my sister's bedroom many months after its disappearance. Sadly, the mystery was solved.

The fish tank required the usual aquarium pump to oxygenate the water. The pump ran all the time. I fed the fish every day and cleaned the tank once a month. All in all, the fish tank was a fairly low maintenance project. When the family was away, we asked a neighbor to feed the fish.

However, when the family traveled to Maine for two weeks one summer, we returned to a rude surprise. While we were away, extremely hot temperatures had evaporated a great deal of water in the fish tank and dropped the water level below the siphon. The neighbors did not know to add water or how to restart the siphon. Instead, they turned the pump off.

As soon as the family drove into the yard, we all knew that something was terribly wrong. The stench that emanated from the house was unbelievable and it was pretty obvious that the fish tank was the problem. I walked to my bedroom on the second floor and saw my beautiful tank full of jet black water, dead plants, and dead fish.

Mom and Dad removed the tank and opened up all the windows to let the smell out of the house. Mom was particularly sorry. She felt that it was our responsibility to take care of the fish, just like any other animal, and we had failed. When the neighbors asked whether the fish had died, we did not have the heart to tell them the whole truth.

Maine Cabin

Family on a Budget

In 1970, when I was three years old, Mom and Dad considered the purchase of a vacation home in Maine. They had a natural affinity for the state due to Mom's experience in Fryeburg, as well as their honeymoon in Kennebunkport. A teacher's income never allowed us to take long-distance or exotic vacations, but a second home within driving distance offered an affordable escape from the daily grind.

Discouraged after looking at small lakefront homes in disrepair, Mom and Dad settled on the purchase of more than a hundred acres of land in the woods of Acton, Maine, midway up Gerrish Mountain. The Salmon Falls River was at the bottom of the mountain and designated the border between New Hampshire and Maine.

The mountainous land had been the site of an old homestead, but the structure had been destroyed by fire many years earlier. The original field stone foundation remained as a big hole in the ground. Fields surrounded the immediate area, with several apple trees, and two Seckel pear trees. The rest of the property was woods that had been logged in the 1950s and regrown to a mature forest that included sugar maples, beech, white birch, pines, hemlock, and balsam trees.

Mom and Dad contracted with a local builder, Warren Crawford, to construct a small 24' x 32' cabin with a vaulted ceiling that included two bedrooms, one bathroom, a kitchen, living room, and a loft over the bedrooms. A full basement had a garage door that opened to the outside. Two sides of the living room were covered in windows. A small porch provided a view of a rambling brook that was spring-fed further up the mountain. The water flowed into the Salmon Falls River several miles away.

Dad wanted to use the homestead's field stone foundation, but the builder warned that we would "never get rid of the snakes." The comment quickly put an end to Dad's idea, which meant that we poured a new cement foundation. Dad also wanted a large picture window to view the mountains in the distance, but the contractor talked him out of that idea, too. Stray bullets from hunters frequently shattered windows in the area. Instead, the contractor suggested a series of smaller windows that created the illusion of a picture window. Mom and Dad both liked the solution. (The contractor was right. Bullets broke the smaller windows several times.)

FIGURE 74:
My mother and sister in an unfinished cabin bedroom.

The family traveled back and forth to Maine to view the progress on the cabin's construction. Most of the time we stayed at a nearby motel. On one trip, we stayed at a cabin on Great East Lake at the invitation of Mr. Crawford. He owned and maintained the lake-front house as a rental property.

The Great East cabin was nestled in a pine grove and had a long dock that extended from the water's edge. The shallow beach was perfect for a small child to swim safely. I was only a few years old and jumped off the dock by myself. Like at the YMCA, I wore my Styrofoam bubble for flotation. Dad had

FIGURE 75:
Jumping off the dock at
Great East Lake in Maine.

his camera with him and took some great snapshots of me, including a mid-air jump and a beaming grin from the water as I looked back at him on shore.

Mom waded into the lake with Doris, who was still a baby. She dipped Doris into the water, as she rocked her back and forth. They stayed in the water awhile, as I continued to jump off the dock. When Mom was ready to return to shore, she lifted Doris out of the water and found that Doris was completely naked. My sister's diapers had disintegrated. White bits of diaper soon floated all around the dock area, and we could do nothing but watch. Over the next several hours, the diaper debris moved slowly away from the cove. Doris was refitted with a fresh covering, and we resumed our lake fun.

Warren understood the requirements of our family on a budget. He completed a minimal cabin structure with foundation, roof, exterior siding, windows, and floor. Interior walls were left framed, but uncovered. He connected a cold-water tank to a pre-existing lead pipe from the original well on the property. Two 100-amp electrical boxes were installed, although only one was connected. The intention was to use the second box for a future hot water heater that took advantage of lower electrical rates at night. A phone line was not installed.

FIGURE 76:
The Maine cabin before it was painted.

The seasonal cabin was not insulated and did not include a furnace. Instead, Mom and Dad purchased a freestanding, wood-burning stove made of sheet metal to keep the cabin warm. Dad used a chainsaw to selectively cut down trees for fuel. Dad liked certain trees and disliked others. He attacked alders with a vengeance and declared them as "junk trees," while he cleared around white birch, beech, and hemlocks to showcase his favorites in the yard. I liked pines and transplanted many seedlings from the woods to the house area. Dad liked hemlocks the best and started a "nursery" of hemlocks that he tended like a garden. Unfortunately for Dad, the porcupines liked his trees, too. The herbivores munched away to decapitate several of his beloved hemlocks.

Dad purchased a red International Cub Lo-Boy tractor with a mower and cart. The tractor was about eight inches lower than the tractor in Connecticut. The lower center of gravity provided more stability for Dad to mow on the hills. We used the cart to move wood and clear brush after Dad cut down trees. All of us helped to load the cart full of wood in the fields and unload it in the basement. Mom, Doris, and I dragged the brush into piles for Dad to burn in late winter or spring when the ground was wet. The family's effort to clear the land around the house kept us in steady supply of wood, although our first wood-burning stove did not last long. The sheet metal wore through, so we replaced the whole unit with a sturdier cast iron version. The new stove had sides molded with a New England scene that contained a cabin and several moose.

While the Connecticut house was furnished with antiques, the Maine house took on an entirely different aesthetic. Friends generously donated household goods to us that they no longer wanted. In addition, Dad enthusiastically cruised tag sales for used household items and rarely paid more than a few dollars for anything. Soon, the Maine house was furnished with beds, tables, chairs, old towels, rugs, plastic plates, and odd silverware that was given to us or purchased at tag sales. Seasonal cabins were frequently burglarized in Maine, so Mom and Dad maintained that we should never keep anything of value at the cabin.

Doris and I perused the sales for old board games or puzzles, while Mom sorted through the books with us. Mom had such a tremendous knowledge of literature that she carefully examined each title and shared her recommendation as to whether we should read it. If Mom recommended a book, then we nearly always made a point to buy it. We rarely paid more than a quarter for anything and amassed a healthy collection of puzzles, games, and books. Jigsaw puzzles were a favorite for the whole family after dinner.

Slowly, Mom and Dad completed the interior walls of the cabin and added doors to the bedrooms and bathroom. The kitchen was outfitted, too. The electric stove was a gift from Mom's teaching colleague, Ella Williams. General Electric had produced pink stoves and refrigerators as an experimental color. The new stoves were installed in Ella's apartment complex in Bridgeport, Connecticut. However, at some point, the apartment complex was converted to condominiums. The new owners did not want the pink appliances and gave them to anyone who wanted them. Ella gave us a pink stove for the Maine cabin. We joked that the unusual pink stove was the only item safe from theft.

Ella also gave us a small white refrigerator with a freezer. An automatic dishwasher was never planned, given that the water pipes had to be drained in winter to prevent their freezing and breaking. We also acquired numerous second-hand electric space heaters to place in areas furthest from the wood stove.

Mom and Dad packed a large cooler of food anytime we traveled from Connecticut to Maine. Perishable items traveled with us, but otherwise we left food in the Connecticut refrigerator and freezer. The Maine food situation was more complicated. We turned the power off to the cabin when we were not there, which meant that we needed to take all the food in the refrigerator and freezer with us and defrost the freezer before we left. We turned the main circuit breaker "on" upon arrival at the cabin and flipped it "off" as the last thing we did before we left.

One year in fall, we arrived at the Maine cabin around dinnertime. Dad switched on the oven to get ready to cook. It was not very long before we all sensed a pungent smell. We looked around the house and discovered that the source of the smell came from the back of the stove.

Dad switched the stove off and pulled it away from the wall. To our surprise, we found that a mouse had constructed a nest between the wires that supplied power to the appliance. When the stove had been switched on, the nest had burned and the mice had been electrocuted!

Mom and Dad cleaned out the mouse mess and returned the stove to operation. We ate dinner as planned, but the putrid smell of the dead mice lingered in the cabin for the next several hours.

The odor reminded us that whatever we ate probably tasted a lot better than a grilled rodent.

Tractors and Travels

To and from Maine, we stopped a few times for meals or bathroom breaks and sometimes visited discount stores to search for bargains. *Spag's* store in Shrewsbury, Massachusetts, became a regular stopover point, although Massachusetts enforced blue laws, so the store was closed on Sundays.

The iconic New England discounter sold products in bulk in a large warehouse with tents in the parking lot for seasonal promotions. We browsed the indoor aisles or tents to find products piled high in their original cardboard boxes, one choice for toothpaste, one for coffee, etc. *Spag's* accepted cash payments only and did not provide shopping bags. Mom and Dad always searched for empty cardboard boxes to carry our stash to the car. The store also had a large hardware and paint section, which Dad utilized heavily as needed.

The drive between Connecticut and Maine usually took us more than five hours. Dad did most of the driving, while Doris and I read books or slept. Mom sometimes sang to us. Her favorites were *(How Much Is That) Doggie in the Window*, *Ta Ra Ra Boom De E*, as well as the first verse and chorus to the *Three Little Fishes*. Mom sang the verses, while Doris and I joined in at the chorus. If we were tired of the car, then Mom and Dad communicated the time that remained to our destination in terms of the number of *Mister Rogers' Neighborhood* episodes.

In Maine, Doris and I worked on numerous arts and craft projects that included drawing, painting, leather craft, model building, woodworking, wood burning, weaving, science kits, and model rockets. Mom invented something new for us to do every day. One time she had us trace ourselves on large pieces of brown paper. We also hiked a lot in the woods, and Mom taught us to read a compass and a map. We read a lot of books in Maine, too, and made regular trips to our favorite used booksellers that lined the coast to serve summer tourists. The musty smell of the bookshops added to the adventure as we explored shelves full of old books. I liked biographies, sea stories, and classic literature, while my sister devoured science fiction. Mom also had us both read the authors she adored who wrote horse stories, including Will James, Marguerite Henry, and Walter Farley.

Dad spent most of his time outside, mowed the fields on his tractor, cleared and planted trees, and worked on the house. Mom had me assist Dad each day, so I learned general carpentry, drove the tractor, and assisted in the various tasks needed to maintain the property. I even learned how to use the chainsaw. (Many years later as an adult I bought a chainsaw to clear trees on my own property. A few weeks after my purchase, my (male) neighbor bought one, too. He came over to visit and told me that, when the salesman asked him why he wanted to buy a chainsaw, he answered, "to keep up with the lady next door!")

Dad loved to ride his tractor around the fields, but pushed the equipment to the point where it broke or rode it into a muddy area where he got stuck. The harsh use of the equipment accounted for most of the breakdowns, but he lacked common sense when it came to driving in wet areas.

"I thought I could make it across," he defended himself. Mom kept a keen watch on Dad's whereabouts in the yard, but we all knew to listen for when the tractor engine quit.

"Did it stop? Did it stop?" Mom asked Doris and me. She could not hear the sounds of the tractor herself and sometimes detected the expression on our faces when we heard Dad and his tractor collide with something or stall and startup again. We all knew when the tractor engine stopped that, it was "time to help Dad." Mom made sure that we embarked on rescue missions with the same expediency as professional first responders.

If the tractor was just stuck in mud, we used a car jack to raise it, and then put wood under the wheels. With enough height and traction, Dad could drive the tractor free of the wet area. Sometimes he was able to drive a broken machine back to the basement. On other occasions, we covered it with a tarp in the field to be fixed in place or towed back to the house at a later time. If Dad knew which part was broken, he spent the rest of the day on the phone to find a dealer with the part in stock, and we all knew to expect an excursion to some remote part of New England in search of the needed item on the following day.

We did not mind the long trips, but Dad must have grown tired of them. At some point, he became infatuated with the idea of a sickle bar mower, sure that the change would solve his tractor problems. I do not think that the rest of us were convinced; but if it meant fewer breakdowns, then that was okay.

After several years of talking about it, Dad finally bought his prized sickle bar and mounted it on the Cub. He drove around the fields in wonderment for a few days and then was back in the basement to take it off to remount the regular mower. He had lost so much maneuverability with the sickle bar that he did not like it. Mom, Doris, and I could not believe it, but we all had enough sense to stay quiet. Secretly, we confided to each other that Dad *liked* to get stuck.

Dad worked up an appetite in the fields. He entered the cabin for a cold lunch and poured the morning's leftover coffee over ice and added milk. Doris and I thought that the cold coffee was strange and always cried "eeew" when he drank it. Dad smacked his lips and proclaimed that Papa had also liked cold coffee. A sandwich and the homemade iced latte satisfied Dad's hunger until dinnertime, when he never ceased to cook an elaborate meal. Similar to Connecticut, Maine farms produced an abundant supply of seasonal produce, and we ate everything that was grown locally. Dad knew how to cook each vegetable to perfection including fiddleheads, which were fern fronds and only available for a short time each year. We also enjoyed boiled lobster!

One year we were disappointed that the local farm did not have any corn to sell. The farmer explained that someone had been stealing his produce.

"Don't worry, next year I'll have it," he promised. Sure enough, the next year the farmer was flush with corn. He had purchased two trained St. Bernards to guard his crops and caught the thieves. The perpetrators were pinned to the ground when the old man called the State Police. Citing the robbery as the jurisdiction of the local police, the farmer scoffed at the rebuff. The town was too small to have a police force or even a single police officer, so the state police was effectively ignoring the matter.

"Fine," said the farmer. "I'm going out to shoot them. Send someone to pick up the bodies." The abrupt sign-off prompted the State Police to investigate with urgency, and they deployed their resources to the small town. They apprehended the men who had been stealing the corn and determined that the thieves had made a business of selling the corn to tourists by the roadside near the coast.

Several farms offered pick-your-own strawberries and high-bush blueberries. In southern Maine, July was strawberry season, while August was blueberry season. We loved to go to the farms with our own buckets to pick the fresh berries. The blueberry farm hired teenagers to ride dirt bikes between the rows of blueberry bushes to scare away the birds, which looked like a fun job.

We gorged ourselves on the fruit and showed off our colorful tongues to one another. Mom baked cobbler, fruit pies, and Grandma Sibley's shortcake with the fresh berries. Dad made strawberry or blueberry syrup to go with pancakes that he cooked for us in the morning. We also bagged a lot of the fruit to freeze for use throughout the winter and carried an extra cooler with us to Maine to return our stash to Connecticut.

If it was warm enough, then Mom took Doris and me to Mousam Lake each day for a swim. Dad would go with us if he had worked up a sweat in the yard and wanted to clean off. We did not yet have a shower at the cabin, so daily dips in the beautiful lake were the best way to ward off dirt. We stayed in Maine for one or two weeks at a time during the summer, usually returning to Connecticut for a proper shower before we stunk too badly. The public beach at the lake was a popular swimming area. I often wore a mask to explore underwater, but never saw much more than a few minnows. However, once I floated around on a raft with a tiny window to view the water's depths and came eyeball-to-eyeball with a large one-foot turtle. I'm not sure who was more surprised, the turtle or me, but I fell off the raft, and the turtle quickly swam away.

Once we stayed a little longer in Maine than we usually did, and Mom decided that we should all wash our hair outside at a pitcher hand pump that Dad had installed in the old well. The mountain water was pristine, but quite cold. My sister volunteered to go first. She stuck her head under the pump's spout, while one of us worked the pump handle to get the water flowing. She shampooed her long hair, but quickly complained that the water temperature was too cold to continue. My mother insisted that she finish, although Doris clearly wanted to halt the exercise.

"Mommy! It's cold!" Doris cried. She was not very happy when she finally finished rinsing her long hair.

Mom decided to go next. She stuck her head under the spout, and we started to pump again. Like Doris, it was not very long before Mom shouted for us to stop. We ignored her and kept the water flowing. If Doris had survived the cold-water temperature, then we assumed that Mom could, too. Before long, Mom stood up to get away from the water.

"That's cold!" she yelled. We all laughed. Dad went into the house to get a thermometer. We measured the water temperature in the forties. Mom and Doris had indeed experienced some very cold water. By the time it was my turn, although I had short hair, a shampoo and rinse under the hand pump lasted only a minute. We never tried to wash our hair in this manner again. Dirt was better than a brain freeze.

Blue Water

FIGURE 77:
Petting the Bartlett's baby goats.

There was plenty to do in Maine around the cabin, although we also liked to visit the neighbors that we had gotten to know. Dr. David and Jeanne Bartlett lived up the street on Tamarack Farm. Dr. Bartlett was an optometrist, while Jeanne was a gifted artisan. Over time, they raised goats to sell milk and cheese, Angora rabbits to sell woven clothes with the wool, and a Welsh pony to race.[58]

208

Mrs. Bartlett brushed the rabbits for their wool in her lap, spun the wool into yarn, and wove the high-end women's clothes herself, mostly hats and scarves for visiting tourists. Dr. Bartlett competed with the pony at a nearby racetrack, Pinebrook Raceway.[58] The racing event required the large pony to pull a two-wheeled cart and maintain a trot throughout the race. Both adults, naturally talented and hard working, had lots of projects in progress at any given time. Doris and I loved to see the animals and the only time that we went to the racetrack, Dr. Bartlett took first place. Mom and Dad lost the opportunity to win any money, however. They were both against gambling and had refused to place a bet.

Across the river in Milton Mills, New Hampshire, was Griswold's Store. Mr. Griswold was a kindly, gray-haired man, who greeted us warmly each time we visited. The tiny shop provided staple groceries for the local residents. Mr. Griswold also catered to children and maintained a candy counter, including some treats for a penny, which was a bit of a throwback from a bygone era. Doris and I spent our loose change and could leave with a bag of candy for less than a dollar. Mr. Griswold also liked trains and had built an impressive model railroad in the apartment that he lived in above his store.

FIGURE 78:
Mr. Griswold in front of his store in Milton Mills, New Hampshire, 1979.

Lastly, we visited Dennis Long and his wife Virginia who lived in a small cabin on the shore of the Salmon Falls River. Dennis was born in 1907 and had grown up in Maine. He played semi-professional baseball until a motorcycle accident ended his career as a ballplayer.

With a college degree in education, he worked as both a teacher and as a principal. An accomplished taxidermist, he owned a gun shop for twenty years and worked for a number of mills in the area until retirement. He also played the saxophone and trumpet in professional bands and collected hundreds of instruments.[59]

At his home in Maine, Mr. Long had built an extension on to the house to serve as the "music room." With an assortment of musical instruments, sheet music, music stands, and the mounted head of an American Buffalo, Mr. Long was known as the "Acton Music Man" and gave free music lessons to anyone who was interested. I regularly joined sessions when Mr. Long assembled a group to perform at a local event. I usually played the C melody saxophone and covered a flute part, which was also in the key of C. Mr. Long could play almost any instrument, but could not play a flute due to his dentures. Since the groups were small, Mr. Long usually played with us. He mostly picked up a tenor or alto saxophone, but did not necessarily play the saxophone part in the same key as his instrument. Instead, he played a part for an instrument that was missing in the makeshift ensemble. He transposed the music in his head *as* he was playing!

I spent a great deal of time at Mr. Long's house during the summer and played a variety of his instruments. On one July 4th, Mr. Long assembled a group to perform on Great East Lake. Someone he knew had a flatboat, and we all climbed aboard with our instruments to create a floating tour group. We motored into coves and serenaded lakefront residents with American classics to celebrate the holiday. The spectators waved and cheered for our band from their docks as we passed by. We also performed at the local church, county fair, and other venues, as requested.

The family never spent all our time in the immediate vicinity of the cabin and made plenty of trips to the Maine coast. Mostly, we visited beaches that were off the beaten path from tourists, although there were plenty of occasions when we braved the crowds at popular destinations, such as Ogunquit Beach, Maine. The temperature of the ocean water ranged widely throughout the summer. We swam in tolerably warm water one visit and returned to agonizingly cold water during the next visit when the currents had changed.

Large parking lots for tourists required a much longer walk to find an available patch of sand to claim for the day. This hindered our family a bit as Doris and I were only capable of carrying our own small beach bags until we got older. We never packed lightly and carried beach towels, rubber rafts, shovels, pails, picnic lunch, and drinks.

We all liked the ocean for different reasons. Mom liked to stroll along the beach for exercise and watch the waves. Dad liked to collect interesting rocks and explore the tidal pools at low tide. Doris and I spent as much time in the water as we could to surf the tiny waves with our rafts. At low tide, when the waves were not as big, we retreated to the beach to build sand castles, catch small crabs, search for seashells, or accompany Mom and Dad on one of their excursions.

At the end of a long day at Ogunquit, we headed back to the car with our pails full of interesting things that we had collected along the beach when Mom and Dad noticed that Doris and I did not have our shoes. They had just bought us each a new pair of shoes a week earlier. Doris and I looked at each other and remembered that we had buried our footwear in the sand.

"Go back and find them!" roared my father. "We're not leaving until you find those shoes!" We put everything into the car and returned to the beach to search for the buried items. Luckily, we located and reclaimed our shoes without too much trouble. After the incident, Mom and Dad made sure that Doris and I wore only cheap flip-flops to the beach. Flip-flops could be replaced inexpensively, if needed.

Although Dad preferred to stay at the cabin, Mom planned a lot of day trips for us to take together as a family. Using the cabin as home base, we explored Maine and New Hampshire within a few hours' driving distance. In Maine, we ventured from the outlets in Kittery to the state house in Augusta. We learned about arctic exploration at the Peary-MacMillan Museum at Bowdoin College, shopped at L.L. Bean in Freeport, toured art and history museums, and took train rides, trolley rides, and boat rides. We visited a plethora of beaches and lighthouses, including Old Orchard Beach, which had a seaside amusement park, complete with carousel, souvenir stands, fried dough, fried clam shacks, and an arcade with skeeball.

In New Hampshire, we explored shops in the old ski resort of North Conway and made the rounds of the tourist attractions in the White Mountains, including Story Land, Santa's Village, Clark's Trading Post, Flume Gorge, Castle in the Clouds, Attitash Mountain Resort with the alpine slide, and the famous Old Man of the Mountain, a rock formation on Cannon Mountain that resembled the jagged outline of a man's face. The iconic image was used on the state's road signs and license plates. (The Old Man of the Mountain collapsed in 2003.) A few times we visited Portsmouth to see the USS *Albacore* submarine, or historic houses of the seacoast, including the John Paul Jones house, and Strawberry Banke Museum.

The New Hampshire State Fish Hatchery was within a short drive of the cabin and provided an easy-going form of entertainment. The fish were grouped by size in large cement, rectangular tanks that looked like a miniature Panama Canal. The fish were moved from one tank to the next as they grew. Visitors were allowed to feed the fish, and the hatchery sold food pellets out of bubblegum-like vending machines. We threw the pellets to the fish and watched as they swarmed to get the food. We were particularly delighted if any of the fish jumped out of the water.

On one visit, Mom perceived the water as a deep blue color.

"Can't you see it?" she asked excitedly. She described the blue water as strikingly beautiful and angled Doris and me around the fish pools so that we could see it for ourselves. Neither Doris nor I saw the purported blue water. Mom eventually gave up trying to convince us and retired to a picnic table in the shade to sit with my father, while Doris and I continued to feed the fish.

A few minutes later, Doris and I heard Mom and Dad laughing uncontrollably. Mom had sat down at a picnic table and taken off her sunglasses. The magical "blue water" was gone. It was her sunglasses! "Blue water," developed into a Jansson euphemism for "it's not there!"

Penny Pincher

In August each year, the family enjoyed the Acton Fair, which attracted people throughout southern Maine and New Hampshire. The fair hosted livestock competitions, horse shows, horse pulling competitions, tractor pulls, craft exhibitions, vegetable competitions, commercial exhibitions, musical entertainment, midway, and a pig scramble. We looked forward to the event all year and watched the fairgrounds intently for activity in advance of opening day.

We toured every bit of the fair and made sure that we saw every animal, every vegetable, every piece of art, every commercial display, and every competition that was scheduled during the time of our visit. Mom and I attended the horse shows. She narrated the activities and explained everything about the riders, their horses, and the event's objective, as she tried to predict the winners.

I liked the horse-pulling competitions, where a team of horses worked together to pull sleds of concrete blocks. I was amazed at the combined strength of the large horses, although felt uncomfortable that the animals only started to pull at the crack of a whip. After we made the rounds at the fair, we always went to the midway.

Doris and I enjoyed the midway attractions until we used up the book of tickets that Mom and Dad usually purchased. One year, Mom and Dad took a different approach. They decided to give us each a certain amount of money instead of buying a book of tickets. With a few dollars in our hands, they explained that we could keep any money that we did not spend.

The offer presented a dilemma for me. I was in the habit of saving any money that was given to me (usually for birthdays or Christmas) and had convinced myself that I was on a path to great wealth. Papa had contributed all those quarters to my savings, and I had a respectable balance in my bank account to show for it. Furthermore, my savings account passbook from the *Newtown Savings Bank* had "Save 10 % of what you earn and watch your savings grow," printed neatly across the bottom of each page. I was certain that I could beat the system if I saved ninety percent and spent only ten percent. Little did I know that *total income* had more to do with savings than anything else, although I would not learn that lesson for many more years.

Why would I ever spend money if I could save it and put it in the bank? Never in doubt, I pocketed my midway dollars with plans to add the bills to my great fortune of coins. Doris, however, wanted to go on the rides. I eventually joined her in the fun, but Doris paid for *my* tickets out of *her* money. I went home with exactly the same amount that I had been given at the beginning of the adventure. Doris went home with nothing, and Mom and Dad never let me forget it.

Visitors

Mom and Dad frequently invited friends and family to visit the Maine cabin. Ella Williams visited often, and Grace and Harold Peer joined us for a week every year in August. Dad's brother, Lawrence Jr., visited us one year in Maine, too.

A passionate fisherman, Lawrence Jr. lived in Minnesota and sent us pictures of enormous fish that he had pulled from the rich northern lakes. He arrived in Maine with all his angler's gear and immediately scouted for fishing locations. Doris and I tagged along with our small rods. To ensure that I caught the biggest fish, I tied an enormous hook to the end of my line and was disappointed when I had not caught anything at the end of the day. Afterwards, I learned that the fish at our location were quite a bit smaller than what I had seen in my uncle's pictures. I had thrown the equivalent of a boat anchor into a small pond.

FIGURE 79:
*Ella Williams getting
ready for a swim.*

Grace and Harold, my grandparents' generation, enjoyed slower-paced day trips to visit museums or enjoy the beautiful New England scenery. We took them on a boat tour on Sebago Lake, visited the Canterbury and Sabbathday Lake Shaker Villages, and drove the length of the Kancamagus Highway. We always traveled with a picnic lunch and found forested areas in which to relax and eat. Harold never let us pass an ice cream stand and treated us to banana splits as much as my parents allowed.

Grace particularly liked our visit to the Maine Wildlife Park in Gray, Maine, to see wild animals that were native to the region. The park rescued animals that were injured or orphaned and released them back into the wild upon successful rehabilitation. If

FIGURE 80:
Grace (Bissonnette) Peer and Harold Peer in Maine, 1980s.

the animals were seriously injured, the park served as their permanent home. The family had enormous sympathy for an eagle that was blind in one eye, and we enjoyed seeing the other animals at close range.

Grace also loved birds and equally enjoyed our trips to Lake Winnipesaukee in Wolfeboro, New Hampshire, to soak up the scenery and feed the ducks. We carried several loaves of bread and strolled the shores of the largest lake in New Hampshire. The ducks were popular with the tourists, and we did our share to keep them well fed. (Wolfeboro no longer allows people to feed the ducks. The ducks roosted in docked boats and made a mess for the boat owners.)

Grace was less than thrilled when we pushed her into the famous "Skimobile" to ride to the top of Cranmore Mountain. The ski lift consisted of small cars that ascended a wooden platform that was a few feet off the ground. A cable under the track pulled the cars. The contraption had been developed in the 1930s as one of the first ski lifts and had since become a summer tourist attraction.[60] Grace reached the top safely and admired the gorgeous view of the White Mountains. Shocked at the mode of transportation we had used, she had to give herself some credit for bravery.

FIGURE 81:
Riding down the skimobile at Cranmore Mountain.

Dad was always challenged to cook for Grace. She was a terribly picky eater and had the appetite of a small bird. There were a lot of things that we knew Grace did not eat. Most significantly, she did not eat cheese, although Dad constantly tricked Grace into sampling dishes that contained the detested dairy product. Grace praised Dad's cooking, but as soon as he revealed the forbidden ingredient, she pushed her food aside. Grace also insisted on piping hot soup. She was a bit irritated when a local restaurant misunderstood her request and loaded her soup with hot pepper.

Helen Bissonnette, Dad's aunt by marriage to Tina's brother, visited the cabin as well. Helen had spent her childhood in Ashland, Maine, *waaaaay* up north by the Canadian border. She was completely comfortable in the outdoors and taught me the name of any plant, tree, or bush that I could find in the woods. In the kitchen, Helen's specialties were Welsh rarebit (a cheese dish) and popcorn balls. Aunt Helen also had an encyclopedic mind for Maine folklore, both fact and fiction.

FIGURE 82:
Helen (Walker) Bissonnette, 1987.

Helen liked to walk around the cabin to admire nature as I played in the brook by the cabin to capture frogs and salamanders. The brook was also full of water bugs, which skimmed the surface of the water and darted from one side of the brook to the other, never staying in one place for very long. I had tried to catch the bugs many times before without much luck and had long since given up until Aunt Helen told me that each water bug would spin a penny in my hand if I could catch it. She suggested that I try to catch the bugs again. Always interested in money, I imagined the coins that I could accumulate and spent the next several hours in the brook trying to collect the creatures. With few bugs ever captured, I felt less than accomplished in the get-rich-quick scheme. I never saw a penny and learned the hard way that the family's most gifted storyteller had fooled me.

The brook never lost its magic, though. By the time I read *Huckleberry Finn*, I was even more captivated by the small waterway in our Maine backyard. I decided to replicate the Huck's adventure and made plans to build a raft to float down the brook to the river below. I cut down small trees and lashed them together with webbing from an old deck chair that I found in the cabin's basement. After several days of work, I had finished. I dragged the raft from the woods to the brook and heaved it in. To my amazement, I had built a bridge. The raft was twice the width of the three-foot brook.

Creepy Crawlies

Water was all around us in Maine. The large Salmon Falls River at the foot of our mountain provided a home to a great deal of wildlife including moose, otters, and waterfowl. A small, sandy area where cars pulled off the road served as a popular nesting spot for birds. In spring, lots of baby ducks and goslings made their way into the world as a stream of human spectators stopped to admire their cuteness.

As the owner of a new camera, I decided one year that the Maine geese and goslings would provide excellent subject material for a few quick pictures. Mom and I drove down the street and left the car on the opposite side of the road from the river so as to avoid early detection. I sneaked up to the water's edge and snapped a few great shots of the birds in the water.

I moved closer until my position was given away by a slight sound underfoot. The geese turned their heads and saw me immediately. I expected the birds to flee and continued to take pictures before I realized that the geese were swimming *toward* me.

Startled, I jumped up from my hiding spot and ran across the road to the parked car where Mom waited for me. I hopped into the car as quickly as possible, but the road was soon entirely blocked by geese as they had continued to follow me. Mom and I stared at each other, completely dumb-

FIGURE 83:
The geese running toward me!

founded. It took a few minutes for the birds to clear the road and return to the water. Mom and I had a good laugh and drove back to the cabin.

We found out later that people on the street often stopped to feed the geese, so the animals had expected food when I had only wanted to take their picture. We were glad that the neighbors had not fed the bears!

Mom, Doris, and I liked to see any animal that made its home in the Maine wilderness. Dad, on the other hand, drew the line at snakes. Dad was an animal lover, but he never liked the crawling reptiles. Yet we saw snakes quite frequently, slithering in the fields or sunning themselves on rocks. Even with the knowledge that there were no venomous snakes in Maine, Dad did not want anything to do with them.

When he was not on the tractor, Dad walked through the fields and "did the dance," when a snake crossed his path. As a mischief-maker, I often shouted "snake" just to see Dad's reaction. He jumped on one foot and then the other foot as if performing a jig, while he scanned the grass to determine if a snake was really there or if I had just been teasing him again. I was reprimanded for my pranks, although I had plenty of opportunity to witness the real encounters.

On one occasion, I was helping Dad in the basement while the garage door was open. He wanted to pour gasoline from a large can that was half-full into a smaller one. I held a funnel in the small can on the basement floor, while my father stood and poured gasoline from the larger can into my smaller can. As the gas flowed, I happened to glance out the garage door and observed a very large snake crawling across the entrance. Nonchalantly, I remarked, "Snake."

Safely in the confines of the basement, my father turned his head very casually and probably expected another false alarm. Instead, he observed the huge snake. I have no idea whether he was more surprised by the snake or by the fact that I was not teasing him. Shocked, he let out a huge yell. The gas can flew into the air and crashed onto the cement floor with a loud noise. His reaction startled me such that I yelled, too. Mom heard the commotion and ran down the cellar stairs to find out what had happened. She was in a panic that one of us was hurt.

We all calmed down and realized that the spilled gasoline was probably the worst thing that had happened. After a moment, the three of us went outside to look at the snake. It was a huge, three-foot Black snake, completely harmless.

Mom decided that we should move the snake across the street to get it away from the house. We often moved snakes that intruded into Dad's work zone. Mom knew how to handle snakes from her experiences in Texas with Teacher. Over the years, we had developed a system to move the snakes for Dad. I pinned the snake to the ground with a metal rake, while Mom picked up the animal with work gloves after she had gripped it safely behind its head. We had done this many times before, but not with such a big snake.

FIGURE 84:
My mother holding a small garter snake. The back of the original picture is labeled "Mother holds garter snake for children to see, June 1974."

It did not take very long to realize that we were dealing with a lot bigger animal than usual. I could not pin it to the ground, and Mom had trouble picking it up. The snake was so strong that Mom could not control it, either. It escaped her grip and clamped its mouth on her work gloves, while she fought to maintain control of the rest of the snake's body. She walked across the street as quickly as possible and threw the snake into the woods. Mom and I watched the snake move away from us as Dad stood at a safe distance.

Never tell your father that there is a snake nearby when he is pouring gasoline.

Animals

First Puppy

Over the years, the family had numerous pets. A black Labrador puppy joined the family when I was about two years old. Dad had learned from his colleagues that a litter of puppies needed homes. The puppies had belonged to a registered breeder in the area, but the purebred Labrador mother had escaped to mate with a neighborhood half-breed rather than the intended purebred male.

Seeking to avoid further humiliation, the owner gave away the puppies as quickly as possible. As a result, our puppy was still quite young when Dad brought her home. The animal suffered for several days and weakened to such an abysmal state that Dad called the local veterinarian, Dr. Bath, for assistance. The consultation concluded with the doctor's recommendation for Dad to get the puppy to the veterinary office without delay. However, Connecticut had just been pummeled by a major snowstorm. Our house had lost electrical service, and our street was impassable. Only major roads had been plowed.

The next day, the dog was worse and failing fast. Dad called Dr. Bath again. The veterinarian recognized the severity of the situation and offered to drive to a main intersection if Dad could meet him there with the puppy. With a plan in place, Dad bundled up the sick animal, laid her in a cardboard box on a sled, and pulled her through the snow to the designated meeting place. Dr. Bath met Dad on the side of the road, collected the puppy, and told Dad to call him the next day. The doctor made a cautious U-turn on the snow-covered state highway and headed back to his office.

The family did not expect to see the puppy again, but anxiously awaited an update. When Dad finally called, the doctor immediately relieved the tension.

"I think that she's going to make it," he reported. The puppy had been loaded with worms, which was a dangerous condition for such a young animal. She stayed at the veterinarian's office for about three days for treatment and recovery, by which time the storm damage had been cleared and our road was drivable again.

When the black puppy with a white bib returned to our home, we named her Shadow. She nudged her way into our lives and seemed to wear a permanent smile on her face, as if to say "thank you" to her rescuers. The dog exhibited a great deal of independence, however. She liked to sleep on the porch in the evening, but dashed off into the darkness the moment Dad called her in for the night. Shadow came back when *she* was ready.

FIGURE 85:
Shadow and me.

224

Shadow maintained her independent streak and often surprised us with her unpredictable behavior. The first time she got loose in the chicken coop, we were alarmed. However, instead of chasing chickens, Shadow ate the chicken poop.

"Ugh, she's never going to be a good dog," Papa grumbled in disgust.

Papa may have been Shadow's biggest critic, but he always arrived for his weekly visits with a handful of chuck steak bones for the dog. Shadow stood on her hind legs and spun in circles with delirious ecstasy as Papa rolled up the long driveway in his big blue 1972 Cadillac. Papa barely had time enough to get the car door open and one leg out of the door before Shadow snatched the meat bones from his hands and retreated to the backyard to gnaw on them for the next several hours. My father's brother drove Papa's Cadillac to the house one day, and Shadow growled in protest. Shadow rarely growled, but Lawrence Jr. should not have driven Papa's car.

As long as they were not driving a blue Cadillac, Shadow readily accepted other visitors. John Mitchell was a Newtown resident and a good family friend. He was also a General Electric repairman and could fix any appliance problem. At the time, we had a stacked washer and dryer, with the washer on the bottom and the dryer on the top. Both units opened to the front.

Since we were regular customers, General Electric knew to assign John to all our service calls. He arrived at the house one day to fix the washer. John knew his way around, as he fixed every appliance we owned. He carried his tools with him into the bathroom and proceeded to work on the washer.

A few minutes later Mom heard John yell for help. She rushed into the bathroom and found the rear ends of both John and Shadow protruding from the washer. Both their heads were stuck inside. John had looked into the washer to find the problem, and Shadow poked her head in at the same time. Neither one of them could get out. John tried to back up to free himself; but as soon as he moved, the dog moved too, and they both got stuck again. Mom rescued both John and the dog. John fixed the washer and always remembered that Shadow "helped" him with the repair.

Shadow remained a loyal canine member of the family until she died of heart failure when she was about nine years old.

Cows, Apples, and a Bull Running Loose

The farmland across the street from our Connecticut home contained a large barn with more than ten acres of pasture. The owner kept a few dozen cows and a young bull. Because the animals were less than a year old, the farm was really more of a nursery. The bull was small enough so that he was not very intimidating. The cows had access to the entire pasture to graze, but the baby bull was cordoned off in a smaller pen.

We often fed the cows apples that we picked up off the ground. Our large yard had many different types of apple trees. If the apples were out of reach, we used apple pickers on long poles to reach the fruit on higher branches. I was also allowed to climb the trees to shake the branches that were even higher. We gathered the apples in big wooden baskets and carried them into the house for a family production line to peel, core, and cut. We made lots of applesauce, apple pies, apple betty, and other treats.

Mom and Dad made sure that we picked up the rotten apples on the ground so that we could mow the lawn around the trees. The rotten apples attracted bees, which made mowing a bit precarious. We collected the rotten apples in a wheelbarrow and dumped them across the street for the cows. The cows ran toward the apples as soon as they saw them.

One time, we dumped several loads of apples into the cow pasture. After a few hours, we noticed that the cows were wobbly. Dad became concerned. The cows did not belong to us, and they looked sick after eating our rotten apples. Worried that something was wrong, Dad called our neighbor, Ellen Orosz, who had grown up on a farm. The consultation did not last long.

"The cows are *drunk!*" she laughed. The rotten apples had started to ferment, so we had effectively given the animals alcohol. The boozed-up cows burped and staggered around for the rest of the day. None of the cows was old enough to produce milk, but I could only imagine what the milk might have tasted like that day.

While the cows were a source of amusement across the street, the baby bull proved a frequent visitor to our yard. He escaped from his pen on several occasions, including when a crew of painters was working on our two-story farmhouse. The bull ran through the yard and knocked over everything in his path. The painters yelled, and there was a lot of commotion. One of the painters was high up on a ladder and later explained his dilemma. He had been especially frightened that the bull would tip over his ladder and was not sure whether it was better to stay on the ladder or face the bull on the ground!

Ellen Orosz rescued us again. She captured the bull and drove him back into the pen across the street. The painter, who had been on the ladder, was thankful to reach ground level safely.

Never paint a house on a ladder when there is a bull running loose.

Gray Cat

When a neighbor's cat had a litter of kittens, Doris and I were given the opportunity to pick out the family's first feline pet. Dad's cat, Zipper, had died after being hit by a car in the road. Mom and

Dad took us to the neighbor's house and let us play with the kittens, while the adults kibitzed in the living room. By the end of the evening, we had settled on a little gray, tiger-striped kitten that we named "Lollipop."

We ceremoniously drove the short distance to re-locate the kitten from the neighbor's house to ours. Mom and Dad took on the responsibility to housebreak the kitten and established a healthy diet of Kitten Chow. Mom taught us how to make toys for the kitten out of paper and string. Lollipop occasionally chased the toys, but gained much more satisfaction from love pats and kisses.

Lollipop settled in to her own routine. Her affection, however, was reserved entirely for Doris, as she retreated more and more frequently to my sister's second floor bedroom. Before long, the rest of us rarely saw the creature, and Mom and Dad could not change the cat's behavior. Lollipop's heart belonged to Doris, and that was the end of it.

Within the confines of Doris' room, Lollipop lived a pampered existence. Doris smothered the cat in love. If Doris slept, Lollipop curled up next to her chest in bed. During the long hours of my sister's evening homework, the cat sprawled across the top of Doris' desk, such that my sister could only see her homework papers in between the cat's four legs. Lollipop allowed for the readjustment of papers if she received affection to ease the interruption. On special occasions, Doris fed her adoring feline a few pieces of cheese.

Lollipop's lethargic existence did not afford her much exercise, and she grew quite rotund. Her belly hung down from her mid-section, although Mom and Dad attributed the hanging flesh to a botched spay operation where her tummy muscles had been injured. Whether true or not, Lollipop's size and shape caused visitors to inquire whether the "fat cat" was pregnant. Since the answer was always "no," the cat became an easy target in which to tease Doris. Doris was so offended by "fat cat" comments and the pregnancy questions that Mom and Dad finally insisted that we call Lollipop "pleasingly plump" rather than "fat." Doris was not satisfied.

"Not pleasingly plump, just *pleasingly*," my sister implored.

While Lollipop lived with Doris, the cat relegated the rest of us to servitude status. We amusingly attended to Lollipop's needs with the exacting and prompt attention that she required. I fed her a can of 9Lives tuna each night. The cat refused to allow any substitutes, so her diet never changed. We all hastily opened the outside door when she demanded bathroom breaks. Lollipop disliked spending a single minute outdoors longer than needed and climbed the window screens in summer to let us know that she was ready to reenter the house. Any time he saw the cat mid-window, Dad hollered that Lollipop had already torn multiple screens to shreds.

Lollipop called the shots and did not appreciate any disruption to her preferred routine. During the school year, I had "put-the-cat-out duty," as I was the last one to leave in the morning. Lollipop had several hiding places, and her favorite was the back of Doris' closet. I frequently opened the closet door to find the cat staring back at me with a look to kill. Too lazy to run away, she hissed in protest as I hoisted her into my arms to carry her downstairs to the outside door. More than once, she swiped her paw across my face. A small scratch was not so unusual, but on one occasion I bled enough that the school bus driver asked me what had happened.

"Had to put the cat out," I blithely answered, as I climbed aboard the bus.

Lollipop mostly stayed hidden, although made an appearance when it suited her. Dad came across some baby mice while he was working in the barn one summer. He had disturbed the nest and suspected that the mother would probably abandon the babies. He put the baby mice in an empty fish tank and brought them inside the house for Doris and me.

My sister and I were thrilled with the science project and decorated the enclosure to emulate the natural living conditions of field mice. We entertained ourselves by watching the mice for a while and then wandered off. A few hours later I revisited the glass container, and the mice were gone. Lollipop sat atop the glass tank with a particularly broad grin as she smacked her whiskers in a most delicious fashion. 9Lives tuna had finally been displaced. The menu du jour had obviously been mice for lunch.

Surprisingly, Lollipop's pleasure from the baby mice as a delicacy did nothing to awaken her hunting instincts. As all New England homes have mice, Lollipop could easily have supplemented her diet and contributed rodent control skills to the household at the same time. Instead, the cat killed a mouse only once, as she leapt off her perch to catch one that ran right in front of her in broad daylight. Lollipop could not tolerate such brash disrespect from a mouse; but as long as they stayed hidden from view, she did nothing to seek their destruction.

FIGURE 86:
Lollipop in my sister's suitcase, 1986.

As Doris and Lollipop grew up together, they became more and more inseparable. Lollipop was traumatized when Doris left for a sleepover, camp, or any other overnight activity. As soon as Doris started to pack a suitcase, the cat jumped in the suitcase to protest. By the time my sister left for college, the cat was so neurotic with separation anxiety that Doris somewhat seriously

considered whether she should forgo college to "take care of Lol'."
When Doris left home for school, Lollipop was lost in loneliness.

The cat's unhealthy mental state persisted until she finally ventured out of Doris' empty room to seek attention from Mom and Dad in the evenings. As they relaxed in the family room, Lollipop situated herself on an empty sofa within full view, but out of arm's reach. Mom occasionally gave the cat a love pat for reassurance, but Dad never forgave the cat's snootiness and kept his distance.

Years later, I traveled to France to stay a week at the home of a French family. Since I was an adventurous eater, my hosts prepared a plate of French cheese and pâté hors d'oeuvres. I eagerly sampled my way through the specialties to the delight of my hosts, until I arrived at a pâté that I could never have touched. My sudden lack of experimentation proved an embarrassing moment. I simply could not overcome my aversion to put that particular pâté in my mouth. It looked normal enough, but smelled exactly like the cans of 9Lives tuna that I had opened for Lollipop many times. After so many years, the gray cat still commanded my attention.

Lollipop died two weeks before her twentieth birthday. Doris never lived at home again after she left for college, so the cat's last years were sad and pathetic. Still, it was hard to forget the gray cat that had been part of our family for so long.

Lost Cat

Whereas Lollipop's arrival proved anticlimactic, our next feline filled the void. Lollipop had already disappeared to Doris' room when my father discovered a stray kitten that had wandered into our garden. It was a beautifully warm September afternoon, also my birthday. My father had been in the garden with relatives to pick a few last vegetables before the growing season ended.

Fully aware that Lollipop was Doris' cat, Dad called me to the garden to discover the lost kitten for myself. I spied the tiny black creature immediately amidst the tall green plants. The kitten was starved and had a broken tail. In an instant, I had her in my arms and carried her back to the house where I poured her a bowl of milk.

The kitten drank so much milk that my parents worried that she might get sick. As she cried pitifully for more, I sat with her on the porch until my bedtime. I did not want to leave the kitten and begged Mom and Dad to let me take her into the house for the night. They insisted that she remain outside on the porch. Unconvincingly, they argued that she would not run away.

The next morning I raced downstairs to find the kitten right where I had left her on the porch, just as my parents had predicted. I fed her more milk plus a few bites of Lollipop's Kitten Chow. She drank and ate everything that I placed in front of her. She gained more strength over the next several weeks and transformed into a curious kitten that chased strings, explored empty paper bags and cardboard boxes, climbed furniture, and asked for attention indiscriminately among the family members. Although Lollipop only hissed at the intruder during their brief encounters at dinnertime, there was no question that the new kitten had won our hearts.

With the kitten formally adopted, we needed a name. I wanted to call her "Little Black," a reference to the title of my favorite children's book *Little Black, A Pony*, by Walter Farley, while Doris preferred the name "Cherry." Without much debate, my parents made us compromise, and the black kitten was named "Little Black Cherry." In jest, the neighbors who had given us Lollipop referred to the black cat as "crooked tail."

Little Black Cherry endured several trips to the veterinarian to recover from her shaky beginning. When she stayed overnight for tests, I went with Mom to pick the cat up the next day. We walked into the office where the receptionist asked me the name of my pet. As I proudly declared "Little Black Cherry," the receptionist smiled.

"I know just the cat," she said. "We have only one cat named Little Black Cherry." The long and unusual name forever distinguished our special cat with the veterinary staff.

Little Black Cherry explored every part of our 1700s farmhouse, including the old iron, claw-foot tub. Bubble baths were routine for Doris and me. We soaked and splashed in the tub and played with bath toys under Mom's watchful eye. One time I was in the tub with Bubble Bath suds when Little Black Cherry decided to visit.

The black kitten surprised Mom and me as she jumped up on the side of the tub to investigate our fun. However, the smooth enamel surface challenged the kitten's footing. Off-balance, she teetered awkwardly for a moment and then started to slide down the tub wall. With her feet outstretched in terror, she plunged head-first into the bubbles and water.

Mom hurriedly scooped the black kitten out of the bath. Cute Little Black Cherry was transformed into a massive bundle of soap bubbles. Her yellow eyes peered out at us with innocent feline astonishment amidst the suds. Mom toweled her off and freed the kitten outside of the bathroom to continue her house adventures.

As much as Little Black Cherry was curious and sought human contact, she also enjoyed the fertile hunting grounds of our two-acre New England yard. She often left a half-eaten mouse, a few feathers, or the tail of a small snake on the doorstep. Once she brought a live baby rabbit into the house and dropped it on the floor. The frightened bunny ran under the radiator and promptly got stuck. Mom wore work gloves to extricate the animal and let it go in the backyard. I held Little Black Cherry in my arms until the rabbit got away.

While the wildlife around us provided ample hunting opportunity, Little Black Cherry seemed to take little notice of the chickens that we raised for eggs. Each spring, a new batch of chicks hatched. Sometimes we kept the young chicks in the house and put them in a box with a light bulb to keep them warm. At one point, we had a box of new chicks on the floor by the back door, and I saw a perfect opportunity to play with them without my mother's normal supervision. I carefully lifted a chick out of the box and into my lap. With good intentions, I was startled when Mom saw me and gasped.

In a split second, Little Black Cherry sprang from the nearby chair and seized the chick in her jaws. I was left empty-handed as if the chick had simply vanished. Mom chased Little Black Cherry into the kitchen and wrestled the chick out of the cat's mouth. The chick survived and was returned to its cat-proof box. I learned that Little Black Cherry really liked chickens after all.

If Little Black Cherry was not hunting in the backyard, she might have been dressed up in doll clothes and wheeled around the house in a baby buggy by Doris. With a baby bonnet tied around her head, the cat sat upright in the child-sized carriage, fully aware of her exalted status and enjoying every minute of the activity.

Little Black Cherry made a sweet "brrrp" sound when she jumped up on a chair or sofa, as if she politely announced her arrival. Her more famous vocalization kept us up at night. Any time we left for several days, mostly to go to Maine, the cat let us know that she was happy to see us. She prowled the upstairs hallway on the nights of our return and cried a vociferous yell that pierced the still summer

FIGURE 87:
Little Black Cherry exploring my bedroom, 1983.

nights. None of us slept through the racket, which is likely what she intended, although uncharacteristic of her sweet personality.

Little Black Cherry also showed an affinity for a small wood-burning stove in our Connecticut dining room. During the summer, when the stove was not in use, she used it as a perch, a black cat atop a black stove. In the winter, she liked the stove's warmth and situated herself underneath it, regardless of the intensity of the heat. We often joked that Little Black Cherry was "cooking her brains" on these occasions, but she never appeared less clever as a result of the excessive heat treatment.

Little Black Cherry wanted to be near the family at all times and followed us around the house or yard. In the summer, she streaked across the lawn and tempted us to play with her by dashing to the side of our feet. In the winter, she climbed the trees to chase the falling snow or swatted at miniature snowballs that we tossed up in the air for her to catch. She slept at the foot of my bed until the alarm rang in the morning. Sometimes, she slept on my head.

The black cat never brought bad luck. We were fortunate that Little Black Cherry had been lost in our garden and provided so much joy in our lives.

A Puppy from the Pound

A year after Shadow died, the family decided to get a new dog. Mom, in particular, did not want to be without a dog for too long. She insisted that Doris and I needed to be raised around animals, so that we would know how to interact with them safely and would not be afraid of them. Dad wanted to take Doris and me to the dog pound, but Mom was sure that we would fall in love with every dog in sight. She suggested that Dad survey the options in advance.

When Dad showed up at the dog pound, the dog warden directed him to a female Labrador-mix puppy that had been picked up as a stray. Dad barely got within view of the animal before she jumped up and down with excitement. Once inside the cage, Dad was greeted with kisses from the puppy that offered affection as much as she craved it.

"Now, *there's* a dog for children," the warden proudly proclaimed. Dad agreed that the dog's friendly disposition was a perfect match for our family, but the puppy was not yet available for adoption. The dog pound had a mandatory three-day waiting period after a newspaper ad publicly announced that the dog had been found. In the absence of an owner's claim, adoption was possible. The black puppy was near the end of that process, with only one day left in the waiting period.

The next day, the dog warden called. No one had responded to the newspaper ad. The black puppy was officially available.

"We are just going to look at it," I overheard Dad say to Mom.

"You know you will come home with it," Mom mused. With great anticipation, Doris and I hopped into the car with Dad. We were not quite sure where we were going, but had a hunch.

As soon as we entered the dog pound and had closed the outside door behind us, the dog warden let the black puppy out of her cage. From the end of the kennel hallway, we could see the small animal bounding toward us with unbridled excitement. Doris and I instinctively kneeled to greet the dog. She jumped into our arms and smothered us with wet kisses. It was a puppy-child love fest. The puppy could not get enough of us, and we could not get enough of her.

Both Dad and the warden knew that we were not leaving without that puppy! Dad filled out the necessary paperwork to complete the adoption. The dog was too young to have received all her shots,

236

so the paperwork required that the new owner commit to take the dog to a veterinarian.

The puppy was black with a white bib, very similar to Shadow, except that she had long curly hair. The dog warden speculated that she was likely part Labrador and part Cocker Spaniel. He emphasized that the Cocker Spaniel influence had contributed the curly hair and predicted that the puppy would grow to the size of a Cocker Spaniel. Doris and I listened, but did not care. It was much more important that we had a new puppy! We found out later that the Cocker Spaniel theory was completely bogus. The dog grew to the full size and shape of a Golden Retriever, but remained black in color. The veterinarian attributed the curly hair to a much larger breed, Irish Setter!

When we returned home with the puppy, Mom was thrilled with the choice. The dog was so full of energy that she had a "full body wag." More than just tail wagging, her whole head and rear moved in one direction, while her mid-section moved in the opposite direction. We named her "Wiggles" based on this unusual, worm-like motion.

FIGURE 88:
Wiggles in the backyard.

As much as Shadow was independent, Wiggles was loyal. She never ventured too far away. She accompanied us on numerous walks in the Maine woods and explored the terrain in close proximity, in our sight at all times. If we ever had to call her at a distance, she ran to us immediately.

Wiggles always wanted to be with us. She jumped in the car as soon as a car door was opened, even if we were not going anywhere. We sometimes dragged her out by the collar, but otherwise left the door open until she decided to get out by herself. As soon as we started to pack the car for a trip to Maine, she claimed her usual spot at the rear of the station wagon, whether we were ready to leave or not. Wiggles sometimes sat in the car for several hours before we left, and no amount of prodding convinced her that we would not leave her behind.

Wiggles was not the smartest dog in the world. We discovered over the years that my nickname for her as "amoeba brain" was not so far from the truth. She never learned to swim or walk up or down stairs. If we swam in the lakes, she waded into a few inches of water and cried for us to come closer. We tried to coach her into the water, but the dog steadfastly refused any swimming lessons we offered. The Maine cabin also presented a challenge for the dog as it had three steps that led to the front door. Wiggles entered the cabin with a running leap to clear the height of the steps. Later in her life, when she could not make the jump, Dad built a custom dog ramp.

The few times that the family traveled outside of New England, we boarded Wiggles at a local dog kennel. The very first time we retrieved her after a trip, the kennel owners explained how stubborn Wiggles had been when she first arrived. They could not move her from the office to the lower-level kennel because she refused to go down the stairs! They finally figured out that the stairs were the problem and walked Wiggles around the outside of the building to the door at the lower level.

One day as a puppy, Wiggles explored the culvert that ran underneath our road. She went into the culvert and did not have enough room to turn around to get back out. My father heard the puppy whimpering. He had been working in the nearby barn with his uncle, Harold Peer. It took a few minutes for the men to realize where the dog had gone. They tried to reach Wiggles, but she was frightened and moved further and further into the pipe.

Dad and Uncle Harold quickly discovered that the culvert was blocked on the other side of the road by an enormous stone. With a shovel and a crow bar, they worked together for several hours to try to move it. They finally got the stone to rock back and forth. Without provocation, Wiggles saw daylight while the rock was in motion and squirmed through the small space to safety. Dad and Uncle Harold had not anticipated the dog's action. Another second, and she would have been crushed by the moving rock. A narrow miss, but there were more of those to come for Wiggles.

Wiggles liked to explore the numerous construction sites in the neighborhood. Sadly, the beautiful farmland all around us was developed into suburban homes. It was heartbreaking to see the fields disappear. They had served the farming needs of early Americans for hundreds of years and had been home to an abundance of wildlife. The new houses were standard colonials with two living floors, full basement, and a two-car garage. Each house had two acres of land to comply with Newtown's zoning laws. There were always a few houses in development at the same time, but in varying stages of construction. The contractors came and went and often ate their lunch at the worksites. Wiggles enjoyed stealing any loose items that the workers may have left lying around.

The first time that we knew Wiggles was a thief was when she returned to our house with a full can of beer in her mouth. Dad wrestled the beer away from her, but she bit down on the can and punctured it, spraying Dad with beer in the process. The dog disappeared and shortly returned with a second can of beer. The second time, Dad jimmied the beer can loose without damage. He left it on a nearby stonewall in view of the nearest group of workers in case one of them wanted to claim it. It stayed there for months until Dad finally threw it away.

Wiggles soon had a collection of items on the back porch, including a rubber boot and a few tools. By this time, the workers knew that the dog was the culprit and closely guarded their loose items. When an item vanished, they came to our house porch to retrieve it from Wiggles' stash.

Wiggles' continued as a kleptomaniac, and the construction workers remained on high alert for the puppy retriever. When a new man arrived at the construction site, the regular contractors warned him that he should not leave his tools lying around where they might be stolen. Not provided with an explanation, the man scoffed at the warning. Who was around to take his tools? A short while later, his entire tool belt was gone. The other workers laughed and laughed before they confided that they knew "who" had taken it. They led the baffled contractor to our back porch to retrieve his property.

Although a hardened criminal, Wiggles also had a conscience. When she did something wrong, she cowered in a corner and beat her tail loudly against the floor. The loud tail thumps were a dead giveaway to the confession of a crime and led us to investigate her wrongdoing. More often than not, we found the garbage spread all over the kitchen floor.

Wiggles may have had a conscience, but dog brains often made for bad decisions. She poked around the Christmas tree one year and encountered Dad's prized antique manger scene. The display had a wooden barn structure. Mary, Joseph, the shepherds, wise men, and animals were made of a delicate *papier mâché*, while the little baby Jesus was made of wax. The Jesus figurine was quite tiny, only a little over an inch long.

It was unclear how the dog could have acted with such precision, but without warning, Wiggles *ate* the little baby Jesus. Witnessing the act, we jumped out of our chairs to get the figure out of her mouth, but Wiggles had swallowed it before we pried her jaws open. Wiggles was in the proverbial doghouse again. Dad was extremely angry about the incident, but continued to display the manger scene without a baby Jesus. Reluctantly, after several years, he replaced the lost baby Jesus with a plastic substitute.

Wiggles' undiscriminating appetite seemed to get her into the most trouble during holidays when new foods and decorations were available for doggie taste testing around the house. For several years, Mom and Dad took us to the cabin in Maine to celebrate Easter. We dyed several dozen eggs in different colors. Doris and I woke up to find them hidden around the cabin on Easter morning.

Mom and Dad went to great lengths to hide the eggs in hard-to-find nooks and crannies, but were always worried that some eggs remained hidden. Their fear of a rotting egg forced us to keep egg tallies, although somehow none of us could ever remember the count or how many we had eaten. While the egg hunt was obviously the main attraction, Mom and Dad also filled our Easter baskets with candy and small toys.

Chocolate was always a big hit with Doris. One Easter, her basket was brimming with Hershey kisses that had different Easter-colored wrappers. Admiring her holiday haul, she laid out her candy on the kitchen table and organized it by the color of the aluminum foil wrappers.

Sometime later in the day, the family went out for a few hours. When we returned to the cabin, the candy was gone! There was no sign of it anywhere, but we all suspected that the dog must have eaten it, as there was no other explanation. A little while later our suspicions were confirmed. Wiggles spent the rest of the afternoon throwing up chocolate. Although terribly sick, she survived her gluttonous behavior.

The story of the Easter chocolate became Jansson lore, although everyone who heard the tale found it hard to believe that the dog had eaten not only the chocolate, but also the aluminum wrappings. Charlotte Knaur, family friend, decided to test if the dog would really eat a Hershey kiss with a wrapper on it. She called Wiggles over to where she was sitting and tossed a silver-wrapped Hershey kiss into the air. The dog jumped for the treat and gulped it down without hesitation. She had not even chewed it.

"Well, that answers that!" exclaimed Charlotte, with a grin on her face. We all agreed that the data spoke for itself.

New England seasons resulted in wardrobe changes that also piqued Wiggles' curiosity. Winter obviously required more clothes, and skiing required specialized equipment. Mom encouraged skiing as a family affair once both Doris and I reached elementary age, and Dad decided that he wanted to learn, too.

We took several trips to Northern New England and had great fun skiing together. Mom and Dad both learned to ski as adults. Mom was pretty adept, but Dad was rather awkward. Dad "took his time" going down the easy trails. I joked that he spent more time skiing across the mountain than down it.

Certain that we all wanted to continue skiing, Mom and Dad decided to make the investment in equipment for all of us. My parents bought new skis and jackets at a local ski shop. Doris and I were outfitted with used children's skis and clothing from the annual ski swap. We had great fun ahead of us!

Not long after the new purchases, the family drove to Maine for a ski trip. Somewhere along the Massachusetts Turnpike I heard a noise that came from the back of the car. I turned around in my seat to discover that Wiggles had chewed a basketball-size hole in the back of my father's brand new ski jacket. Uh oh!

My father was so mad that he immediately stopped the car on the side of the road. He opened the tailgate, dragged Wiggles out of the car, and spanked the dog furiously in plain sight of passing cars and trucks. The dog deserved punishment, but Dad was brutal.

When we got to Maine, Dad examined his coat more closely. The dog had chewed through the back of the coat, including the insulation and the liner. Determined to salvage the purchase, Dad spent the next day sewing. He constructed a patch from random pieces of cloth to match the size and thickness of the area that Wiggles had chewed and sewed the weird-looking patch onto his jacket. In the end, he achieved a solution that held together for the remainder of the ski season, although the jagged repair looked as though a giant shark had attacked him on the slopes.

Wiggles barked violently at any visitors who approached the house. Anyone who knew the dog ignored her behavior, but a stranger thought twice about entering until one of us grabbed her collar and gave her a chance to settle down. After a few minutes, her ferociousness subsided and she transformed into a pest. She nudged guests with her nose until they made amends for their intrusiveness with a certain quota of affection.

While strange humans were always suspect, Wiggles' bravery dissipated rapidly in a thunderstorm. As soon as she heard claps of thunder, she jumped into my father's lap and whimpered in fright. Dad always had to be ready for the big fifty-pound dog to land in his lap when there was a storm. He preferred her to sit on the floor next to him with her head in his lap.

If there was something that Wiggles *should* have been concerned about, it was porcupines and skunks. The first time she tangled with a porcupine was when we had just arrived in Maine at night. As soon as we opened the car door, the dog jumped out and ran into the darkness. A few minutes later, she returned with quills in her face, ears, mouth, and paws, clearly in pain. Mom, Doris, and I settled into the cabin, while Dad raced off to a 24-hour emergency animal clinic with Wiggles.

The veterinarian sedated the dog to remove the quills. Unless an animal had a quill in the eye, infection from the quills was the biggest health risk. Wiggles returned to us after the emergency procedure and remained groggy for several days due to the anesthetic and antibiotic medication.

A dog's encounter with a porcupine in New England was not such an unusual occurrence. The porcupine population was quite healthy, as the adorable creatures loved to feast on the tops of hemlock trees. A hemlock tree with no top or upper branches had almost certainly been the food and home for a porcupine, and the tree would often die as a result. We often saw porcupines in a tree or slowly walking across the field. They are not afraid of humans, which allowed us to get close to them on a number of occasions.

Unfortunately, Wiggles did not learn her lesson about porcupines. The next time we went to Maine, the same thing happened. Wiggles jumped out of the car and returned within minutes with a mouthful of quills. Once again, Dad raced off to the veterinary clinic with the dog. When we picked up our hapless pet the next day, Dad grumbled about the veterinarian bill, but we all felt sorry that Wiggles had suffered. Still, the dog did not learn, and the porcupine drill was repeated, yet again, for the third time. After that, Wiggles received a by-the-collar escort in Maine if we arrived at night.

If our Maine property had porcupines, then the Connecticut property had skunks. The skunks wandered through the yard with their pointed noses in the ground to look for either plant or animal

244

material that satisfied their omnivorous diet. Skunks were usually an amusement for onlookers. The "wood pussies" of New England never bothered anyone unless someone bothered them first. Wiggles did just that.

The family was gathered in the living room for the visit of family friends from New Haven, Jim and Joyce Fillmore. We all smelled a skunk at the same time and looked around the room for Wiggles. The dog was not in the house. The smell increased, and a few seconds later we heard her lunge onto the back porch. It did not take a genius to know what happened: Wiggles had stuck her nose where it did not belong. We bathed Wiggles in tomato juice per the old New England tradition but could not "smell" an improvement. A few more baths in soap and water did not help, either. The dog was banished to live outside the house for the next several weeks.

Wiggles did not like being separated from the family. She much preferred her usual spot in the living room of the Connecticut house or by the wood stove at the Maine cabin. She liked the heat from the wood stove in Maine, as much as Little Black Cherry liked the wood stove in Connecticut. Wiggles relished the warmth and sat as close to the wood stove as possible.

In Maine, Dad kept the stove full of wood at night, but we also relied on electric space heaters to keep the house warm on particularly cold nights. Mom and Dad were constantly worried that the electric heaters would start a fire. Doris and I knew to keep the curtains, papers, shoes, and pretty much everything else away from the electric heaters. The danger was ever present, though, as household items were constantly moved around.

As we relaxed in the cabin one cool evening, my father bolted upright from his position on the couch and sniffed the air.

"What's that smell?" he asked with concern. He sniffed again, but it was not obvious what the smell was or where it was coming from.

"Something is burning!" he exclaimed. The family sprang into action. We ran to check the electric heaters, kitchen stove, electrical outlets, and anything else that we could think of that could cause a fire.

The dog sensed the commotion and got up from her comfortable position by the wood stove. As a trail of smoke streamed after her, my father saw the problem.

"Oh no! The dog is on fire!" Dad cried. We turned our focus to Wiggles, but as soon as the dog sensed that she was the center of attention, she wanted to play. The family fire brigade chased her with blankets and buckets of water as Wiggles played a game of "hard to catch."

"Put the dog out, put the dog out!" Dad hollered. Finally, we extinguished the dog's smoking hair.

After the excitement, we inspected Wiggles to determine whether she had been seriously hurt. Her hair was singed on the side where she had lain against the stove. Her normally long curls had been reduced to the length of a crew cut. The short hair had burned to different lengths and left the impression of the New England scene that was molded on the side of the stove like a hair tattoo. She wore the art proudly for about a month until her hair grew out.

Wiggles was the only dog I ever knew that sat close enough to a stove to catch on fire.

Number One

Mom and Dad avowed that they loved their "children" equally, but declared a rank order if for no other reason than to provide a consistent signature on Christmas cards. Humans were ranked by age, dogs ranked higher than cats, and other animals were ranked according to the date of their arrival in our home. Rank order shifted upon departure from the home or upon death. In the Jansson home we ranked as follows: Kelley-1, Doris-2, Wiggles-3, Lollipop-4, Little Black Cherry-5.

As the older child, I discovered that the number one position had absolutely no privileges associated with it. Nevertheless, Mom and Dad amused themselves and announced that Doris had moved to the number one position when I left for college. Three years later, Doris left for college, and Wiggles inherited the number one spot.

Wiggles, Lollipop, and Little Black Cherry all passed away after Doris and I left home as adults. The pets had been the last "children" in the house, so Mom and Dad became true empty nesters. Retired, the house was quiet, and it seemed to me that my parents could benefit from a new pet. A dog was probably too much for them to take care of in their golden years. A cat, the right cat, might offer some companionship.

I raised the idea of a new cat, but both Mom and Dad quickly dismissed the idea. They strongly communicated that they did not want to take care of another animal. They thought that they were too old and that the animal might outlive them. I listened to their objections, but could not help thinking that consummate animal lovers needed a pet.

As luck would have it, a family friend from Maine, Joanna Torow, had a relative with a litter of kittens that needed homes. Secretly, I arranged for Joanna to pick out a kitten for my parents and mailed a check to her to cover the veterinarian costs. My parents knew about the litter of kittens, but continued to insist that they did not want one.

Joanna and I plotted the surprise long distance and arranged for "kitten delivery" when I visited Mom and Dad at the Maine cabin. We planned for Joanna and her boyfriend, Kris Berglund, to come for dinner and bring the kitten with them. As I talked over the details with Joanna on the phone about the dinner, Dad became suspicious.

"No kittens," he trumpeted. *"No kittens!"*

Joanna heard Dad's protest in the background and paused to question whether we should follow through with our plan.

"I don't want this to be the end of my friendship with your parents," she fretted.

"Don't worry," I assured.

When Joanna and Kris arrived, they had the kitten in a cat carrier in the back seat of their car. The kitten was sound asleep and oblivious to her surroundings. We left the kitten in the carrier in the car and rolled the car windows down so that she had fresh air.

Joanna and Kris entered the cabin and greeted my mother and father as if they were there for a normal visit. We chatted through dinner and dessert, with no mention of kittens. If Dad suspected anything, he likely abandoned his concerns after so much unrelated discussion. He must have assumed that Joanna and Kris had heard his strong objections about the kitten and decided not to force the issue.

As the evening neared its natural conclusion, Joanna, Kris, and I made our way outside to check on the kitten in the car. Adorably, she was still sound asleep! Joanna picked up the kitten, while Kris and I gathered up a small pile of cat supplies, which included a litter box, kitty litter, food, and a few toys. We walked back to the cabin with the kitten and cargo. Mom and Dad were wide-eyed with astonishment. The routine visit had fooled them and they recognized the trickery immediately. Joanna handed the small, gray kitten to my mother, while Kris summarized the list of supplies and handed Dad the vaccination records.

Mom cuddled with the irresistible kitten. Dad was shocked and repeated, "Oh my gosh, oh my gosh," like a broken record. Kris declared that there was a two-week return policy if Mom and Dad really decided that they did not want the kitten. Joanna and Kris already had two cats, including one kitten from the same litter, called Gus. They were ready to adopt the second kitten if needed.

The adults were mesmerized by the kitten's cuteness as she awkwardly ventured around the room. She seemed to know that she was the center of attention. By the time Joanna and Kris were ready to leave, the kitten was back in my mother's arms. The instantaneous bond between Mom and the kitten led Kris to joke, "…the two-week return policy had already expired."

It was Sunday night. Joanna and Kris left for their home, and I planned to return to my own house as well. I packed my car with my weekend luggage and went back inside the cabin to tell Mom and Dad that I was ready to leave. They were both staring intently at the kitten.

Since it was nighttime, Dad walked me to the car with a flashlight to say goodbye. Mom stayed inside the house. She stood at the bedroom window with the kitten in her arms and waved goodbye with the kitten's paw. At that moment, I knew the kitten had a permanent home. The return policy was never mentioned again and even became a taboo subject.

Mom and Dad were pet owners again and doted on their new kitten that they named "Caper." With great fanfare and silliness, they informed me that the kitten had secured the new number one rank in the household.

"Number *one*," my father emphasized, as he gestured to the cat.

"Fine," I said in good humor. "If the cat is number one, and number one is better than number two, then I am POINT 5." Unknowingly, I had given myself the nickname that I still carry to this day.

"It's POINT 5," Dad announced when I called on the phone, or "we need to ask POINT 5," Mom referenced me when she needed help with something.

Caper was spoiled from the start. She entered a home with two animal-loving, retired adults and took full advantage of the situation. Mom and Dad loved the fuss and did everything possible to attend to the needs of their precious new "child." Most importantly, Caper demanded a schedule that allowed her to indulge her ravenous appetite.

CAPER'S SCHEDULE

6:30 a.m.:   1st Breakfast, 1/3 can Fancy Feast (seafood preferred), 1 handful dry food

6:45 a.m.:   Explore outdoors, drink from puddle, hunt

7:00 a.m.:   2nd Breakfast, dry food, 6-9 hairball treats

7:15 a.m.:   Lap time

9:00 a.m.:   Combing

9:30 a.m.:   3rd Breakfast, more dry food

10:00 a.m.: Explore outdoors, hunt

5:00 p.m.:   Dinner, 1/3 can Fancy Feast (seafood preferred), 1 handful dry food

6:00 p.m.:   Lap time

9:00 p.m.:   Petting, snack time (vanilla ice cream preferred)

Caper developed some unusual habits as a kitten. She never drank from a water dish, but rather preferred to drink fresh rainwater from an outside puddle. One of the stones in the Connecticut walkway had a small depression. If it rained, Caper walked straight out of the house to the puddle in the stone and drank the water. If there was no rainwater available, she jumped up on the sink in the bathroom and meowed until Mom or Dad turned on the cold-water faucet.

Caper slept lying on her back with her four legs in the air. She looked a lot like the drawings by Simon Bond from *101 Uses for a Dead Cat* that was popular in the 1980s. It did not matter whether she was outside or inside, on a sofa, on the ground, or in Mom's lap; Caper slept upside down.

The cat also demanded attention whenever she needed it. If she felt ignored, she jumped on tables and pushed anything that she could find onto the floor. Magazines, newspapers, pens, pencils, tissue boxes, and anything else were systematically cleared from tabletops until she received the attention that she desired.

My parents kept a comb in a drawer of a table in the living room. Caper jumped on the table and paced back and forth whenever she wanted to be combed. The cat spun in raptured delight when Mom or Dad drew the comb through her thick hair. She paused to give them a kiss every so often and walked away when she had had enough. Guests often remarked that they had never seen a cat that liked to be combed so much.

FIGURE 89:
Caper.

Caper fully explored the houses in both Connecticut and Maine and particularly liked places that were off limits. She sneaked into the attic and barns in Connecticut and prowled the basement in Maine. Somehow she managed to get into the smallest of spaces but, unlike Wiggles, she never got stuck.

One time in Maine, Mom was in the process of making her famous shortcake to serve for dessert. We had picked fresh strawberries earlier in the day and looked forward to strawberry shortcake for dessert. For some reason, Mom left the kitchen for a few minutes with the shortcake mixture on the counter. When she returned a few minutes later, the kitchen was covered in flour. It did not take much detective work to identify the guilty party. The tiny flour paw prints led right to Caper. Mom recovered from the setback, and we enjoyed delicious shortcake that night. It was no surprise; *kittens are no help in the kitchen.*

In Connecticut, Caper preferred to sit underneath the piano bench or in a patch of sunshine that shone through the window. In Maine, she sat on the edge of the loft and looked down at the activity on the main living level or escaped to the basement to sleep in the round seat of Dad's tractor. If a new shopping bag or box entered either home, Caper dashed into it to claim the spot for a few hours of rest. Once, she even slept in an empty litter box. Mom found a cat toy in the litter box one time and could not stop laughing, comparing the incident to a person who read a newspaper on the toilet.

Caper had favorite spots to nap and equally as many favorite spots to hunt. She reliably killed several small animals each week. The mouse, rabbit, bird, frog, and snake populations suffered for her instincts, while chipmunk populations were summarily decimated. More often than not, Caper dragged dead or half-dead animals into or near the house. Sometimes they were half-consumed or regurgitated. Caper meowed with pride when a human family member discovered her hunting trophies.

The New England rock walls that surrounded our homes in both Connecticut and Maine proved fertile hunting ground for chipmunks. If Caper found a chipmunk hole in the ground, she lay down on her belly and extended her front leg into the hole to search for rodent flesh hours at a time. One afternoon, I relaxed on the sofa inside the Maine cabin and heard a commotion outside. I dashed out the door with Mom to discover that Caper had cornered a chipmunk. The rodent was wildly running back and forth across the house foundation. We caught Caper and left the chipmunk to escape on its own.

An hour later, I heard the same disturbance. Caper had another chipmunk, maybe even the same one, in the same situation. Mom picked up Caper again, but the chipmunk was so confused that it started to chase *me*. I ran about ten yards before the chipmunk stopped and ran in a different direction.

Relieved, I returned to the house, unsure as to whether I would ever admit to having been chased by a chipmunk. It was possible that the chipmunk may have gotten a little satisfaction from the feat, but only if it lived long enough to ponder its heroism. Chipmunks that were caught once usually paid the price with their lives; a second time just tempted fate.

Caper liked to disappear after dinner, before she sought lap time from Mom or Dad. If we were in Maine, then she almost always slept in the tractor seat. When she finally made her appearance for the evening, we always checked her mouth to make sure that she had not caught a mouse in the basement. She usually walked around the room a few times, knocked a few things off the tables, inspected the status of her food dish, and then sought Mom's lap for the rest of the evening.

On one of these nights, she circled the living room with purpose. We all reached down to pet her as she passed by our feet. I sat on a chair with my legs outstretched on an ottoman. Caper walked underneath my legs, between the chair and the ottoman. Before I saw her reappear on the other side of my legs, she had pulled an enormous, adult-size chipmunk from underneath my chair and held it in her mouth. The chipmunk had obviously been dead for some time, although it appeared that Caper had "stored" it in the living room.

We wrestled the dead chipmunk away from Caper and were a bit worried that she may have used the house as a rodent graveyard, similar to a dog that buried bones in the yard. We searched under the sofa, chairs, and tables, but did not find any other dead animals. After that, we never assumed that Caper had a bad hunting day, and we checked under the chairs, tables, and sofa often, just to make sure.

Caper may have been a prolific hunter, but she did not always win her battles. Once she stalked wild turkeys in the backyard in Connecticut. She may have expected to kill a turkey when she suddenly found herself enclosed in a circle of turkeys that would not let her pass. She made a movement toward the perimeter of the circle, and the turkeys moved to block her escape. The terrified cat only broke through the circle when Mom and Dad, who had watched the whole episode from the inside of the house, decided to scare the turkeys away. Caper appeared to have learned her lesson that turkeys were too big for her to hunt. She never pursued them again, although growled (yes, a cat can growl!) at them through the windows of the house.

While the turkeys only scared Caper, a fox took a bite out of her belly as if she had been sleeping unaware, upside down on her back. Besides the turkeys, the fox was the only animal to get the better of the cat. Although she lived through the experience with a heavy dose of antibiotics, the veterinarian suspected that there was a fox in the neighborhood that was blind in one eye.

Caper's status as "number one" achieved further significance when we abandoned reference to her as the "cat" or the "kitty."

Animals

❖

Mom and Dad were both devoted fans of the English sitcom *Keeping Up Appearances*. The 1990s comedy featured an eccentric, snobbish, female character, Hyacinth Bucket. The character pronounced her surname Bucket [buhk-it], as Bouquet [boō-kā], as a means to associate herself more closely with high society. Mom and Dad declared that both "cat" and "kitty" were too middle-class for Caper. She assumed the classification as a Kitté [kit-tey] to signify her exalted status in the household.

Caper's birthday was June 21ˢᵗ and marked on the family calendar for observation, which usually meant Atlantic salmon for dinner. Caper's brother Gus, in the care of Joanna and Kris in Maine, received a birthday card each year.

To Yellowstone and Back

In the summer of 1982, Mom hankered for the family to explore the western United States via a cross-country expedition. We had traveled extensively by car throughout New England and camped as far away as Quebec, Canada. Other than short trips to New York City, Hyde Park, and visits to Grandma and Uncle George in Texas by plane, the family had rarely set foot west of the Hudson River. The Jansson family had done nothing to rival the magnificent spontaneity of westward travel as Mom had trekked years earlier with the various Smith family members, Cynthia, Cynthia Lee, and Judy.

It must have been hard for Mom to convince Dad that we needed to indulge in such an expedition. To Dad, there was never any reason to leave his beloved six New England states. He also worried about money and expenses, but when Mom made up her mind to do something, that was that. Mom repeated her mantra that Doris and I, "...needed to see the world," and Dad complied. As for Doris and me, we were more excited about the fact that Mom had proposed Yellowstone as a destination, and we wanted to see the bears that she had talked about so often.

To travel inexpensively, Mom and Dad prepared to buy a small motor home for our temporary use. We crawled through the classified listings in the newspaper, and Mom and Dad test-drove several vehicles. We settled on a Winnebago that included a small kitchen with dinette to seat four, a miniature bathroom, and a sofa. The sofa folded down into a double bed for my parents. I slept in the dinette area, which collapsed into a single bed, and Doris stowed away in a large overhead area above the cab.

Our camper did not exactly fit the model of luxury travel. Mom and Dad had skimped on quality to save money, and the camper had many problems before the end of our trip. Still, it allowed the family to travel comfortably with plenty of room. Mom and Dad took turns driving, although neither of them had any experience with large vehicles. As we scouted for campgrounds each night, Dad insisted that we look for pull-through campsites. He did not want to have to back up the camper.

We headed west on I-80 through Pennsylvania and camped in Youngstown, Ohio, on the first night of our adventure. In my travel diary, I noted that we had stalled on the road once, set out a flare, and lost a hubcap. The problems with the camper had just begun.

We reached Indiana Dunes National Lakeshore and walked a short distance to swim in Lake Michigan. As we approached the water, another family was just leaving.

"It's cold!" they warned. Doris and I swam for a long time and thought that the water was quite temperate. The other family had obviously never been to the Maine coast. In my travel diary, I recorded more troubles with the Winnebago, "...air conditioning broke down... repairman said he found blown fuse and got it working again."

We crossed the Mississippi River on our third day of travel. Mom made sure that Doris and I stopped whatever we were doing in the camper to fully devote our attention to the majestic waterway. I scanned the muddy banks and imagined Huckleberry Finn rafting down the mile-wide river. There was a lot of water on which to float, much more than the three-foot brook in Maine. Huckleberry Finn had an unfair advantage!

We visited Herbert Hoover's birthplace in a two-room cottage in West Branch, Iowa, and camped for the night at the Iowa State Fairgrounds in Des Moines. The camper's air conditioning had stopped working again, but was fixed at night by a local repairman.

We drove more than 350 miles and camped in Chamberlain, South Dakota. Doris and I played mini-golf for $0.50, although the course's simplistic design greatly disappointed us. I wrote, "…they had about three different kinds of holes…they just should have said 1-6, 7-12, 13-18." We stood in line to use a shower and washed our clothes at the campground laundry. With flies everywhere, we happily escaped the campground the next morning.

As we rode along in the camper, I mostly read books until Mom insisted that we look out the window at something of interest. I had lots of books with me on the trip due to the summer reading requirements for Honors English at Newtown High School. With a long list of books to choose from, I picked roughly a half dozen to fulfill the maximum requirement. When the school year started, I was expected to write essays on each of them in class. In addition, I had to read either Homer's *The Iliad* or *The Odyssey*. Mom suggested that I read *The Iliad* as "…it was the story of the Trojan horse." Likely, Mom had read, or maybe even taught, most of the books on the list. At a minimum, she was familiar with the titles.

I was halfway through *The Iliad* and perplexed that the Trojan horse had not yet been mentioned.

"When am I going to get to the part about the horse?" I asked Mom.

"Keep reading," said my mother. Almost to the end, I teased Mom that there were only a few pages left for the famous horse to make its entrance in the story. I finished the book without having read any mention of the Trojan horse.

"It must be in *The Odyssey*," corrected Mom. So, I read *The Odyssey*, which related the travels of the great Odysseus as he returned to his home in Ithaca *after* the Trojan War. The book mentioned the Trojan horse, but provided few details. My mother had no explanation the second time, so I continued to read the other books on my book list.

When we made it back to Connecticut, we researched the story of the Trojan horse to find it in *The Aeneid* by the ancient Roman poet Virgil. Mom bought me a beautiful hardcover copy of *The Aeneid* to make amends for her erroneous guidance, and I still cherish it today. "When will I get to the part about the Trojan horse?" is a Jansson family euphemism for "You've led me astray!"

As we entered the geological wonder of Badlands National Park, our real indoctrination to the American West began. We looped the park to admire the forces of deposition and erosion that began millions of years ago when it was completely underwater.[61] We continued west to the famous tourist destination of Wall Drug Store, observed the beauty of Mount Rushmore, and camped for the night in Rapid City, South Dakota. Although man-made, Mount Rushmore reminded me of The Old Man of the Mountain in New Hampshire.

We banged along, but had more trouble with the camper's air conditioner. The heat was unbearable, so we stopped at a gas station to have the system rewired by a mechanic. The rest may have been fortuitous, because the next part of the road trip included steep mountain roads with switchbacks that wound up and down the mountains. Dad had driven through the White Mountains of New Hampshire and the Green Mountains of Vermont, but nothing prepared him for the windy roads with switchbacks in the American West. With nothing between the camper and a many-thousand-foot precipice, Dad gripped the steering wheel in fear, unable to judge the small distance between the camper and the side of the road. We reached Worland, Wyoming, with Dad exhausted. We all agreed that he needed a rest and ate at Pizza Hut to give our chef a night off.

The next day, we saw a herd of buffalo by the side of the road, Devil's Tower, and the Buffalo Bill Historical Center. We reached Yellowstone National Park and toured Old Faithful, the hot springs with bubbling mud pots, waterfalls, and a mountainside of obsidian. The rocks were a mineralogist's dream, although they were off-limits to collectors, including Dad and me.

FIGURE 90:
*Dad, Mom, and Doris with
Devil's Tower in the background.*

We watched for animals and spotted an adult female moose with a baby moose, male elk, deer, and more wild buffalo. We kept our eyes peeled for bears, but disappointment reigned, as we learned that the animals had been moved out of the campground areas. Mom had promised us bears in Yellowstone, and we never saw a single bear!

To complete our Yellowstone experience, Mom insisted on a trail ride. Mom, Doris, and I signed up for a guided horseback tour, while Dad rested in the camper. The horse trail, away from the roadway, gave us a unique view of the park's majestic landscape. As the horses hugged the mountain trail, we looked down thousands of feet and snickered that Dad was much better off in the camper.

At the end of the day, I recorded the horseback ride in my travel diary, "...it was terrific, although Dad was too scared to go. I'm dying to get back to Connecticut and ride again on a regular basis. After the ride, my allergies started up." The mention of allergies proved to be understated. Medical tests later revealed that I had become allergic to horses, in addition to the dog and cats that lived with us in Newtown. The short jaunt around Yellowstone on horseback may have renewed my interest, but my riding days were over.

Still in the vicinity of Yellowstone, we experienced a hailstorm during the night before we drove all day to Salt Lake City. We stopped only to see the Idaho Lava Beds. The camper's air conditioning had stopped working again, so we left the vehicle for repair and took a cab into the city, where we toured Temple Square, heard an organ concert, viewed the city from a 26th floor observation deck, and went for a swim in the Great Salt Lake. The lake was far saltier than the ocean and provided unnatural buoyancy that allowed us to float without effort. The novelty did not disappoint us, but the rotten egg smell created by the unusual ecosystem ensured that we would not repeat the experience. A shower after a swim never felt so good.

Salt Lake City marked our farthest westward destination. Dad was happy to turn the camper toward home, but handed over the driving to my fearless mother as we entered the Rocky Mountains. I rode shotgun with Mom. She steered the camper around the steep turns without fear as I admired her unfailing confidence. We plotted a course for Colorado Springs, another must-see destination according to Mom.

Dad stayed in the back of the camper so that he could not see the road. Bored, he rummaged through some of the maps and tourist brochures that we had collected along the way. Mom and I had navigated the whole trip. Dad knew only that we were on the way home, but he had not really grasped where we were. In a burst of sudden comprehension, he yelled from the back of the camper, "We're going the wrong way!"

Mom and I laughed. *We* knew where we were going, but poor Dad had only just realized that a trip to Colorado Springs diverted us from the most direct route home. We had been on the road for nearly two weeks and were still all the way across the country. With his beloved New England home so far in the distance, he pouted in the back of the camper all the way to Colorado Springs. It did not make sense to abandon the planned excursion, but Dad would rather have headed home. Fortunately, he softened his mood as we rode to the top of Pike's Peak on a cog railway. Dad liked trains.

We steered for Nebraska and stopped in Kimball to see Father Kimmett. The priest was Dad's friend and chaplain from Turner Field in Albany, Georgia, during the war. The kind priest welcomed us

FIGURE 91:
Dad and Father Kimmett.

into his home. Dad and Father Kimmett reminisced about the military, Turner Field, and the many rowboat excursions they took to explore the surrounding swamps.

The camper had finally provided a few days of reliable transportation before having other problems. We camped in Goodland, Kansas, where it rained during the night. The camper's roof leaked over the bed where Doris slept and flooded her sleeping area. Doris moved into my bed and consumed the bedding, so I moved onto the floor. According to my journal, the shift in sleeping accommodations clearly irritated me. No one seemed to care that I was the one sleeping on the floor when it was my sister's bed that had been flooded. In the morning, Dad discovered that the camper's previous owners had drilled a hole in the roof for a CB (Citizens Band) antenna. The antenna had loosened during the trip and opened a gap for water to leak through.

We traveled through Kansas to see the Eisenhower Presidential Library and Museum. Touring the President's boyhood home, we saw a movie about his life. Famously, someone had predicted that Dwight Eisenhower would become the president of Yale, while his elder brother would become president of the United States. Oops!

Mom charted a different route home, and we picked up our pace of travel through Missouri, Illinois, and West Virginia, and reached our last stop in Hershey, Pennsylvania, where we toured the Milton Hershey School. The school's history interested all of us and, in future years, we learned that at least one person from Newtown had attended.

We also indulged ourselves in the chocolate plant tour, which offered a special promotion on Reese's Pieces. The peanut butter candy had been introduced in 1978 and had achieved stardom after product placement in the film *E.T. the Extra-Terrestrial*, where the alien in the film eats the candy. The plant offered a free T-shirt with the purchase of five large bags of Reese's Pieces. I wanted the T-shirt badly enough that Mom and Dad bought the candy. I gorged myself on the chocolate and felt sick the rest of the way home. According to my diary, we arrived home in Newtown around 10:30 p.m., unpacked the camper's refrigerator, and went to bed.

The next day, Mom and Dad unloaded and cleaned the camper. Within days, the camper was relisted for sale in the classified section of the local newspaper. Dad moved it out of the driveway and parked it in the field by the old horse barn. However, because the field was wet from rainfall, the camper sank in the mud and tipped onto its side so that its roof crashed against the side of the barn. Dad cursed!

He made several failed attempts to extricate the camper, which only increased the damage to the barn. Giving up, he called for help from a neighbor, Don Tenney, who was a professional truck driver. Mr. Tenney took the keys from Dad and maneuvered the camper to dry ground in seconds. Dad had driven the camper thousands of miles without incident, only to collide with his own barn.

After a few weeks, Mom and Dad sold the Winnebago for two hundred dollars more than what we had originally paid for it. Mom calculated that the extra money had covered the cost of gas for our trip. Mom achieved the educational experience that she had desired for Doris and me and hailed our cross-country adventure as a splendid success. She would never get Dad to take another big trip until after they both retired. Dad should have been worried; Mom's short list for travel destinations included Egypt and Greece!

The Computer Age

Amidst the science, history, and travels, Mom and Dad collaborated to introduce Doris and me to computers. Before the IBM PC (Personal Computer) had been introduced in 1981, Dad's school (Dad moved to Nathan Hale Middle School in Norwalk, Connecticut, in 1971) had purchased a number of Commodore PET (Personal Electronic Transactor) machines to teach computers as a class. The principal encouraged the teachers to take the machines home with them on the weekends. He reasoned that teachers who learned more themselves would be in a better position to teach the students. Dad volunteered to try the new technology.

The Commodore PET included the computer motherboard with 8-bit microprocessor, power supply, monochrome monitor, and keyboard, all built into one unit. The complete system weighed more than forty pounds, and Dad could hardly get his arms around the machine to pick it up. On Fridays, I anxiously waited for Dad in the afternoon to see if he had hauled the computer home with him. If he had the computer, then he usually had new software, too. The computer teacher at Nathan Hale provided him with all the latest programs that the school had purchased.

Computers were new to everyone at the time, and we all learned together. The computer teacher wanted feedback on all the software that we tested, whether educational programs or games. We particularly liked an airplane game that challenged us to drop bombs on targets in which the whole family competed individually against one another. Another game challenged us to mow a lawn in a pattern in the least amount of time. Dad's extensive real-life experience with lawn mowing did not help his score. He was better at flying simulated planes.

Mom enthusiastically enrolled in a community college class to learn the Fortran programming language. She shared her assignments with me as she progressed through the semester. Using the school's equipment, she created punch cards with keypunch machines to input her code into a mainframe computer. Each card contained a line of code for the computer to execute. Mom liked the class, but regretted that she was not a better typist. One wrong hole punched, and the whole card needed to be typed over again!

I enrolled in the BASIC (Beginner's All-purpose Symbolic Instruction Code) programming class that was offered at the high school as soon as I had room in my schedule during my sophomore year. The class used Apple II Plus computers and a Wang machine with a card reader. The Wang mark sense cards were similar to the punch cards that my mother had used, but instead required a #2 pencil to fill in an array of bubbles to indicate various numbers, letters, or symbols. The tedious process was still prone to mistakes, but it was a lot easier to erase a mistake than to start all over again with a punch card. Still, any type of cards had to be fed into a machine in the right order. Cards that were dropped required a manual effort to resort them. The Apple II Plus was much easier to use as we entered our BASIC programs directly into the computer with the built-in keyboard and typed "RUN" to execute.

The introduction of the first computer class at Newtown High School had been controversial. The school system had no plans to teach computers until a local company offered to donate the Wang machine. While most people did not understand the concept of a computer and some argued adamantly against it, Mom asserted her influence as a Board of Education member to insist that Newtown accept the gift. The first computer programming class at Newtown High School was installed in the 1978-79 school year as a result, years ahead of many other school systems.[62]

As a newly minted computer geek at Newtown High School in the early 1980s, I met with similarly-minded friends before class. We watched the industry develop from afar and relied on technology magazines, Beagle Brothers catalogs, and the *New York Times* for information. We pawed over the newspaper's special Tuesday section that was dedicated to computers and read the latest advertisements for computers and computer parts with interest. Predictably, 42nd Street Photo in New York City offered the lowest prices anywhere.

As the personal computer phenomenon swept the nation, Mom took me to visit the new computer stores that had cropped up in Danbury, Connecticut. Both Apple and IBM machines were sold through authorized dealers.

The dealer for Apple had a rainbow-colored apple logo on the window, offered a cheery atmosphere with lots of machines on display, and salesmen more than willing to demonstrate the capabilities of the Apple II series machines. The store also showcased a wide variety of software that included word processing, spreadsheets, games, and educational programs that made the computers attractive to students and home consumers alike. The store buzzed with customers.

In contrast, the Danbury dealer that sold IBM equipment maintained a much smaller retail space with salesmen in dark business suits. The store displayed the IBM-authorized dealer sign on the window, as well as a wall-sized image of Charlie Chaplin's Little Tramp character with an IBM PC. Mom and I visited the IBM store, where a salesman happily demonstrated the equipment for us. We were probably the first mother-daughter pair who had ever entered the shop, and Mom already had enough knowledge in the area to ask intelligent questions. The polite, dark-suited man was likely as intrigued by us as we were of the mysterious PC. Mom had me sit at the computer throughout the demonstration, and the salesman let me type on the iconic PC keyboard that clicked loudly at every key press. The PC certainly had a lot of functionality, although it looked a lot more like office equipment than something fun for the home.

Mom and I absorbed the knowledge gained from the visits to both stores and compared notes with everyone we knew who had any knowledge of the subject. In general, the consensus viewed the IBM PC as a machine for business, whereas the Apple was considered best for a home consumer. The PC was more expensive than the Apple, which also suggested that it was aimed at corporate buyers.

Eventually, Mom and Dad decided that they wanted to buy an Apple, but learned that there was a less expensive option available if they purchased an Apple clone. Clone manufacturers produced computers that were software compatible with the brand-named machine, either Apple or IBM, by copying the designs. After a great deal of comparison shopping, Mom and Dad settled on the Franklin Ace 1000, an Apple II Plus clone.

The Franklin Ace 1000 had been designed and manufactured by the Franklin Computer Corporation and compared favorably to the genuine Apple II Plus. The Franklin motherboards were very similar to Apple and copied the Apple software to maintain compatibility. (Note: Eventually, Apple Computer, Inc. would sue Franklin Computer Corporation for copyright infringement. Apple won, and Franklin was forced to withdraw its clones from the market.) Whereas both machines relied on an 8-bit 6502 MOS Technology microprocessor with roughly 1 MHz clock speed, the Apple II Plus had 48 KB of RAM (Random Access Memory) and had a 24-row by 40-column text display with only uppercase letters. The Franklin computer offered 64 KB of RAM and had both upper and lower case letters in the same display size, as well as a numeric keypad. Mom and Dad thought that we would all benefit from the letter flexibility for schoolwork. At high school, I shared the amount of memory that our new computer had with my math and computer teacher, Mr. Frank Tomaino.

"You'll *never* use all that!" he exclaimed.

Along with the Franklin machine, we also purchased a floppy drive, monochrome (green) monitor, dot matrix printer, DOS (disk operating system) software, a word processor called WordPerfect, and a box of floppy disks to save files. We all used the word processing software, although Mom did most of the typing. Dad wrote out tests for his classes for Mom to type, and I pounded out drafts for English essays and term papers on a manual typewriter before Mom helped me to enter them into the computer. While the software did the job, amazingly, it took three keystrokes just to delete a single character.

We also played games, which came to us through a network of friends who also had Apple compatible computers. Some of our friends had invested in machines that were not compatible with Apple, such as the TRS-80 sold by Tandy Corporation or the Commodore 64, which was a follow-up to the Commodore PET. I also programmed in BASIC and experimented with sample code from computer magazines. Once, I typed for several hours and was unable to save my efforts to a floppy disk as I had forgotten to format it before I started. Every disk required "formatting" before it was recognizable by the computer's file system, and there was no way to format a disk once another application was in use. The requirement was annoying, but I had to make the mistake only once before I got in the habit of formatting blank disks as soon as they were purchased.

Throughout my high school years, I received more and more computer peripherals as birthday and Christmas gifts, including a second 5¼" disk drive, 80-column card, 300 baud modem, and a joystick for games. The 80-column card expanded the number of characters on a single row from 40 to 80. The installation instructions were quite simple, but required modifications to the motherboard. I held my breath and hoped for the best, as I used wire cutters to disconnect various components and connect others. Luckily, the instructions worked flawlessly.

Amidst the 1980s computer hype, Newtown High School added a second year of computer instruction to teach the Pascal programming language, and I completed the inaugural class. With the additional exposure, computers became more and more a focus of a long-term career possibility.

My parents had always wanted me to go to college, although their reasons were more practical than noble.

"You need to go to college to get a skill and put food on the table," Mom must have said a thousand times. She also insisted that a *technical* field would provide better options for financial security. She stressed the importance of science and math, although English was always my favorite subject.

"You'll starve as an English major," she said, referring to her own background. I had heard "we can't afford it" so many times as a child that I assumed there was a good deal of truth in her statement. Fifty years after the Depression, its lingering effects on my mother shaped my future. She wanted something better for me.

To a certain extent, I had assumed I would pursue a career in chemistry throughout my youth. My mother had spoken so frequently of her father's ambitions to learn the subject, as well as her own attempt to pursue a chemistry major in college, that I was inspired to complete the journey. However, I had interests in other science areas, too, notably geology (due to the rock collection) and botany (due to the plants in my bedroom). When I mentioned geology as a possibility, Mom was less than enthusiastic.

"You'll end up working for an oil company," she warned about the field. My Texan mother obviously knew which companies employed geologists.

In spite of the overwhelming push for math and science inside my home, I received little encouragement at school, which I attributed mainly to my gender. Computers, on the other hand, were still new, and no one knew enough about them to say whether a girl should study the field or not. With no role models in the science field other than my father as a teacher, computers seemed like a safe bet for a secure financial future. I had no interest whatsoever in teaching, did not want to go into a field where I was not wanted, and had no desire to starve.

Mom and Dad took me to see various colleges as I re-focused on computer science or computer engineering as a major. Many schools were not prepared for the influx of students interested in computers due to the home computer phenomenon and struggled to answer questions about the field. If that was the case, I lost interest in those schools. On one visit to a prestigious New England college, a tour guide showed us the school's computer lab that consisted of one pitiful machine shoved into a corner. The facilities paled in comparison to the large room full of computers at Newtown High School. I was disappointed by several of the colleges' computer labs, but in some ways was not surprised. My mother had been a driving force in the Newtown school system to push forward into new academic areas. In large part, I had my mother to thank for the high quality of my public education.

The Dawn of Girls' Soccer in Newtown

I had played soccer in Monroe on a boys' team for several years when the Newtown Soccer Club finally formed a girls' league. Newtown's population had grown, and lots of people moved into town from other states. The newcomers had higher expectations for girls' soccer and pressured the town to form a league. With the creation of a middle-school age girls' team, I was one of the players recruited to become part of the new travel squad, even though I was already playing on a boys' team in Newtown after having played in Monroe for several years. The Newtown girls' team included an age span of four years to fill a full roster.

I was usually among the oldest, so I sometimes played with girls who were several years younger. I was also one of the strongest players, not only due to my age, but also due to having played so many years on a boys' team. I settled permanently into the center-halfback position and gained a reputation for having superb dribbling skills and a booming kick.

I played on both the boys' team and girls' team for several years. The boys' team played on Saturdays, while the girls' team played on Sundays in the tradition of other travel teams. The girls' parents shared the driving, as we traveled up to an hour away to find other girls' teams to play. On a few occasions, we traveled over the border to New York and played in towns that I had never even heard of before. Mom was one of the workhorse drivers and carried a full station wagon of players to and from the away games. Mom never missed a game and anchored the cheering section with a number of other devoted soccer parents.

Our new team compared similarly to other newly-formed teams in surrounding towns. Bigger towns, such as Westport and Stamford, with more established girls' leagues, beat us badly. The Westport team was so strong that we managed to get the ball past half-field only a few times in one of the games.

Coaches stepped forward to lead the girls' soccer team. Our first coach was a young policeman in town, Adrian Stroud, whose parents were from Great Britain. Parents, some with European ancestry, volunteered to coach in subsequent years. We were lucky to have enough parents who knew soccer, as the sport was still fairly new in the U.S. My mother sometimes partnered with a few of the men to split the team's coaching responsibilities. The men coached on the field, while Mom managed the team's logistics, which included the coordination of practice times, game schedule, drivers for carpools, and the overall time-consuming task of team communication via phone calls.

The growing interest in girls' soccer led to the idea for the formation of a girls' soccer team at Newtown High School. The head of the girls' league introduced the concept to the Superintendent of Schools to lukewarm reception. Newtown was still not ready to fully embrace girls' soccer.

Over time, the girls' advocates heard a myriad of excuses to block the formation of a high school team, including the cost, field availability, coaching staff, and equipment needs. The dissenters even challenged whether girls wanted to play soccer or even *should* play soccer. Contact sports were still considered by some as suitable for boys only.

Despite the objections, the idea for a high school team gained momentum. The Superintendent agreed to take the issue to the Board of Education if the supporters could raise $1,000. My mother sprang into action. Although she had resigned from her Board seat a number of years earlier, the Board of Education was still her bailiwick. When my mother lent her organizational skills and voice to a political cause, she was a force to be reckoned with, a Newtown political titan.

My mother arranged for me to meet with several business leaders in town to explain the goals for the team and ask for donations. As I sat across the desk from Eleanor Mayer at the Connecticut National Bank, I was stunned when she wrote a check for $100. I had never seen so much money, but learned that the lifelong Newtown resident was no stranger to either women's issues or civic activism. She was not only the vice president of the bank, but also a highly regarded member of the community. Ms. Mayer encouraged me to continue the fight for a team, while her financial contribution publicly signaled to other business leaders in town that she supported the cause.

Bob Tendler, owner of Bob Tendler Realtors, added a similar donation to the coffers. My teammate, Kate Stark, and I visited Mr. Tendler at his office. A *Newtown Bee* photographer took our picture and reported the donation in the sports section of the newspaper. Soon, other business owners followed. I marched from business to business in the Sandy Hook section of town to ask for donations. Warmly received, I could not believe that so many businesses were willing to donate.

"Don't worry," said Mom. "They love the publicity." I was dumbfounded that I had received donations for anything other than altruistic reasons, but did not complain. Secretly, I hoped that the business owners genuinely supported our goals. I am sure that most did. Finally, the team met our $1,000 objective, and the Newtown Soccer Club that presided over the girls' soccer league matched our fund-raising with another $1,000.

Still, the reality of a girls' team for the high school was far from certain. Roadblocks were thrown up everywhere. Aside from the money, the school determined that there were not enough playing fields at the high school to accommodate a girls' team. The three boys' soccer and football teams, including varsity, junior varsity, and freshman teams for both sports, as well as girls' field hockey, consumed the high school playing fields. The best alternative available for girls' soccer consisted of busing the participants a short distance to nearby Treadwell Park, a relatively new facility with a soccer field. The field had been scooped out from a hillside. Spectators benefited from a naturally sloped perimeter. The transportation requirement was not optimal, although certainly feasible.

In the background, the implications of Title IX loomed. Title IX, passed in 1972 as part of an education amendment, required any school that received federal funds to provide an equal number of sports for boys and girls. Newtown High School was a public institution and therefore subject to comply with the federal legislation. At the time, the school offered boys' football, soccer, cross-country, swimming, basketball, wrestling, baseball, and track. Boys' ice hockey was offered as a club sport. Girls' teams included field hockey, volleyball, cross-country, swimming, basketball, softball, and track. Boys' sports totaled eight, while girls' sports totaled seven.

After a muddy practice on June 14, 1983, our recreational girls' team walked the short distance from the practice field to the superintendent's office to attend the Board of Education meeting that determined the fate of a girls' soccer team at Newtown High School. In a packed room with the dirty players and their supportive parents in attendance, the Board of Education seemed rather surprised at the turnout.

My mother was conspicuously absent and sat in the family station wagon that was parked outside. She felt strongly that it was inappropriate for a former Board of Education member to publicly confront the current board's membership. It is possible that her presence in the room may have been perceived as bully tactics, but she had already exercised her influence. The Board knew what was coming, whether they liked it or not.

Parents spoke in support of the team one by one. Our core cheering section was out in force, including both fathers and mothers, who wanted their daughters to have the chance to play soccer as a high school sport. I spoke, too. In my short, extemporaneous speech, I emphasized that I really did want to play soccer. I wanted the Board to hear my conviction directly and not continue to question the commitment of girls to the sport of soccer.

The superintendent reported on the status of funding, although a coach had not yet been identified. The members debated in the public forum; some clearly supported the team, while others did not. As a high school student, I found it hard to follow the discussion, but when one board member spoke I heard every word he said.

"I cannot support a girls' soccer team because it would take away from boys playing football," he bellowed. Even by 1980s standards, the statement seemed utterly preposterous. His words drowned the discussion and dampened my spirits. Did his opinion reflect the majority? Like the rest of the team's supporters, I could only sit back and wait for the vote.

The Board moved to introduce the girls' soccer team at the high school as a Junior Varsity sport for the 1983 fall season, subject to the availability of a qualified coach, successful negotiations with the Newtown Federation of Teachers for a coach's salary, and the matching $1,000 donation from the Newtown Soccer Club. The vote began, and I held my breadth. I heard ayes and nays. When the votes were tallied, the movement had passed by a narrow margin. Newtown High School would introduce girls' soccer as a junior varsity sport in 1983 and add a varsity team in 1984. The audience cheered!

The Board of Education paused the meeting to allow the players and their parents to exit the meeting room. With spring in our step, I am sure that we may have inadvertently left a little mud behind. I ran to my mother in the car and shared the magnificent news. Eager for all the details, I repeated everything that I could remember as my mother beamed the largest smile that I had ever seen.

Less than a week later, the Newtown High School Athletic Director, Bob Sveda, offered to coach the team. Klaus Ertl, a policeman in Newtown and father of our goalie, Chris Ertl, became the assistant coach. During the fall season, two men worked together flawlessly and drilled the team with precision. Some of the team members had played together for as many as five years. We were no longer a rag-tag bunch, but a committed group that benefited from everyday practice sessions that were organized by seasoned and skilled coaches.

The team found its footing in the inaugural 1983 season, albeit as a junior varsity team. In 1984, we made our varsity debut in the

Western Connecticut Conference (WCC) and competed against Weston, New Fairfield, Bethel, and Brookfield. No other towns in the WCC had yet established high school girls' soccer teams. Even Monroe, where I had started soccer almost a decade earlier, lacked a team. Mr. Sveda filled in the schedule with as many games as possible outside the WCC, although some of the competition represented schools much larger than Newtown High School. At the time, Newtown had approximately 1,200 students in the high school with grades nine through twelve.

The inaugural varsity team included four seniors, seven juniors, four sophomores, and two freshmen. I continued to play center halfback, flanked by midfielders Kate Stark and Shona Curtis. Kate's

FIGURE 92:
Newtown High School inaugural varsity girls' soccer team, 1984.
Back row: Assistant Coach Ertl, Jacque Grenier (manager),
Megan Kearns, Jennifer Nitray, Kate Stark, Kristin Burke,
Nancy Watkins, Courtney Lehmann, Rebecca Birkett (manager),
Coach Sveda, Middle row: Laurel Whelan, Carrie Lish, Patty Hensel,
Louise McCullough, Wendy Leitner, Debbie MacDonald,
Front row: Sue Knapp, Chris Ertl, Kelley Jansson (me), Shona Curtis.

mother and Shona's father had both been outspoken advocates for the team. The wings exhibited track star speed, while the center forwards had a knack for being in the right place at the right time. The aggressive play of the fullbacks trapped the opposing team off-sides with steady frequency. Breakaways against us were almost anomalies due to their strong play. Chris Ertl's sure-handedness in goal, as well as her presence as a team leader, anchored the defense.

In our season opener, we played against Weston, at Weston, in a WCC conference game. The varsity season had finally arrived; and due to poor play we lost 1-2. I walked off the field in a daze. The loss stung, but served as a wake-up call. We re-grouped to knock off conference rivals New Fairfield and Bethel, and upset Danbury 7-1, a much larger town than Newtown. I remember that the Danbury team was so frustrated that their center halfback lowered her shoulder and launched me into the air with an illegal football-style tackle. I cannot recall whether the offender was ejected from the game. I was slow to get up, and the referee was very kind to give me a few minutes to catch my breath. It must have been humiliating for Danbury to lose to "little" Newtown.

We beat Weston the second time that we played them and obliterated the weakest team in the WCC, Brookfield. Other non-conference teams proved more formidable, as we lost to Shelton and Ridgefield. At the end of a 7-win, 1-loss, conference schedule, we tied for the conference lead with Weston, having split games with them during the regular season. To decide the championship, the league scheduled the teams to play again at a neutral location to break the tie.

On an extremely cold November afternoon, with temperatures in the forties, the first varsity girls' soccer team to represent Newtown High School took the field at Joel Barlow High School in Redding, Connecticut, to compete for the first WCC championship. Mom was in the stands with the usual Newtown cheering section

FIGURE 93:
Kicking the ball on the soccer field. Go Newtown!

along with other spectators who had turned out for the big game, including members of the boys' soccer team. The parents were wrapped in blankets, while someone had brought sleeping bags for our team's substitutes to keep warm on the bench. My father came to watch, too. While my mother had never missed a game, my father had mostly seen me play in the backyard.

The wind howled at the coin toss. Connecticut's windy weather often challenged the game of soccer and meant that it was hard to move the ball against the direction of the wind. On the day of the WCC championship, November 2, 1984, the wind blew lengthwise across the field with gusts over 30 mph.[63] The coin toss determined which goal each team defended for each half of the game. Soccer rules dictated that the teams switched sides at half time. Due the weather conditions, the coin toss also determined each team's field position relative to the wind. Our team had consistently chosen to play with the wind in the *second* half of the game. I nearly choked when we lost the coin toss.

As I stood in the middle of the freezing field with the captains from both teams and the referee, I knew that the wind mattered. In an instant, my fears were allayed. Weston *chose* to play with the wind during the *first* half. We had lost the coin toss, but won our favored position. I walked to Mr. Sveda in disbelief and told him about the Weston team's decision.

"If your horse is second in the race and the horse in front of you falls over dead, then keep running and don't feel sorry about it," he chirped. His expedient response resonated with me, and my thoughts swiftly returned to the game.

We beat Weston 4-1 to win the first Western Connecticut Conference championship for girls' soccer. Mr. Sveda had always said, "Three goals should be enough to win any game." I knew that we had won when we reached that mark and felt a little sorry for the Weston team as they struggled to move the ball against the wind near the end of the second half. When the final whistle blew, the team piled on top of one another in a midfield celebration before we dashed to the bus for warmth. We sang Queen's *We Are the Champions* all the way back to Newtown High School where our parents picked us up. Mom declared that I had played a "brilliant game." I always relished her compliments, even though I knew that she was completely biased. In this case, she felt her praise was warranted, as Mr. Sveda apparently agreed in her assessment. He was quoted in the newspaper as saying, "…Kelley Jansson…efficiently distributed the ball to the forward and wings. Jansson, in particular, took command of the center of the field and continually pushed the ball into the attacking zone. Kelley controlled the midfield and the game."[64]

With the win over Weston, our team was seeded eleventh in the state tournament's L Division. We played two games as part of the tournament, but were eliminated in a loss to the sixth seed from Newington. Including the tournament loss, we had scored 83 goals in the season, with only 21 goals against us, a ratio of almost 4:1. Four of us were selected to the WCC all-conference team. As an added honor, the Western Connecticut Soccer Officials Association awarded us the Bill Walsh Sportsmanship Award. We may not have won the state title, but the recognition for our conduct on the field was significant. I went on to play soccer for more than twenty years after high school and never had more pride in a group than the 1984 championship team from Newtown.

1984 Newtown High School Girls' Soccer Season Results

DATE	OPPONENT	SCORE
9/13	at Weston	1-2
9/14	New Fairfield	3-0
9/21	at Bethel	7-0
9/24	Danbury	7-1
9/28	Brookfield	14-0
10/5	Weston	1-0
10/9	Wolcott	10-0
10/11	at Wolcott	5-1
10/12	Shelton	2-3
10/16	at New Fairfield	2-0
10/19	Bethel	4-0
10/22	at Danbury	4-4
10/23	at Brookfield	10-0
10/31	at Ridgefield	1-5
11/2	Weston (WCC Championship)	4-1
11/6	Torrington (State Tournament)	5-0
11/8	at Newington (State Tournament)	3-4

I graduated from high school the following spring with a varsity letter in soccer, but yearned for more of a high school playing history. Because I never had a chance to compete for the record books, I endured a sense of loss. What could I have accomplished if the team had existed when I was a freshman? My only consolation was the satisfaction to have been part of the political process that established the high school team for future students. My kindergarten pursuits and third grade petition had set a chain of events in motion that changed the course of girls' athletics in Newtown.

The high school team dominated the WCC conference for the next ten years. Mom followed the team with interest and mailed *Newtown Bee* clippings to me in college so that I could read about the team's accomplishments from afar. The team and its players collected accolades as Mom and I silently cheered for the next generation of Newtown players.

A Yankee in Texas

When it came time for me to consider college choices, I was keenly aware of how much my mother loved her own college experience at TSCW (Texas State College for Women) in Denton, Texas. She had made lifelong friends and discovered horseback riding. To Mom, it was important that I considered a college far enough away from home so that I could get a new experience. Like Yellowstone, she wanted me to see a different part of the country and encouraged me to explore options beyond New England. I looked at schools in Washington, D.C., Virginia, and Pennsylvania, as well as New England, but when my grandmother suggested, "Kelley, why don't you go to a school in Texas?" my undergraduate planning changed course.

I can still hear my grandmother's sweet Texan accent as she argued her case, but the fact of the matter was that I loved the possibility of discovering my mother's roots. The stars aligned, and I left Newtown for college in Texas. For almost eighteen years, I had lived in the same house, on the same street in Newtown, Connecticut. In the fall of 1985, I had a new address for the first time in my life.

Shortly after I arrived at school in Texas, I planned to try out for the women's soccer team during the first week of school. My mother had prepared a booklet that profiled my accomplishments in high school and sent it to the coach before the semester started. The coach had been a player at the university herself a few years earlier and looked forward to my arrival after receiving the material from my mother. Even though I had seen the campus before, I was dazzled by the school's sports facilities. New England weather meant that I grew up playing soccer on crabgrass and dirt. I had never seen a soccer field so perfect, completely covered by soft, green grass.

At the onset of my engagement with the team, I joined the other athletes for warm-ups. We went through the usual stretching drills and proceeded to do sit-ups in the grass. However, in just a minute or two, I was covered in bugs. Once again, I had discovered some new breed of insect by rolling in its home. My teammates said that the bugs were chiggers, but I was not convinced. I still remembered my experience with Texas ants in the second grade and simply did not trust that ants were not the culprits on the soccer field.

The coach excused me from practice so that I could run a quarter mile back to my dorm and wash the bugs off in the shower. I returned to the field after changing my clothes and was warned that I had to be careful where I sat on the grass. The team thought it was funny that a kid from Connecticut did not know that already. It was so obvious to the Texas natives.

I earned a starting position on the varsity team as a freshman. The school participated in the NCAA (National College Athletic Association) Southwest Conference, which mixed play between Division I and Division III schools. Women's soccer was still a new sport, and there were not enough teams to maintain separate divisions.

Mom visited Texas to see me play. She sat nearly alone in the large stadium, but cheered just as loudly as if she had been with the parents group from Newtown. She witnessed my involvement in several scoring plays and declared my role on the team as invaluable. Mom was always partial to my performance, but I swelled with pride that she had made the trip. Soccer had been a large part of my life, and we both recognized the long, hard road taken for me to arrive on the NCAA stage.

Many years after I graduated from college, a newly formed U.S. national women's soccer team garnered attention. They captured the first Olympic gold medal in women's soccer in 1996 and defeated China in a 5-4 shootout to win the 1999 Women's World Cup title in front of more than 90,000 fans at the Rose Bowl in Southern California.[65] Little girls playing soccer finally had their heroes. Some may have been in Newtown.

A Truck and a Shower Curtain

In college, I visited my grandmother and Uncle George in Texas on long weekends and holidays, but flew back to Connecticut for Christmas and the summer breaks. Unfortunately, my grandmother passed away in January of my sophomore year in 1987, but I know that she would have been proud of me at graduation.

Toward the end of my sophomore year, my uncle gave me a 1974 Ford pickup he had used on farmland that he maintained as a hobby. The big, baby blue truck had an eight-cylinder engine, an

AM radio, waist-only seatbelts, and a cap over the truck bed. Conveniently, I used the covered truck bed to store my belongings during the summer between my sophomore and junior years in college. I stuffed in a small sofa from a college friend who also needed summer storage space. My uncle kept the loaded truck in his garage for the summer and started it on occasion to keep the battery charged.

At the start of the fall semester, I returned to Texas and collected my truck from my uncle's garage. Moving off-campus for the first time, I drove to meet my roommate to sign the lease for our two-bedroom apartment with rented furniture. We signed the papers in the middle of the day and lugged a few things in from our vehicles before the excessive August heat slowed our efforts. We decided to wait for cooler temperatures in the evening before we moved anything else.

Even with the little that we had done, I exerted myself enough to work up a sweat. I wanted to take a shower before I realized that the apartment unit was not furnished with shower curtains. I went to the apartment office to inquire where I could buy one, and they gave me directions to the local Sears store. I headed to the store in my truck, which was still full of my stuff as well as my friend's sofa.

Dressed in a T-shirt, shorts, and Docksiders, I was in Sears only briefly to buy the shower curtain. When I returned to the parking lot, I could not find my truck. Confused, I assumed that I had walked out a different mall entrance than what I had entered and went back inside the mall to get reoriented. I walked in and out several times, but still could not find the big baby blue truck that Uncle George had given me.

Without a better idea, I walked around the outside of the entire mall several times. The truck was large and would have towered above most of the cars. In addition, the mall was closing for the night, and the parking lot was nearly empty. After three complete laps around the giant Texas-size mall, my feet ached terribly. Embarrassed, I made my way to the mall's security office and explained that I could not find my truck and was probably twisted around.

"Was it a Silverado?" asked the guard flippantly.

"No, it's a 1974 Ford pickup," I answered dryly, which certainly was not a new car by 1987 standards. The guard was surprised by my answer, but shrugged in acknowledgement.

"Well, it's probably in Mexico by now. Let's take a ride."

I got in the security buggy with the guard, and he drove me around the mall's perimeter. I looked for the truck, although the parking lot was pretty empty given the mall had closed for the night. After one complete loop, the guard declared the obvious.

"Yup, it's gone," he said. I could not believe it.

We went back to the security office, where I filled out a bunch of paperwork for the police. I was still in complete shock when I called my roommate to pick me up. As we returned home, I felt deflated. I had been excited to move into an apartment for the first time. A few hours later, my jubilance had turned to dismay. I clutched my new shower curtain on the way back to the apartment. I still needed it, but it felt like a booby prize. Fortunately, I had unloaded my suitcase and computer earlier in the day, so I still possessed a few days of clothes and my most critical asset for engineering school.

I called my uncle to let him know what had happened. Like me, he could not believe it. There was nothing either of us could do to help, as the police said that the truck had probably been taken for a joy ride. They estimated that it would be recovered in a few weeks.

School started, and I was able to hitch rides to and from the campus. Without a long-term transportation solution, my uncle and I went car shopping and found a fairly inexpensive Volkswagen. I prepared to make the monthly payments by picking up additional part-time work. I had worked continuously through my summer breaks so far and earned more than $4,000 for each of the 1986 and 1987 calendar years. I also had a long history of part-time work to earn whatever I could to save for college. Even before I was sixteen and eligible to work, I had earned money as a softball umpire, basketball referee, and papergirl with the *Bridgeport Post*. I had also worked part-time at a machine shop after high school in my senior year, where the plant was close enough to school to walk and my Dad could pick me up at the end of the day. Mom had politely encouraged that I should do whatever I could "...to help Mom and Dad with finances." I had certainly done my best.

Due to my student income level, my uncle agreed to co-sign the car loan. However, when the time came to complete the paperwork, he offered to pay the whole amount. To this day, I am amazed by Uncle George's generosity. I wonder if he knew that a college student would have had trouble making car payments. I worked part-time anyway, but applied the money toward tuition and living expenses.

About a month after the truck was stolen, I received a call from the police that they had recovered the vehicle. They explained that I could claim it at the city's auto impound. I immediately felt guilty because I had just taken possession of the Volkswagen. I called Uncle George to give him the news, and we arranged to meet at the specified location to claim the truck.

We arrived at the auto impound, registered at the front desk, and received a ticket that we gave to a bus driver who would take us to the truck. As we pulled out of the administrative area, we both sensed the huge scale of the facility. Thousands of cars were lined up in rows as far as the eye could see. There were about ten people riding with us on the trolley-like bus. Every few minutes the driver stopped and let a few people off, presumably at their vehicle's location. The impound lot seemed endless, and we descended further and further into the auto abyss.

After about fifteen minutes, we were the only two passengers who remained on the bus. I asked the driver whether he forgot us.

"No, you're in the *back* lot," he answered. Neither of us had any idea what that meant, so we stayed seated. As we passed by the rows of cars, we noticed that the vehicles appeared to be in progressively worse condition. At the beginning of the bus ride, the cars had looked in good condition. A little further, and the cars had showed signs of fender benders, minor collisions, and then major accidents. Where was the truck? The police never said what condition it was in, and I had assumed that I could drive it home. I had brought the keys with me.

After a few more minutes, the landscape turned black. We exited the section with smashed cars and entered a new section with torched vehicles. In shock, we remained on the bus until it stopped. Uncle George and I looked at each other. Neither of us saw the truck or anything like it.

"There it is," announced the driver. We re-focused our eyes in the direction of the driver's hand to see the metal frame of the truck lying on the ground. The cap over the truck bed was gone, along with all my stuff and my friend's sofa. In fact, it looked like the truck bed had been swept clean. The wheels and tires were gone, the doors were gone, and the engine and hood were also gone. Even the gas cap had been stolen. A truck, which had once dwarfed other vehicles suddenly, looked pathetically small.

The driver did not want to leave us in "the back lot," but gave us a few minutes to grasp the magnitude of the loss. Sympathetically, the driver loaned me his screwdriver to take off the truck's front license plate as a souvenir. The back license plate with the recently renewed registration had been stolen. I took some pictures and climbed back on the bus with my uncle. We made the long ride back to the auto impound office in silence.

The office administrators asked us whether we wanted to claim the truck for a fee, which we obviously declined. A truck

FIGURE 94:
Uncle George with the 1972 Ford truck that was stolen (and somewhat recovered by police), 1987.

frame had no use to either of us. The administrator explained that the city sold unclaimed vehicles (or parts!) at auction. We left the impound lot in disbelief as to what had just transpired. I went back to school driving the Volkswagen and once again felt fortunate that my uncle had come to my rescue.

Even to this day, I panic in a parking lot when I do not see my car right away. I also purchase a shower curtain *before* I move into a new apartment.

Engineering for Sound

I studied engineering in college and focused mostly on computers, which was still new in the 1980s. (Giving my mother credit, I graduated with several students who had gone back to school to earn a second degree in engineering. Their first degree was in geology, and they had not been able to find a job!) Engineering students often joked that when we went home, all our friends and family wanted us to fix their televisions or VCRs (Video Cassette Recorder). It did not matter what type of engineering any of us had studied, it just seemed that the world expected us to fix things. Remote controls and the blink of "12:00 AM" on the VCR were apparently beyond the average person's understanding. We felt smart and always helped out when we could.

My mother had particularly high expectations in my ability to solve technical problems. She frequently doodled her ideas for a new gadget on paper and mailed it to me. In particular, her hearing had gotten worse, and she wanted a better solution. She had relied on hearing aids for most of her adult life, but the available technology proved inadequate for someone with a profound hearing loss.

"Why can't you invent a better hearing aid, so that I can HEAR?" she asked repeatedly, to which I tenderly explained that audio was processed by analog electronics, whereas I studied digital electronics. The two disciplines were fairly separate, and a specialist in one usually did not have much knowledge or expertise in the other. My mother persisted in her encouragement. She peppered me with her ideas for new devices that could help people with a hearing loss and pestered me to "design a better hearing aid."

When I was a year or two out of college in the early 1990s, my mother called me with news.

"I have a new hearing aid," she said. Pausing for effect, she finally revealed, "it's *digital*." The words sank in, as neither of us spoke for a moment. The analog-to-digital revolution had taken root, and she obviously benefitted from the transition. I tried to explain that I had not studied much digital signal processing, which was the method by which digital electronics manipulated an analog input. My mother laughed it off. If her daughter could not design a better hearing aid, at least someone else had done it!

At the tender age of seventy-nine, my mother received a cochlear ear implant in one ear. She had followed the technology ever since its inception and desperately sought its benefits. Since her overall hearing had deteriorated to less than ten percent in one ear and less than one percent in the other, a surgeon in New York agreed to perform the operation.

After a long surgery and several weeks to let the wound heal, an audiologist switched on Mom's cochlear device at its lowest setting. Even with minimal amplification, tears streamed down Mom's face as she heard the audiologist speak to her for the first time after the implant. The doctor continued to tune it regularly throughout the next year and gradually increased its amplification.

Mom discovered the sound of water running from the kitchen faucet, the click of the keys on a computer keyboard, and the ticking of my father's watch. The watch drove her crazy, though. Dad and I could only chuckle, as neither of us could hear the watch tick unless we held it to our ears.

"Mom has a bionic ear," I joked. Mom also had fun when Dad and I teased her by whispering between us.

"I heard that!" she said, as she scolded her tormenters. Mom wholeheartedly appreciated the gift of hearing that she had been given at such an advanced age. She relied on her cochlear implant to enjoy life to the fullest for the rest of her years.

The End
of our
Family Unit

—— Saying Goodbye ——

My mother passed away in February 2012, less than eight weeks after I had given her my original book of stories. Two days before she died, she whispered to me in the hospital "…we've had some good times together." It was only luck that I had decided to write about those good times a few months earlier. Any kind of procrastination on my part and it would have been too late to share my gift with Mom.

Although my mother died at eighty-three in Danbury Hospital, her mind was very much intact at the end of her life. She munched on small bites of hospital Jell-O and retold the story from her youth in Texas when she had been hospitalized due to pneumonia and woke up in a private hospital to receive a hot meal at a time when her family had so little to eat. Whereas today's hospital food is generally known to lack taste, Mom wanted me to know that, in certain circumstances, lemon Jell-O tasted just fine. She smacked her lips to emphasize her point.

Mom also laughed at the doctor who had been stumped by her answer for an acuity test.

"What was your first job?" the doctor had asked.

"Riding fence," stated Mom confidently as she straightened up in her chair.

"Huh?" said the doctor. Mom explained her job on the Texas ranch and followed up by assuring the doctor that she "...had all her marbles." On the inside, she was surely laughing at someone who did not understand the life of a Texas horsewoman.

Mom also reflected on our adult trip, just the two of us, to Roosevelt Campobello International Park. I took off work for a week so that Mom and I could make the trip that she long desired. We had only been in the museum for a minute or two before she was overcome by emotion.

"We were hungry and he gave us food to eat," she spoke softly with tears in her eyes. After so many years, the pains of hunger during the Great Depression remained a vivid memory for my mother. We had traveled to Roosevelt's home in Hyde Park, New York, so many times. Campobello Island was the missing pilgrimage to pay homage to the president whom she so deeply respected.

I teased her about the famous lists that she left for me on the countertop when I was a teenager that contained day-long tasks such as "mow the lawn," or "paint the barn."

"I knew that you would do it," she beamed broadly with a twinkle in her eye.

"Take care of Dad," she requested. Mom did not have to write her last to-do list for me.

"I will," I promised.

"I know you will," she smartly acknowledged. Even at the end, she knew that I would "get it done."

My mother was a remarkable person and a pillar in the community. Her obituary noted her many accomplishments as an equestrienne, educator, and elected official. Her political activism was extremely well known throughout Newtown. She stood up in public meetings and spoke for the people. She wrote letters to the editor in the local newspaper and advocated for numerous causes. She gathered petitions, endorsed candidates, campaigned in public areas, or worked the phones to build solidarity.

Most notably, Mom attended town committee meetings to voice her opinion during the "public participation" agenda item. Eyes of committee members might have rolled, but Mom stood her ground until they heard what she had to say. Unabashedly, Mom confronted her political opponents with heavily researched facts. If elected officials tried to fabricate their own truth, then politely and firmly, she set the record straight. Always, Mom put Newtown first.

Shortly after Mom died, I knew exactly the type of memorial service that would celebrate her life appropriately. I wanted to bring the family, friends, and community together to remember my mother. Craftily, I added a last line to her obituary notice that read, "In honor of Ruby's public service, the memorial service will include *public participation*." The invitation was serious, but the town understood the humor.

With more than a hundred people in attendance, my mother's friends and colleagues shared their stories. At the reception, when someone said to me, "Thank you for the laughs as much as the tears," I knew that I had accomplished the perfect tribute to my mother. Shortly, another person gripped my arm.

"You are your mother's daughter," she said. I could never have received so high a compliment.

The complete text for my mother's obituary and my eulogy to her follows in the next sections.

———— Obituary for Ruby Kelley Jansson ————

February 17, 2012

Ruby Kelley Jansson, lifelong advocate for Newtown, dies at the age of eighty-three.

Ruby Kelley Jansson, of Sandy Hook, loving wife and mother, devoted friend and lifelong advocate for Newtown, passed away February 16, 2012, at Danbury Hospital, with her family by her side.

Born in Houston, Texas on September 7, 1928, Ruby spent her youth in San Antonio, Texas. An accomplished equestrienne, Ruby won the New England Championship for Jumping in Fryeburg, Maine. Ruby's love of travel took her to Egypt, Russia, and Europe as well as a cross-country trip with the family in a Winnebago to Yellowstone.

Ruby pursued her education with the tenacity that would become her trademark. She graduated from the Texas State College for Women in 1949 with a double major in English and history, and earned her Ph.D. from New York University in Linguistics in 1966. Ruby became a leader in education. She served on several boards, such as the Commission of English Language, published two texts and numerous articles, and was asked to demonstrate the effectiveness of Inductive Teaching in Linguistics before the National Council of English Teachers in Washington, DC.

It was Ruby's passion for education and the potential that she saw in every individual that guided her to serve on Newtown's Board of Education. During her tenure, Ruby advocated for: the building of Head O'Meadow Elementary School, the addition of dinosaur fossil tracks that once roamed Connecticut to Sandy Hook Elementary School's courtyard, the addition of calculus and computer science to the high school curriculum, and the addition of a swimming pool to Newtown High School. She was instrumental in the formation of the Newtown High School girls' soccer team in 1983.

A staunch advocate for those with disabilities, Ruby was instrumental in the installation of telecoil hearing loops in Newtown's Municipal Building, Newtown Middle School and High School. Ruby helped establish The Friends of Fairfield Hills and served as a member of the Legislative Council. A visionary who saw the wisdom in strategic planning, she was a respected voice at numerous board and committee meetings.

Ruby is survived by her husband of 45 years, Kenneth H. Jansson, and daughters Kelley and Doris Jansson.

The family will receive friends and family at Honan Funeral Home, 58 Main Street, Newtown, from 3 p.m. to 6 p.m. on Sunday, Feb. 19, 2012.

Memorial services will be held at the Newtown United Methodist Church, 92 Church Hill Road, Sandy Hook, Monday, Feb. 20, 2012, at 11 a.m., with a reception following in the church's lower-level meeting room. In honor of Ruby's public service, the memorial service will include "public participation." The family invites attendees to share a personal story of Ruby.

In lieu of flowers the family requests contributions be made to the Ruby K. Jansson Memorial Scholarship, Newtown Scholarship Association Inc., PO Box 302, Newtown, CT 06470.

My Eulogy for my Mother

My mom was very special and will be deeply missed. I have lived away from Newtown since high school. During trips back, people would often ask if I knew what a special person my mother was. It was always an easy question to answer. YES, I KNOW.

I want to share with you three things that defined my mother to me. First, Mom was a lifelong educator, and everything was a lesson. It is fitting that her memorial service is in *this* church (Newtown United Methodist Church). My first memory of the church is when Mom took me out of Sandy Hook Elementary School for a day to watch the church being moved across the street.

"It's not every day that a church moves across the street," Mom said. So, we stood with others on Church Hill Road and watched as the church moved across the street. It was an early lesson that learning from life is important and that we do not always learn from books. At least, I cannot imagine ever reading a book titled "How a Church Gets Moved Across the Street."

My day began with lessons, too. Mom would wake us up singing and clapping as she came down the hallway to rouse us from our beds in the morning. Mom would share her Texas heritage by singing *The Eyes of Texas are Upon You,* or on a special day, more emphatically state "It's April 21st, the Battle of San Jacinto (1836)...RISE and SHINE." Or, on Sundays, as we got ready for Sunday school, "count your many blessings, count them one by one," a regular anthem here at the Methodist church.

Before my freshman year in high school, the family took a trip out west, driving in a Winnebago to Yellowstone National Park and back. Somewhere in the Midwest, on a highway in the middle of nowhere, my mother insisted that we pull off to the side of the road.

"Look at the HAY," exclaimed my mother. My dad, sister, and I found ourselves staring at a recently cut field. In the field, were large rolls of hay. My mother then proceeded to explain that while we were used to bales of hay in neat little bundled rectangles, other parts of the country *rolled* their hay. That was my mother, always sharing knowledge and wanting us to learn.

Second, Mom stressed the importance of being a good communicator, whether writing, or public speaking. Again, my training came at a young age. I was scheduled to present at kindergarten show-and-tell at Sandy Hook Elementary School. I remember that Mom made me rehearse. I stood on one side of the living room, while she stood on the opposite side of the house.

"Now speak up," she commanded. I started to speak.

"Louder!" said Mom. I started again.

"You need to speak up, because someone in the back row could be hard of hearing like me. ENUNCIATE!" Training complete, I went on to give my show-and-tell in kindergarten, but have used that lesson in every presentation I've ever made, both at school and at work.

Writing was also important to my mom. A stickler for good grammar, she read every school paper I ever wrote. They would come back to me covered in red ink. Over time, I learned never to use the passive voice, use the possessive before 'ing verbs, and for goodness sakes, never confuse the use of "bring" and "take." When I wrote letters home from college, they would be returned by mail, with the same red ink. There was always more to learn, even in informal writing.

This past Christmas, my gift to my parents was a story book about my childhood memories. I wanted to capture the funny things that had happened, the types of stories that a family re-tells again and again to get a good laugh, but that is funny only to them. Initially, I thought that I would write about ten stories, but by the time I was done, I had written more than seventy.

But, I am no fool. I did not want to hand my parents a bound copy on Christmas Day inscribed with "To Mom & Dad with Love, Christmas 2011." *No*, instead I printed out a black and white draft, handed it to my mother a week before Christmas and said "Please, proofread your gift." I watched as she read the document in her chair, red pen in hand, laughing out loud as she re-lived the special family moments.

"You are a wonderful writer," she said. After a brief lesson in pitch, rise, and juncture, she handed the document back to me with very little red ink. After more than forty plus years, all those lessons had sunk in. I had finally gotten it right. More than the book itself, my *learning* to write was perhaps the greatest gift that I had ever given her.

Finally, I have one last story to tell you. My mother was an activist in the community. She believed in the political process and taught me that taking the initiative was the key to change.

I was in kindergarten when one of the boys brought a little round black and white ball to class. We chased after it endlessly. It was 1972, and the game that I was playing, was soccer. By third grade, I began to ask my mom why there was not a team to play on.

"You'll have to write a letter and petition for a team to the Head of Parks and Recreation," explained Mom. So, with my mother's guidance, I sat down as a third grader and started writing. The next day, I had all the little third graders sign my first petition.

By the time I was in the fourth grade, a recreational team had been formed. But, the coach did not want girls on the team. He would let me play, but not *any other* girls. *My mother was livid!*

"Unacceptable!" she said, and very quickly, I was enrolled to play youth soccer in Monroe, where they accepted *both* boys and girls. Newtown eventually formed a girls' travel team while I was in middle school, and I transferred back to town to play on the new team. By the time I entered high school in 1981, the girls' travel team was still the only option to play soccer. Newtown High School had a varsity, junior varsity, and freshman *boys'* soccer team, but *NO* girls' team.

By this time, Title IX, the federal Equal Opportunity in Education Act, had been enacted almost ten years earlier. Yet, as *my mother* pointed out, Newtown High School did not have the same number of athletic teams for girls as for boys. A girls' soccer team was missing. Well, *that* was about to change. *With my mother* as the ringleader, the club team began its march on the Newtown Board of Education demanding the creation of a girls' soccer team. With intense lobbying and fund-raising, the issue was finally going to be put to a Board of Education vote in the spring of 1983.

The meeting was scheduled at a time that corresponded with the end of a regularly scheduled soccer practice at Hawley School fields. The entire team, muddy cleats and all, headed over to the Superintendent's office with their parents to attend the critical Board of Education meeting. The room was packed. I remember one parent after the next standing up and advocating for the team. I spoke, too. After all, I was my mother's daughter, and "public participation" was the way to have my voice heard.

Once the audience members had been heard, the Board members deliberated among themselves in the public forum. I could not follow a lot of what they were saying, but what I remember *the most* was that one board member bluntly declared that he "…could not support a girls' soccer team, because it would take away from boys playing football." The Board moved to vote and we held our breath. By a narrow margin, we *won* our team. The team would be installed at the Junior Varsity level in 1983 and would move to Varsity in 1984. *My mother had won another victory for the community.*

I played *one* year of varsity soccer before graduating in 1985. The inaugural team won the Western Connecticut Conference championship and subsequent teams went on to claim the title *six times* in the next ten years. The *Newtown Bee* hailed the girls' soccer program as "a dynasty."[66]

Still, I was able to play only *one* year of varsity soccer. But, *as my mother would say*, someone in the political process *needs to be first*.

"It's the trailblazers who make the sacrifices," she would say. "Political change can impact generations to come." She lived by that philosophy.

I am proud to say that my mother and I watched a Newtown High School girls' soccer game together this past fall (2011). Almost thirty years since the political battle in my high school years, the girls on the field belonged to a new generation, one that has *grown up* with soccer in Newtown and expected girls' soccer as a high school varsity sport. *These girls never knew my mother, but they are one of her many legacies in Newtown.*

My mom was very special and will be deeply missed. She was an educator, communicator, and activist. She was a trailblazer. I love my mom with all my heart.

In Lieu of Flowers

FIGURE 95:
My mother's graduation photo from TSCW, 1949.

My father, sister, and I were at my mother's bedside when she passed away at the hospital. The nursing staff was very nice and prepared us with a list of items to handle in the wake of her death, such as people to notify, funeral home arrangements, and what to request "…in lieu of flowers."

At mention of the last item, my father immediately suggested a scholarship. He knew that my mother had received a scholarship to go to college, and he wanted to honor her by giving another child the same opportunity. The idea sounded perfect to my sister and me. With the help of the community, a scholarship fund in my mother's name was established in a matter of hours.

Over the next day or two, I looked through my mother's photo albums and the scrapbooks from her youth. My sister and I had planned to fill several poster boards with pictures from all phases of my mother's life that would be shown at the calling hours, as well as the reception after the memorial service. I was in charge of gathering the early photos to scan.

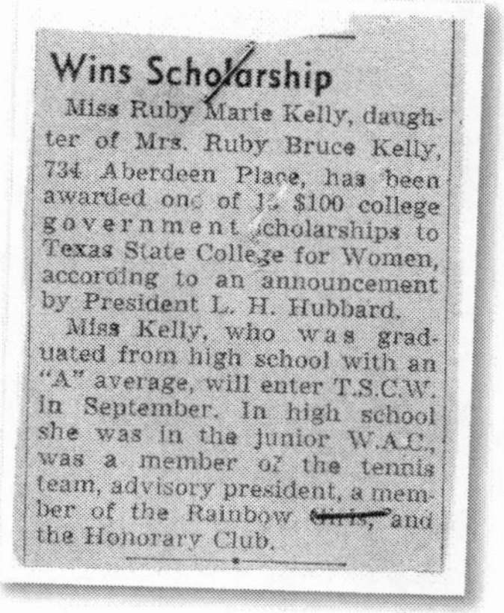

As I leafed through the pages of my mother's high school years, I came to a stunning picture of Mom at the time of

Wins Scholarship

Miss Ruby Marie Kelly, daughter of Mrs. Ruby Bruce Kelly, 734 Aberdeen Place, has been awarded one of 15 $100 college government scholarships to Texas State College for Women, according to an announcement by President L. H. Hubbard.

Miss Kelly, who was graduated from high school with an "A" average, will enter T.S.C.W. in September. In high school she was in the junior W.A.C., was a member of the tennis team, advisory president, a member of the Rainbow Girls, and the Honorary Club.

FIGURE 96:
The San Antonio, Texas, newspaper article that announced my mother had won a scholarship. Her last name was misspelled.

her college graduation. Next to the picture was a small newspaper clipping from 1946 that announced Mom's scholarship to the Texas State College for Women. I am sure that my grandmother had contributed the content to the newspaper, as much as she had proudly pasted the clipping into my mother's scrapbook.

A few months later, my mother's memorial scholarship was awarded to a Newtown student at the graduation ceremony for Newtown High School. There was another student who had been given the opportunity of an education, another clipping in the newspaper for someone to save, another proud parent.

I wrote this book for both my mother and father, but it was my mother who taught me to read, write, and love literature. If you have liked this storybook at all, then please consider a donation to support the education of the next generation of Newtown students at the address below.

RUBY K. JANSSON MEMORIAL SCHOLARSHIP
Newtown Scholarship Association Inc.
PO Box 302
Newtown, CT 06470
www.newtownscholarship.org

Please donate online, or make checks payable to "Ruby K. Jansson Memorial Scholarship," at the address above.

The Newtown Scholarship Association, Inc. (NSA) was established as a nonprofit organization in 1937 to promote and advance the education of secondary school graduates residing in Newtown, Connecticut by providing need-based financial aid to Newtown students.

The Newtown Scholarship Association, Inc. has been a 501(c)3 exempt organization since 1963. A tax identification number is available upon request.

Cast of Characters

———— Family Tree ————

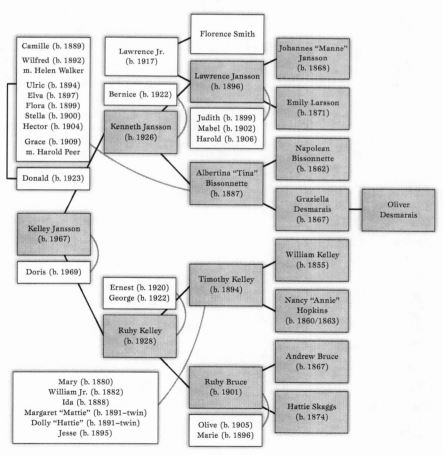

Florence Smith

Camille (b. 1889)
Wilfred (b. 1892)
m. Helen Walker
Ulric (b. 1894)
Elva (b. 1897)
Flora (b. 1899)
Stella (b. 1900)
Hector (b. 1904)
Grace (b. 1909)
m. Harold Peer

Donald (b. 1923)

Lawrence Jr.
(b. 1917)

Bernice (b. 1922)

Kenneth Jansson
(b. 1926)

Lawrence Jansson
(b. 1896)

Judith (b. 1899)
Mabel (b. 1902)
Harold (b. 1906)

Albertina "Tina"
Bissonnette
(b. 1887)

Johannes "Manne"
Jansson
(b. 1868)

Emily Larsson
(b. 1871)

Napolean
Bissonnette
(b. 1862)

Graziella
Desmarais
(b. 1867)

Oliver
Desmarais

Kelley Jansson
(b. 1967)

Doris (b. 1969)

Ernest (b. 1920)
George (b. 1922)

Ruby Kelley
(b. 1928)

Timothy Kelley
(b. 1894)

William Kelley
(b. 1855)

Nancy "Annie"
Hopkins
(b. 1860/1863)

Mary (b. 1880)
William Jr. (b. 1882)
Ida (b. 1888)
Margaret "Mattie" (b. 1891–twin)
Dolly "Hattie" (b. 1891–twin)
Jesse (b. 1895)

Ruby Bruce
(b. 1901)

Olive (b. 1905)
Marie (b. 1896)

Andrew Bruce
(b. 1867)

Hattie Skaggs
(b. 1874)

305

———— Pets ————

Bim Bam Boom ....Pony
Brownie ....Dad's dog, German shepherd
Caper.........................Mom and Dad's cat, aka "Number One"
Cotton Candy...Pony
Fanny ....Donkey
Jet...Mom's dog, cocker spaniel
Little Black Cherry..Cat
Lollipop..Cat
Nipper..Dad's squirrel
Omega Dandy ....Pony
Rose ....Donkey
Shadow...Dog, Labrador mix
Snooky ....Tina Bissonnette's dog
Topsy...Dad's cat
Wiggles ....Dog, Labrador mix
Zipper...Dad's cat

———— Friends of the Family ————

Spike Babcock ....Instructor pilot, Florida
Dr. Fred Bath..Newtown veterinarian
Dr. David Bartlett.....Maine neighbor, married to Jeanne Bartlett
Jeanne Bartlett.....Maine neighbor, married to Dr. David Bartlett
Captain Richard M. Bauer.........U.S. Army officer in Philippines
Ed Beardsley ....Newtown neighbor
Howard Beardsley...................................Newtown neighbor
Kris Berglund...Family friend in Maine
Donald Bissonnette ....Dad's cousin, World War II B-17 pilot
Robert Boynton...Mom's co-author

Cast of Characters

Frank Keating..Newtown neighbor,
married to Madeline Keating
Madeline Keating ....Newtown neighbor,
married to Frank Keating
Charlotte Knaur ....Family friend, married to Karl Knaur
Karl Knaur........................Tutor, married to Charlotte Knaur
Steve Kovacs...Newtown contractor
Helen Lewis...Stratford politician
Dennis Long.............Maine neighbor, married to Virginia Long
Virginia Long............Maine neighbor, married to Dennis Long
Elena Lorenzen...........................Married to Stanley Lorenzen
Stanley Lorenzen......................Principal, Staples High School,
married to Elena Lorenzen
Patrick Lynch ....Newtown landowner
Mr. M.......................Teacher, Sandy Hook Elementary School
Helen Martin ....Tina (Bissonnette) Jansson's friend
Peggy Mason ....Newtown realtor
Eleanor Mayer ....Vice President, Connecticut National Bank
William McAllister ...Horse farm owner, Southbury, Connecticut
Dr. John Miller ....Stratford dentist,
married to Shirley (Mott) Miller
Shirley (Mott) Miller ....Married to Dr. John Miller
Ellen Orosz ....Newtown neighbor, married to Frank Orosz
Frank Orosz ....Newtown neighbor, married to Ellen Orosz
Mrs. P......................Teacher, Sandy Hook Elementary School
Truman Parsons.........Civil War veteran, Stratford, Connecticut
Alice Rafferty ....Teacher, Sandy Hook Elementary School
Ruth Reeves ....Mom's co-author
Mae Schmidle...Newtown politician
Grandma Sibley....................................Nelle Smith's mother
Elizabeth Small...........Stratford resident, married to Tom Small

Cast of Characters

Tom Small...........Stratford resident, married to Elizabeth Small
Betsy Smith.......................Daughter of Ward and Nelle Smith
Cynthia Smith...................Mom's friend, sister to Ward Smith
Cynthia Lee Smith...............Daughter of Ward and Nelle Smith
Earl Smith ....Newtown lawyer
Judy Smith.......................Daughter of Ward and Nelle Smith
Nelle Smith.......................................Married to Ward Smith
Ward Smith ......Cynthia Smith's brother, married to Nelle Smith
Kate Stark ....Newtown soccer player
Adrian Stroud...........................Newtown girls' soccer coach
Bob Sveda.....Newtown High School, head coach for girls' soccer
Julius Szalay ....Monroe soccer coach
Edith Tenney.........Newtown neighbor, married to Don Tenney
Don Tenney.........Newtown neighbor, married to Edith Tenney
Alfred E. "Tommy" Thompson...................Assistant Principal,
Staples High School
Frank Tomaino.......................Teacher, Newtown High School
Joanna Torow ....Family friend in Maine
Ruby Wheeler..........................Teacher, Stratford High School
Richard Whiting....................................Instructor pilot, Texas
Leon F. Whitney...................Veterinarian, Orange, Connecticut
Ella Williams................Teacher, Long Lots Junior High School
Kay Williams..Niece of "Teacher"
Mary Branche "Teacher" Williams...............Texas ranch owner
and college riding instructor
Will Williams ....Shetland pony breeder in Texas
Paul Wilson...Newtown bus driver
Maurice Zowidowski........Pie truck driver, Frisbie Pie Company

Acknowledgements

More than anyone, I have my parents to thank for the content of this book. They did not know it at the time, but each night I called to check on them in their advanced age, I was baiting them with questions about their family and childhood. At the other end of the phone, I was typing furiously to capture their stories in genealogy software that I was using to create a family history. I had no idea at the time that I would ever write a book. However, those notes proved invaluable in understanding my roots and the timeline of facts that contribute to this book.

When I started to write this memoir, I spent more long hours with my father, listening to his stories, writing them, and reading my work to him, so that he could add or correct information. He always found plenty of mistakes once he saw how I expressed his words. Where his memory failed him, I researched historical facts to construct an accurate timeline.

My mother's story was harder, as she had passed away before I decided to write this lengthier family memoir. For her history, I relied more heavily on the notes I had taken during our phone discussions, my own memory of her stories, stories from friends who had known her before she met my father, various papers, photo albums, military records, and scrapbooks that she left behind, as well as her own writings. I had often begged my mother to write about her life, as I thought her experiences and accomplishments were so interesting. How often does a Texas woman born into poverty in 1928 survive the Depression, World War II, and go on to become an accomplished horsewoman, earn a Ph.D., and contribute so much to town politics? Although her childhood was a rather painful subject to her, she had clearly made a few attempts to document her life as I found a precious, few scribbled pages in her file cabinet after her death. I've quoted her writings where appropriate.

To fill in the blanks of my mother's story, particularly the time before she met my father, I am greatly indebted to the help of four women: Susan Jacoby, Cynthia Smith, Cynthia Lee (Smith) Whitaker, and Kay (Williams) Goodman. After my mother's death, Susan Jacoby wrote the kindest sympathy card a person could ever receive— she shared her memories of my mother. Even now, I cannot read it without crying. Susan was the first person to talk to me in-depth about my Texan mother's first steps in Connecticut. Susan even drove me to the address where my mother lived in Trumbull, Connecticut, and pointed out the house's features from the street. She also introduced me to Cynthia Smith and Cynthia Lee (Smith) Whitaker, who had more of the details that I desperately needed to fill in the gaps of my research.

Cynthia Smith, who is pretty much single-handedly responsible for my mother's move from Texas to Connecticut, spent many hours on the phone with me to discuss the circumstances of her meeting my mother in Texas, their friendship, horseback riding adventures, travels, and eventual joint house ownership. Cynthia also provided numerous photos of my mother that I had never seen before. It was a thrill to see snapshots of my mother in her twenties and thirties. Cynthia also proved an excellent reviewer of the manuscript and corrected numerous mistakes that pertained to my mother's history, as well as the local area. Similarly, Cynthia Lee

Acknowledgements

✜

(Smith) Whitaker, who had camped cross-country with my mother during the 1950s, shared her recollection of their travels together.

Kay (Williams) Goodman was only a bright-eyed teenager at the time my mother attended TSCW in Denton, Texas. Kay's aunt, "Teacher," managed the equestrian program at the college. The entire Williams family befriended my mother, and Mom stayed in touch with Kay over the years through yearly updates in Christmas cards. In my email exchanges with Kay, she brought TSCW, the ranch, and especially Teacher to life. She also witnessed Sally Goodin' bucking off Teacher and provided essential detail to the story, in particular that Teacher landed with "legs splayed" and still in the saddle. I could imagine my mother's wonderful experience at TSCW, stables, and big farm, through Kay's words. Kay also provided a personal tour of my mother's old stomping ground when I visited her in Texas. As I toured TSCW (now Texas Women's University) and Teacher's old house, I may have heard the whispers of the ladies from the 1940s who had accumulated so many great memories there.

The genesis for this project would never have come about had it not been for the unwavering support of Karen LaRoche and the San Jose Sketchers (Marilynn Smith, Lolla McMurray, Bobbi Eddy, Lisa Blaylock, Dalene Turner, Sharon Morales, Leah Hayland, Julia Cline, Darlene Tenes, and Mary Lee Baiocchi) who met every Saturday morning to share art experiences, learn drawing techniques, and sketch (mostly) in the great outdoors. It must take a right-brain support group to get the creative juices flowing, because I signed up for art class to learn how to draw stick figures and not only learned how to sketch a little bit, but also wrote this book! Thanks to the group for their friendship, knowledge sharing, and encouragement in all art endeavors.

Many thanks to the reviewers whose feedback made a big impact on my writing, including Jay O'Shea, Jennifer Rodgers, Zehra Zaidi, Teri Temme, and Gary Davis. Jay O'Shea was the very first person to sample an early manuscript and provide incredibly valuable advice as to how to both write and understand the essence of humor. If my book is at all funny, I have to give a shout-out to Jay for setting me on the right path. Jennifer Rodgers offered the key advice that led me to organize my stories into a more narrative form. Jennifer read an early manuscript and provided the brutally honest, constructive criticism that I needed to break through my organizational challenges. Thanks, Jennifer! Zehra Zaidi read a chapter that I was planning to read aloud at the monthly "open mic" event hosted by the California Writer's Club. Zehra helped perfect my pacing and critiqued my reading (aloud) style, which undoubtedly contributed to a successful first public appearance. I would also like to thank Teri Temme, who devoured my manuscript and found mistakes that I doubt anyone else would have caught. In my opinion, Teri is a professional reviewer. Gary Davis also receives much credit, as he edited the eulogy that I wrote for my mother before I delivered it at the memorial service. It is hard to see one's mistakes when writing at such an emotional time, and it was incredibly kind and thoughtful of Gary to help me when I needed it most.

I also owe my gratitude to the organizations that assisted with my research, including the Newtown Board of Education office, Newtown Cyrenius H. Booth Library, Witte Museum, Brackenridge High School Jr. ROTC Department, Kingman Army Airfield Museum, Air Force Historical Research Agency, Westport Historical Society, and Stratford Historical Society. I also appreciate the words of encouragement from early readers, including Dr. Thomas and Doris Bucky, Carol Moore, David LaRoche, Jodie Ostrovsky, Denise Linet, Elizabeth McLaughlin, Karen Pierce, Shirley Licursi, Jim Fillmore, Tuan

Acknowledgements

Nguyen, Jon Forcht, Mark Mickelson, and Debbie Cooper. I also appreciate the help from my cousins Carol Skog, Gunnel Birath, and Denise Kuhl for help with my Swedish family history.

A big thank you to my editor, Louise MacCormack. As a novice, I made a huge number of grammatical mistakes, and Louise patiently corrected each and every one of them. Louise's enthusiasm for memoirs is infectious, and I whole-heartedly appreciated the fact that she felt my family's story was worth the time to write.

I would also like to thank Tom and Tamara Dever of TLC Graphics and their talented graphic designers, Monica Thomas and Erin Stark. They never wavered in their support of a new author and executed my vision throughout the design phase of the project.

Finally, I'd like to thank all of the people who represent the cast of characters in the book. Some are living and some are deceased, but every one of you is special. This book is for all of you, too.

References

[1] Wilcoxson, Wm. Howard. *History of Stratford Connecticut 1639 to 1939*. Bridgeport (CT): Press of The Brewer-Borg Corp, 1940.

[2] "Champion Show Dogs at the Yale Peabody Museum," Yale Peabody Museum of Natural History, accessed August 13, 2013, peabody.yale.edu/collections/vertebrate-zoology/mammalogy/champion-show-dogs-yale-peabody-museum.

[3] "Airships: The Hindenburg and other Zeppelins," Airships.net, accessed August 13, 2013, www.airships.net/hindenburg/lz129-hindenburg-detailed-history.

[4] "Historic American Engineering Record: Merritt Parkway," National Park Service, U.S. Department of Interior, HAER No. CT-63.

[5] Radde, Bruce. *The Merritt Parkway*. New Haven (CT) & London: Yale University Press, 1993.

[6] Larned, Larry. *Traveling the Merritt Parkway*. Charleston (SC): Arcadia Publishing, 1998.

[7] "The Great New England Hurricane," History.com, accessed August 13, 2013, www.history.com/this-day-in-history/the-great-new-england-hurricane.

[8] Knapp, Lewis G., "75 Years Ago This Month – The Hurricane of 1938," Stratford Historical Society > > UPDATE, September 2013.

[9] John D. Calhoun, Lewis G. Knapp, and Carol W. Lovell, *Images of America: Stratford* (CT). Charleston (SC): Arcadia Publishing, 1999.

[10] "World's First Helicopter – Today in History," ConnecticutHistory.org, accessed May, 20, 2013, connecticuthistory.org/worlds-first-helicopter-today-in-history/.

[11] "Sikorsky," Helis.com, accessed May 20, 2013, www.helis.com/timeline/sikorsky.php.

[12] "Ground Observer Corps," Radomes, Inc. The Air Defense Radar Veterans' Association, accessed Oct 19, 2013, www.radomes.org/museum/documents/GOC/GOC.html.

[13] The website Merriam-Webster; accessed May 22, 2013, www.m-w.com.

[14] "Boeing B-17G Flying Fortress," National Museum of the Air Force, accessed May 20, 2013, www.nationalmuseum.af.mil/factsheets/factsheet.asp?id = 512.

[15] Ray, James Ralph, *The Inside Story of the Flying Fortress, Boeing B-17*, Garden City (NY): The Garden City Publishing Co. Inc., 1943.

[16] Krammer, Arnold, *Nazi Prisoners of War in America*. Lanham (MD): Scarborough House, 1996.

[17] Billinger, Jr., Robert D., *Hitler's Soldiers in the Sunshine State*, Gainesville (FL): University Press of Florida, 2000.

[18] "Drew Field with 15 Square Miles, Has 2800 Buildings," *Tampa Sunday Tribune*, May 27, 1945.

[19] Patte, Edouard, International YMCA, Report on Visit to Prisoner of War Camp Drew Field, February 20, 1945, RG 389, Entry 641, Box 2656 and Entry 459A, Box 1609, NA.

[20] Woog, Dan, *Staples High School: 120 Years of A + Education*. U.S.: Woog's World, 2005.

[21] "The Curtis History," accessed June 5, 2013, www.curtispackaging.com/about-us/history/.

[22] Ruby K. Jansson, Letter to Dr. Hinrich Staecker, October 21, 2008.

[23] Ruth G. Neislar, General Services Administration, letter to Ruby Kelley, March 26, 1968.

[24] Luker, Carol, "During war, families keep vigil," *Richardson Daily News*, May 24, 1981.

[25] Army of the United States, Separation Qualification Record for George E. Kelley, October 9, 1945.

[26] *La Retama*. San Antonio (TX): Brackenridge High School, 1946.

References

[27] Deed Records of Bexar County, Texas, 73rd Judicial District Court, Volume 54, Case No. F-43305, Oct 3, 1947.

[28] Enlisted Record and Report of Separation Honorable Discharge for George E. Kelley, October 10, 1945.

[29] Norman, Michael, Elizabeth M. Norman, *Tears in the Darkness.* New York: Farrar, Straus, and Giroux, 2009.

[30] Lt. Col. Duane E. Byrd (Ret.), e-mail message to author, April 11, 2013.

[31] Marise McDermott, e-mail message to author, August 15, 2013.

[32] Department of the Army, Permanent Orders 117-1, August 23, 1985.

[33] Kay (Williams) Goodman, e-mail message to author, April 29, 2013.

[34] Kay (Williams) Goodman, e-mail message to author, March 27, 2013.

[35] Kay (Williams) Goodman, e-mail message to author, April 27, 2013.

[36] Kay (Williams) Goodman, in discussion with author, July 5, 2013.

[37] Kay (Williams) Goodman, e-mail message to author, May 15, 2012.

[38] *Career Colony Summer School and K-Ranch.* Camp Brochure.

[39] Teacher Contract, Board of Education Hobbs (NM), Municipal School District for Ruby Kelley, August 29, 1949.

[40] Cynthia Smith, in discussion with author, February 2013.

[41] Susan Jacoby, in letter to author, February 2012.

[42] Cynthia Lee (Smith) Whitaker, in e-mail to author, February 8, 2013.

[43] Cynthia Smith, in discussion with author, July 2013.

[44] Cynthia Smith, in discussion with author, February 2013.

[45] Cynthia Lee (Smith) Whitaker, e-mail message to author, September 6, 2012.

[46] Cynthia Lee (Smith) Whitaker, e-mail message to author, February 8, 2013.

[47] Cynthia Smith, e-mail message to author, February 27, 2013.

[48] Cynthia Smith, in discussion with author, February 2012.

[49] Doris (Raymaley) Bucky, in discussion with the author, February 2013.

[50] Doris (Raymaley) Bucky, in discussion with the author, October 2013.

[51] Karl Decker, in discussion with author, February 2012.

[52] Ruby (Kelley) Jansson, in letter to author, April 25, 1994.

[53] Doris (Raymaley) Bucky, in discussion with the author, February 2012.

[54] Martelli, Linda, "Newtown school board fills post, ignores GOP nominee," *Danbury (CT) News-Times*, October 30, 1974.

[55] "Sandy Hook's Dilophosaurus" *Newtown Bee (CT)*, September 12, 1975.

[56] Phillips, "It Wasn't a UFO," *Newtown Bee (CT)*, June 23, 1978.

[57] Larry Schwartz, "Eric Heiden was a reluctant hero," ESPN, accessed May 28, 2013, espn.go.com/sportscentury/features/00014225.html.

[58] Craig Bartlett, in discussion with author, May 25, 2013.

[59] St. Laurent, Randy, "Acton man's magic is his music," *Weekender* (*Journal Tribune*, Biddeford, Maine), February 11, 1983.

[60] "The History of Cranmore," accessed June 6, 2013, www.cranmore.com/winter/resorthistory.

[61] "Badlands National Park South Dakota," National Park Service, accessed May 21, 2013, www.nps.gov/badl/.

[62] Recommendation for curriculum/textbook approval at Newtown High School (CT), Newtown Board of Education Minutes, June 13, 1978.

[63] Weather Underground, accessed May 21, 2013, www.wunderground.com.

[64] "Indians Qualify for States," *Newtown Bee (CT)*, November 9, 1984.

[65] "Jul 10, 1999: U.S. women win World Cup," History.com, accessed May 21, 2013, www.history.com/this-day-in-history/us-women-win-world-cup.

[66] T. Wyatt, "Celebrating A Full Decade of Celebration: Newtown High Girls' Soccer Alumni Will Gather, Saturday, To Commemorate Tenth Anniversary," *Newtown Bee (CT)*, July 1994.

Made in the USA
Charleston, SC
10 January 2014